Attention Authors

Manas Publications is fighting a war to tell the world that India can win the battle not only by the bullet but also by pen. We are converting fighters into writers. There is no dearth of intellectuals in our country, however, their knowledge is confined to them only. No sincere effort has been made by any other publisher to channelise their knowledge, that is why the talent of every intellectual remains latent. An author always presents the raw material in the shape of a manuscript and it is the job of the publisher to convert it into a finished product. Manas has been continually motivating intellectuals and publishing their manuscripts for more than three decades and would like to publish your manuscript too. If you or your colleagues have a manuscript ready for publication or are working on it, contact us with a detailed synopsis and list of contents. Manas can also suggest you a suitable title for writing related to your area of expertise. Manas is known for its publishing quality. We take utmost care in production and also give wide publicity to the book and its author through our national and international distribution network.

Intelligence Tradecraft
Secrets of Spy Warfare

Maloy Krishna Dhar, IPS

Former Joint Director: Intelligence Bureau (IB)

Author of Bestselling Book
Open Secrets: India's Intelligence Unveiled

Foreword by
Roger Faligot

Manas Publications
(We Convert Fighters into Writers)
New Delhi-110002 (INDIA)

MANAS PUBLICATIONS

(We Convert Fighters into Writers)

(Publishers for IAS, IPS, IFS, Defence, Judges, Press etc)

4402/5-A, Ansari Road (Opp. HDFC Bank)
Darya Ganj, New Delhi-110 002 (INDIA)
Off. (23260783, 23265523, Res. 23842660
Fax: 011-23272766
E-mail: manaspublications@gmail.com
manaspublications@yahoo.com

website: www.manaspublications.in

© Maloy Krishna Dhar

2nd Impression 2014 (FP - 2011)

ISBN   13 Digits -   978-81-7049-399-0
10 Digits -   81-7049-399-4
₹ 795/-

Designed at-*
Manas Publications

Printed in India at

RK Offsets, Delhi and published by Mrs Suman Lata for
Manas Publications,
4402/5-A, Ansari Road,
(Opp. HDFC Bank),
Darya Ganj, New Delhi-110 002 (INDIA)

Contents

Author's Note

I had written *Open Secrets: India's Intelligence Unveiled* with a view to offer near-side view of what happens and why such things happen in the world of intelligence, which always perplexed the common people. The idea of writing a sequel to the *Open Secrets*, presenting to common readers and intelligence professionals the details of the science and arts of intelligence tradecraft, was seeded in my mind. These are researched in written literature and are taught in foreign universities. In India no such literature is available on India's internal and external security concerns. I nursed and studied the science as practiced by the intelligence agencies of various countries. *Intelligence Tradecraft* is, therefore, a sequel to *Open Secrets*, which tries to explain how the intelligence trade is conducted by the agencies and which instruments they use.

The idea was reaffirmed when I was appointed as the Assistant Director, Training for the Intelligence Bureau. Prior to that my stints as station officer in Manipur and Nagaland offered opportunity to understand the inadequacies in recruitment policy, training and orientation of the cutting edge level officers and certain officers.

While teaching and supervising the instructors I realized that over 95% of the intelligence operators were not equipped and educated enough to teach various aspects of training a recruit and convert him to an intelligence operator. I used the spare time to read whatever books were available in open market sources.

Later, when I headed the counter-insurgency and counter-intelligence matters, many challenges accosted my officers and me. No textbook or classroom solution was there. Discussions with grassroots level officers, subtle experimentations and often bold application helped me in building a structure of theories and practices in these challenging fields of operation.

As Joint Director of the Technical Intelligence branch I received an opportunity to clear up the junkyard of unused and unusable communication equipments and accessories and the TechInt operators were motivated to acclimatize with newer equipment. General duty intelligence operators were encouraged to gain knowledge about the forbidden world of TechInt and some of them developed the aptitude for application of the system tools for intelligence generation. For the first time the forbidden cove of TechInt division, in primary stages of development, was opened up to officers oriented in operational application.

The mysterious world of Signals Intelligence (SigInt) was also in my domain and with the assistance of certain forward looking officers, the wing was revitalized. This was the time when the Intelligence Bureau leapt into the field of Satellite Communication (SATCOM), Computer Communication and Intelligence (ComInt) and certain distant locations of India were connected to the main hub of activities of the Intelligence Bureau.

This fruitful period educated me about application and invention of new methods of applicability of bugging devices, clandestine audio-video operations and application of radio communication during surveillance.

Obviously, technological advancements were intensified from the days the IB was involved in Punjab, Kashmir and Assam operations. I had the fortune of learning from these landmark developments. The TechInt divisions of the Indian intelligence edifices have been revolutionized during the last 15 years and more changes are taking place. Yet, India's position amongst the world intelligence community remains far behind the western countries. More reforms are necessary.

I have a nagging fear that intricate aspects of Intelligence Tradecraft are yet to be researched and applied by the Indian Intelligence agencies. With this path breaking book, I wish other former employees of the central and state agencies would chronicle their experiences on tradecraft for education of future intelligence operators. Unfortunately, India treats intelligence as a taboo area and no specific studies are available on the subject of Intelligence Tradecraft. The western world is much ahead as they realize that openness is the best way to maintain secrets.

I express gratitude to the giants of the Intelligence fraternity with whom I had the opportunity to work and learn. My wholehearted thanks go to the grassroots level Intelligence and Technical operators who always educated me and whom I had the opportunity to educate. Education evolves constant learning and that is the best elixir to survive the war of wits in the mysterious world of intelligence. With this venture, I hope the mission I embarked on with *Open Secrets*, will be partially fulfilled.

Chapter 1

Intelligence Defined

Intelligence in modern world, especially after the First World War and during the Second World War assumed great importance in the lives of the nations and peoples. Nations and states always recognized that Intelligence was as important a part of statecraft as were diplomacy, strategic formulation of external policies, security estimate of the internal situations and even conduct of day-to-day administration. In a vast and complicated country like India, internal intelligence was always given equal importance as the related external intelligence. The internal aspect is again not purely internal. With extensive borders with inimical nations like Pakistan and China and mostly porous borders with Nepal, Bangladesh and Myanmar on the one hand and a vast coastline to defend against unwarranted incursions by hostile elements, the concept of internal intelligence in India was intricately knotted with aspects of external intelligence.

What is Intelligence? Intelligence pundits, scholars and philosophers have tried to define intelligence in the light of their own exposés in the fields of overt and covert intelligence gathering and manufacturing experiences, generalization and often related to Free World's struggle against the Iron and the Bamboo Curtain countries. Somewhere the interpretations have been narrowed down to the experience of the Second World War and later with the extremely hot Cold War.

Western writers often fall back on the Chinese sage Sun Tzu who wrote about the importance of foreknowledge being, "the reasons the entitled prince and the wise general conquer the enemy whenever they move."

Nearer home there are misplaced beliefs that Kautilya's *Arthashastra* was written by Kautilya, alias Vishnugupta alias Chanakya for Chandragupta Maurya, a contemporary of Alexander the Great, 3rd century BC "The temptation to consider the *Arthashastra* to have been composed specifically for the guidance of Chandragupta should be resisted, as the existence of the Empire of Chandragupta is completely ignored in this work."[1] Certain estimates indicate that the *Arthashastra* was composed over the years much earlier to 3rd century BC. The wisdom book received present shape sometime in 10th century. Some historians are tempted to believe the compilers might have been wisecracks like Kautilya and Vishnugupta. It was given the stamp of Chanakya as he had figured prominently in the making of history from the time of Chandragupta Maurya.

Whatever the historicity, Kautilya might have made the summations of intelligence as concept and its tradecraft have been detailed in the *Arthashastra* in chapters eleven to sixteen of the classical book. Starting from appointment of persons in secret service, creation of establishment of spies, the *Arthashastra* enumerated and detailed almost all aspects of intelligence gathering and reporting as an integral part of statecraft, war and peace.

However, defining intelligence has become an obsession with many former sleuths and scholars. It is not worthwhile to get entangled with the punditry of the definition seekers. Whoever and in whichever way intelligence may be defined, the task of intelligence gathering, collation, analysis, dissemination and operations vary from nation to nation. Intelligence makers and producers have to keep pace with the political structure of the country, political regimes and country managers. In a western country like the USA, intelligence is basically foreign policy oriented. The Second World War during the German Abwehr was divided into several branches encompassing internal security, external intelligence and military intelligence. Similarly, the Soviet KGB was also divided into several sections looking after internal challenges, foreign intelligence and it also collaborated with the GRU, military intelligence.

The USA's intelligence system changed considerably after 9/11 attack and global manifestation of Islamic resurgence. Creation of the Homeland Security and other pyramid structures has some way or other drawn a line between external and internal intelligence operations. Britain has a different tradition, where the bureaucracy acts as a strong link between the intelligence community and the political governments. In the USSR and China things were vastly different. In our neighbourhood the ISI and the DGFI have emerged as an integral part of the political edifice of Pakistan and Bangladesh. India had inherited a 122-year old British intelligence system that had a checkered growth right through the days of the thuggee and establishment of the Central Intelligence Bureau, to separation of external and internal intelligence

(Intelligence Bureau and Research and Analysis Wing) and addition of more appendages as the national requirements to cope with the internal fault lines and external threats.

However, it would be worthwhile to take a short journey through the labyrinth of definition making process. "Mark Lowenthal, a distinguished American scholar of intelligence, offers a useful taxonomy, arguing that we can think about intelligence in three ways: first, as process, through which intelligence is requested by policy-makers or operational commanders, then collected, analyzed and fed to the consumers. This is often referred to as the intelligence cycle, second, we can define it as product, once upon a time circulated as paper, but now increasingly distributed through multi-level secure electronic institutions. However, as their name implies, these organisations that provide intelligence service to government also conduct activities that go far beyond the mere collection of information..."[2]

Lowenthal personally defined intelligence in the following words: "Intelligence is the process by which specific types of information important to national security are requested, collected, analyzed, and provided to policy makers; the products of that process; the safeguarding of these processes and this information by counter-intelligence activities, and the carrying out of operations as requested by lawful authorities."[3]

The scholars and many former intelligence high priests have tried to define intelligence according to their own perceptions. According to National Security Act, 1947 of the USA Intelligence was contoured as: "The term 'foreign intelligence' means information relating to the capabilities, intentions, or activities of foreign governments or elements thereof, foreign organisations, or foreign persons."

In 1955, the Hoover Commission described intelligence as: "Intelligence deals with all the things which should be known in advance of initiating a course of action."[4]

Later, with modern requirements and changed global geopolitical and geostrategic requirements of the USA, intelligence was defined by Brown-Aspen Commission. The Commission defined intelligence as: "The Commission believes it preferable to define 'Intelligence' simply and broadly as information about 'things foreign' — people, places, things, and events — needed by the Government for the conduct of functions."[5]

It is surprising that even in 1996 the USA was grappling with a proper definition of intelligence and to award charter of duty to its prime intelligence agencies. One top CIA functionary (Martin T Brown) later tried to define intelligence as: "Intelligence is the collecting and processing of that information about foreign countries and their agents which is needed by a government for its foreign policy and for national security, the conduct of non-attributable activities (*covert operations* — italics by author) abroad to facilitate the implementation of foreign policy, and the protection of both process and product, as well as persons and organisations concerned with these, against unauthorized disclosure."[6]

This definition bunched together the concepts of internal and external intelligence, counter-intelligence and covert operations abroad as sanctioned by the government from time to time. In fact, this definition was sculpted out to suit the role of the CIA that was changed vastly from the original Charter of 1947, when President Truman approved the Bill. We shall discuss about Charter and ethos and functional philosophy of the intelligence agencies, including the Indian agencies in a later chapter.

As far as global studies about definition of intelligence are concerned, we may conclude with the summation made by Michael Warner, who served many years in the history division of the CIA. He is currently the Historian of the Office of the Director of National Intelligence. His most important book is: *US Intelligence Community Reform Studies Since 1947* (2005).

Since India did not have any major intelligence review exercises barring the LP Singh (Home Secretary) Committee Report (not declassified), Indira Gandhi's decision to bifurcate the intelligence behemoth, the IB, and create a separate External Intelligence wing there is very little scope to discuss any reforms bid inside the intelligence fraternity in India. However, during Rajiv Gandhi, regime some functional guidelines were redrafted and redefined. Since the documents are not declassified I desist from incorporating details of these in-house exercises carried out by the Government of India. The latest exercise was done after the Kargil fiasco under GC Saxena, former head of RAW and Governor of Jammu & Kashmir. After 26/11 attack by Pakistani terrorists on Mumbai some lateral movements had taken place and few structural improvements were attempted.

Nevertheless, let us fall back on Michael Warner to sum up the definition of intelligence. He says: "A comprehensive definition of Intelligence — one that says what it is, without also including all sorts of things that it is not — would have several elements. We can say now that intelligence, is that which is:

- Dependent upon confidential sources and methods for full effectiveness.

- Performed by officers of the state for state purposes (this implies that those officers receive direction from the state's civilian and military leaders).

- Focused on foreigners — usually other states, but often foreign subjects, corporations, or groups (if its objectives are domestic citizens, then the activity becomes a branch of either law enforcement or governance).

- Linked to production and dissemination of information.

- Involved in influencing foreign entities by means that are unattributable to the acting government (if the activities are open and declared, they are the province of diplomacy; if they utilize uniformed members of the armed forces, they belong to the military)."[7]

Such labyrinthine walks in defining intelligence were necessitated as the modern nation states (especially democracies) were tied to the string aprons of court intrigues, classical concepts of espionage within and abroad either for consolidation of the ruling regimes or for measuring the barometers of war and peace, trade and commerce competition, empire building and dominating the resources of the underdeveloped and backward countries. The concept of intelligence was mostly 'foreign policy' oriented and intricately linked to diplomatic relations, geopolitical expansion and geostrategic positioning of military forces.

The British Empire was embroiled in competition with the Germans, French, Italian, Belgian, and Scandinavians over expansion of colonial territories and exploiting the resources of the peoples and nations less developed and less prepared for challenging the military prowess of the European nations. These countries required more of foreign intelligence to remain supreme controlling authority in the various areas of influence.

The USA also, before the First World War, was not much bothered about internal security and formulated the role of intelligence as being shadow-diplomatic roles for collecting secret information about the foreign countries and their intentions against American interests abroad.

We propose to discuss in brief the Charter, ethos and functional philosophy of a few selected intelligence agencies a little later. But it can be mentioned here that the Russian system of intelligence and that of China varied vastly from the modern European and American concepts. During the Second World War the intelligence agencies of Germany, Italy and Japan also functioned in absolute authoritarian manner, in which boundaries between internal, external and military intelligence was blurred out. Though this book is not concerned with those aspects of aberrant intelligence pursuits by dictatorial regimes we would make brief comments at appropriate places.

In South Asia—India, Pakistan, Bangladesh and Sri Lanka—the intelligence system emerged as a pan-national concept, much later during the British regime. There are proponents who argue that the ancient concepts of Kautilya a.k.a. Vishugupta a.k.a. Chanakya were followed by the princes and the Mohammedan rulers also followed the existing practices with slight innovation of their own. No purpose would be served by entering into argument about the merits and demerits of the ancient and medieval systems. These were not oriented to protect the people and ensure progress of the states ruled by the absolute princes and sultans and emperors. Intelligence of that variety was more related to the rival princes, enemy encampments, their strength and weakness and sabotage and subversion of loyalties of the subjects ruled by a particular prince. For instance, Robert Clive was shrewd enough to take note of the differences between the Nawab of Bengal and his brother-in-law and his strained relationship with the prominent bankers and traders around him. He exploited these inner contradictions and won Bengal for the East India Company virtually without a war. The same pattern was noticed almost all over India where the British forces were pitted against the local princes. They played one against the other, distributed favour and disfavour to suit their trading and expansionist agenda in South Asia. Following the contours of history and emergence of the British Empire on the skeletons of the Great Mughal Empire is not the thrust area of this volume. However, British requirement for intelligence in South Asia was prompted by consolidation of the Empire and its stability inside India and around its neighbourhood.

The impetus for evolving a proper intelligence gathering institution in British India evolved alongside its military progress and derived greater impetus after the abortive Sepoy Mutiny of 1857, exactly 100 years of British victory-by-Indian-default at Plassey, in 1757. At home the British felt the need for modernizing its intelligence infrastructure and ethos basically out of the Boer War disaster in South Africa between 1899 and 1903. The British went to South Africa without proper knowledge of the white Africaners' tenacity, their capability to live off the ground, expertise in guerrilla warfare. Post-Boer war experiences taught Britain that it lacked in institutionalization of the intelligence agencies, revamping the military intelligence systems and reequipping the internal and external intelligence gathering machineries. The existing British War Office was unable to handle all these national requirements of a vast colonial power. These lessons taught the British government the need for better Human Intelligence (HumInt), Signal Intelligence (SigInt) and other aspects of intelligence tradecrafts.

By 1910 competition started between the European powers over establishing hegemony in different parts of the colonial estates, over the seas and trade and commerce facilities. There was a general 'spy scare' amongst European nations. The ambience of mutual suspicion, rivalries were practically leading the nations to the doorstep of the First World War. Under these circumstances Britain appointed Haldane Committee to enquire into the extent of foreign intelligence against British interest.

The Haldane Committee Report had several components. It created a new Secret Service Bureau (SSB). It took over the Special

Section of the War Office at a national level. Other aspects of Haldane Committee were also the progenitors of the modern intelligence infrastructure in Britain. These new structures were divided into foreign and internal intelligence edifices. The historic MI5 was restructured as Security Services. The SIS was created out of the MI6. After the First World War in 1921 arrangements were made to attach more branches with SIS and Security Service to accommodate new requirements arising out of changing global situation. As the First World War gradually stepped into the Second World War the British system created an analogous body called 'Z Division' within the Directorate of Signal Intelligence Plans and Production. Post-World War II other structural changes were made in the British system. The other important wings of British intelligence systems are the Government Communications Headquarters (GCHQ), and Defence Intelligence Staff (DIS). These establishments work under the umbrella of Joint Intelligence Committee (JIC). The British intelligence agencies were given statutory status by the Security Services Act of 1989 and the Intelligence Services Act, 1994. The USA had provided constitutional status to the CIA in 1947 itself, the year it was created.

India (Imperial and post-independence) has basically followed the British pattern in respect of civilian and military intelligence. Apart from academic discussions on India's indigenous intelligence methodologies there are no recorded histories to indicate that India as a modern nation state had any other source of origin of its intelligence edifices. In fact, the modern concept of geopolitical India had taken shape after the British consolidated their colonial gains on different parts of the country. This volume deals with geopolitical Bharatvarsha and not cultural Bharat.

The British had followed three distinct policies about their intelligence infrastructure: a domestic policy, a policy for European countries and a separate policy for the colonies. India as the prized colony developed its intelligence apparatus along the contours of British internal, geopolitical and military interest in India and in its neighbourhood.

To understand the evolution of the Indian Intelligence Bureau, the oldest surviving intelligence agency of the world, it is necessary to peep into the process of evolution it has passed through. The Imperial government felt the need for organizing a strong military and civil intelligence outfit soon after its victory over the rebellious Indian forces in 1857. The victory had reposed multifaceted responsibility on the burgeoning British Crown and its ever expanding empire in India and neighbouring countries.

It had to effectively suppress the Muslim and Hindu rulers to consolidate and expand its territories; ensure law and order in the directly controlled and administered territories; maintain vigil on the territories ruled by native princes and to gather intelligence about friendly and hostile preparations of regimes in China, Afghanistan and the expanding empire of Russia. Defeat of the Mughal power had also brought about cascading political turmoil in other parts of the Muslim world in the Middle East, Africa and Southeast Asia.

There is a popular belief amongst the intelligence community that the Intelligence Bureau was conceived and set up as the "Central Special Branch" by an order of the Secretary of State for India in London, on December 23, 1887.

Some authors surmised that the first intelligence outfit in India was started in 1885 when Major General Sir Charles Metcalfe MacGregor was appointed Quartermaster General and head of the Intelligence Department of the Indian Army.

It was yet claimed that the Intelligence Bureau should trace its origins to the 'Anti-Thuggee and Dacoity Department' since its inception in 1835. This claim made by certain quarters in the intelligence fraternity is also not accurate.

The British Thuggee (roaming murderous cult group) concerns date back to 1828, due largely to the efforts of Lord William Bentinck, Governor General of India, who had started an extensive campaign involving profiling, intelligence gathering, intercepting and executions of the thuggee groups. The campaign was heavily based on informants recruited (Humint) from captured thuggs who were offered protection on the condition that they told everything that they knew.

By the 1870s, the thugg cult was extinct, but the concept of 'criminal tribes' and 'criminal castes' is still in use in India. A police organisation known as the 'Thugggee and Dacoity Department' was established within the Government of India, with Colonel William Sleeman appointed Superintendent of the department in 1835.

The Department remained in existence until 1904 when it was replaced by the Central Criminal Intelligence Department. It would, therefore, be seen that the Intelligence Bureau had equally inherited its origins to the Thugggee and Dacoity Department and to the 'Central Special Branch' established in London in December 1887.

While on the question of the thugggees it should be stated that even Ziau-d-Din Barni's *History of Firoz Shah* (written about 1356) had mentioned about the thugggee problem and creation of a special force in Delhi that had rounded up over 200 thuggs who were exiled to Lakhnauti (Laxmanabati-Gaur) in modern Bengal. The Emperor had not christened his special force as a Thugggee Department; nonetheless, he used more or less the same tactics as the British did centuries later.

In fact, very minor strand of Indian Intelligence fraternity was born in the womb of the Thugggee Department. It was given criminal investigation, military utility and political mandates from day one, soon after the British Crown set to the mission of consolidating and expanding Empire in India and territories around the first Colony in world history that showered manna on the entire western world. Intelligence was one of the arms used by the British to run their writs in India and other parts of global colonies. In this venture Indian intelligence and army helped the British more than the original sons of the Albion.

The need for the creation of this agency was realized for possessing early and authentic information by the Central Government regarding the political and social conditions of the people especially after the Indian Hindu gentry in Bengal, Maharashtra, Madras Presidency and some parts of the Central Provinces developed national fervour as a distinct aspiration for Indian nation. It was also to monitor the growth and development of popular feeling on issues concerned with security and keeping a watchful control over the inter-provincial activities and movements of criminals, communal affairs and the conditions that predisposed to crime.

The British, from 1906 itself followed some kind of federal structure for its territories in India. Under general supervision of the Governor General (Viceroy) the provinces were administered by the governors or lieutenant governors. The provinces administered their own crime control system and developed local criminal intelligence units, often with nomenclature like Criminal Investigation Department. Alongwith that the concept of provincial intelligence branches was conceived. The Intelligence Branch of Bengal at Lord Sinha Road and the Calcutta Metropolitan Police CID at Lal Bazaar were shaped by British to gather political intelligence and to suppress the nationalists and later the "Swadesi terrorists".

The tasks assigned to the Central Special Branch were to coordinate the working of the special branches of the provincial governments in British India, created under the same order of the Secretary of State, and to guide the new units set up directly under its own charge in the various princely states. The new organisation started functioning as a wing of 'Anti-Thugggee and Dacoity Department', which had attained notable success and renown since its inception in 1835 as an all-India outfit to contain the incipient terrorism of that period and subsequently took over its infrastructure. Since then, the nomenclature of the organisation underwent several changes.

As a result of the recommendation of the Police Commission of 1902–03, the Central Special Branch was remodelled and rechristened as the 'Central Criminal Intelligence Department', which was made responsible for all matters pertaining to national security in addition to its role in prevention of inter-provincial crime, and was designated as the nodal agency of the Government of India.

The word 'criminal' was dropped from the name of the organisation by 1918 as its natural security tasks started to far overshadow its criminal responsibilities. The present name, the *Intelligence Bureau*, was adopted by the organisation in the year 1920.

With the advent of the provincial governments in 1935, the Government of India decided that the Intelligence Bureau should have its own apparatus and arrangements for collecting strategic intelligence in the provinces, to augment the information supplied by the provincial CIDs and special branches.

Field units of the IB were thus organised in 1935, initially at six centres in the country, each under a Central Intelligence Officer, and subsequently elsewhere. The growth of national security problems and their increasing complexities led to the concept of setting up of Subsidiary Intelligence Bureau in the field, under the charge of assistant directors/deputy directors, in the fifties, to organize more scientific and systematic intelligence gathering. In the princely states the Central Intelligence Bureau offices were designated as Office of the Central Intelligence Officer (CIO). This nomenclature was ultimately dropped in early seventies.

The analytical and directional set-up at the Bureau's headquarters at Delhi also gradually grew, with newer and newer challenges and sources of threat to national security being identified over the years. There are several analysis desks, generally headed by a deputy director. The desks are allotted specific subjects and territories to collate, analyse and present the output to the apex point, who shares it with the consumer, the political policy makers.

Since its inception in the year 1887, the organisation has constantly striven to pursue the goal of maintaining the unity and integrity of the country; thwart the machinations of subversive elements, and defeat the forces of disruption and destabilisation. In the years prior to Independence, a good deal of the IB's effort was devoted to tackling problems of securing the boundaries of the country, preserving the basic essential services against disruption, and dealing with sustained militancy of organised groups. It had a cardinal role to play in maintaining communal order in the country especially when communal tempers frayed in various parts on the issue of Hindu-Muslim differences.

The IB was assigned tasks to keep track of the Hindu nationalists, especially the Swadesis, armed terrorist groups and Hindu groups having clandestine connection with foreign powers for procurement of arms and ammunitions. Similarly, consolidation of the Muslim separatist movement, clash of political interest and space between the Hindus and Muslims required the Intelligence Bureau to create separate desks for analysis and study of Hindu and Muslim communalism and impact of Pan-Islamism on Indian Muslims. These 'communal branches' had specific intelligence collection, collation, analysis and dissemination responsibilities.

Around 1925–30 the Intelligence Bureau was tasked to create a strong desk to study Indian communists, the comintern, International Socialist Movement and other related matters. The rise of Russia and its 'sphere of influence' clash with the British Empire had forced the British to strengthen the IB desks dealing with international communism. In brief, it can be said that the original study reports by Indian IB, if declassified, would offer to the world some best studies on international communism and roles of the Indian communists.

It was in this period that much of the formal shape was given to law enforcement on a countrywide scale and the IB played a significant role throughout 1935 in this process. From 1935 to 1947 the British practically ruled India on communal lines, pampering the Muslim leaders and haunting the Congress or Hindu nationalists. Though Congress continued to express belief in secularism the Muslims had rejected it and thus arose the enormous responsibility of the Hindu and Muslim officers of the IB to maintain neutrality and secular convictions. Very often reporting was biased and that created confusion at the analytical desks. However, the Empire was convinced that transfer of power could not be avoided and during and after the Second World War the truth had prompted the British to draw up a plan to transfer most sensitive IB files to London before the IB was bifurcated, Pakistan Intelligence Bureau and the Intelligence Bureau of India.

It was after 1947 that the IB really came into its own as the intelligence arm of new India; steeped in hoary traditions but with a modern outlook, which the new leaders of independent India had cultivated during the freedom struggle. It was soon to prove itself when the new nation-state faced a host of incipient upsurges of domestic nature as well as externally inspired attempts at subversion and external aggression.

Besides the inherent strength of the organisation, the caliber of its first two directors in the post-independence period, Shri TG Sanjeevi Pillai (also the first Indian to occupy that post) and his successor, the legendary 'Father of Intelligence' in modern India; Shri BN Mullik, largely enabled the IB to measure up to these new and unprecedented challenges. Between them, these two pioneers laid the foundation of a vibrant intelligence organisation giving a new dimension and dynamism to the newer thrust areas of its tasks and responsibilities. The IB was thus able to address itself to the complex security needs of a modern, democratic and forward looking nation, successfully withstanding the vicissitudes of time. The groundwork laid by them has enabled a string of their dedicated successors to build up the IB into a sophisticated intelligence apparatus in the succeeding decades.

Today, the Intelligence Bureau has to deal with a myriad of challenges such as terrorism, foreign inspired proxy-war, maoist insurrection, subversion and insurgency on the one hand, and espionage and subliminal attempts to undermine the democratic fabric of the country by external agencies, on the other. The organisation carries out forward and counter-intelligence operations against any incursion from hostile neighbouring countries or any of their client states. It maintains a lonely vigil through penny-packet posts on the Sino-Indian, Indo-Pak and Indo-Myanmar land borders, and also keeps track of developments and movements on the eastern and western sea borders of the country.

In the field of counter-intelligence, the IB has to deal with a far greater number of hostile intelligence agencies than any of its counterparts in other countries. There are no East-West or North-South divides in the area of spying and espionage, and while the nation sleeps, the operatives of the IB have to remain vigilant as a substantial part of espionage activity takes place in the hours of darkness. As for its successes in this sphere, despite the liberal traditions of the country and other handicaps the organisation's record of busting spy rings and capturing espionage agents has indeed been gratifying. In intelligence game it is taken for granted that for one success there could be five failures. Intelligence is not target shooting. Lots of things go in making up of the concept, ethos and functional infrastructures of intelligence collection, collation and analysis.

The responsibility of collection of foreign intelligence was given to the IB during the Second World War period only. Earlier it was mostly with the military intelligence. However the organisation made tremendous strides within a few years in this field and by the mid-1950s concerted intelligence about Pakistan's intentions and capabilities for instance, had achieved a sophisticated dimension. With India developing into a major nation state, strategic intelligence collection outside the country was handed over to a new organisation carved out from the IB, as a whole-time responsibility, in September 1968.

In the sphere of combating insurgency, notwithstanding the initial lack of sufficient experience, the IB had been able to devise, by the late 1950s and more so from the mid-1960s, a counter-insurgency doctrine of its own. It is substantially different from the conventional wisdom based on the Malaysian or Vietnamese experience and has enabled the IB to play a significant role in containing insurgent movements in several parts of the country. In the arena of counter-terrorism, another relatively new field of action, the IB again displayed quick adaptability. Despite major handicaps including its rather thin organisational spread on the ground, the Bureau has striven hard to make its contribution in this major war of the nation against the most serious threat to the country's stability and peace.

The security functions of the IB are perhaps one of the less heralded areas of its tasks. Personnel and document security are today among the most important responsibilities of a security agency in any modern nation state. In this sphere of its tasks, the security checks and vetting procedures of the Bureau and the countermeasures evolved by it have been acknowledged by several foreign agencies as amongst the best in the world, excepting perhaps those possible in a totalitarian or authoritarian society. Security of key industries and vital installations was also an important charge of the IB. Besides its responsibilities relating to conceptualization of threats and devising of countermeasures to protect these national assets against sabotage and other disruptive attempts, the Bureau had a built-in provision for an early warning system whenever portents of serious industrial unrest are present. Later, this execution part of the job was handed over to the Central Industrial Security Force (CISF).

In the sphere of border management IB deployed its check posts all along the Indo-Pak, Indo-China, Indo-Bangladesh, and Indo-Myanmar borders. Negotiating very difficult terrain, hostile living conditions (often in tents) and facing insurgency the young IB officers discharged their duties dedicatedly. Later, the primary duty of physical manning of the Indo-Pak and Indo-Bangladesh borders were given over to a new force 'Border Security Force' raised after Pakistan attacked India in Kachh area. The State Armed Police Forces were not adequate to stop Pakistani attacks and incursions. Following this the Border Security Force was established on December 1, 1965 and KF Rustomji, a pillar of Indian police headed and added more flesh and bones to the new organisation.

In the sphere of VIP security, the IB is responsible not only for the perception and conceptualization of all threats to important personages including the Prime Minister, President and other Indian dignitaries as well as other internationally protected personalities, but also for drawing up the 'Blue Books' and other guidelines for ensuring their security. Later, the VIP security branch of the IB was converted into Special Protection Group (SPG), after the tragic assassination of Srimati Indira Gandhi, in 1985. The VIP security section of the IB still functions as an intelligence generating unit.

In its role as the premier intelligence-cum-security agency of the country, the IB has to service the various ministries and departments of the Union Government with timely intelligence inputs and advice on all aspects of national security. Ever since their inception in 1935 the IB's field units have sought to play a somewhat similar role vis-a-vis the state governments. Such efforts, aimed at an interchange of information to effectively meet any grave threat to public peace and internal security, take place at several levels — regular interactions with chief ministers and governors, maintaining regular liaison with the chief and home secretaries, and direct involvement with the DG Police and state intelligence and police officials.

The purpose of this volume is not to explain different segments, branches, units, operations etc of the Intelligence Bureau, the Research and Analysis Wing (of the Cabinet Secretariat), and other auxiliary units and forces.

However, it must be added here that unlike its western counterparts like the UK, the USA, Germany and France, India has not done much to examine, analyse, retrofit and reboot its intelligence agencies. After the Emergency regime of Indira Gandhi was removed the new government appointed LP Singh Committee to examine the 'alleged shameful and partisan' activities of the IB and RAW. This report has never been made public.

After Pakistan's Kargil attack in 1999 the government had set up Kargil Review Committee under K Subrahmaniam. This report was supposed to point out failures of IB, RAW and the military intelligence directorate. The voluminous report was heavily edited and blacked out for alleged security considerations. Its recommendations have not been published and actions suggested not yet implemented.

The latest exercise was the appointment of Task Force on Intelligence in 2001 under GC Saxena, former chief of the RAW. Its study report and recommendations have also not been made public and recommendations not implemented. There has been some tinkering here and there since 1999 when the post of National Security Advisor, National Security Council (NSC), Advisory Body to the NSC and revamped Joint Intelligence Committee etc had come up. However, at the basic functional and structural level very little has been done to provide the intelligence generating agencies with adequate wherewithal and most modern scientific gadgetry. We would discuss these aspects as and when we proceed with discussions on various departments and tolls of tradecraft of the intelligence community.

References

1. MB Chande, *Kautilya's Arthashastra*, Atlantic Publishers and Distributors, Delhi, p. 21.

2. Christopher Andrew, *Secret Intelligence, A reader*: Routledge, p.1.

3. Mark M Lowenthal, *(2002), Intelligence: From Secrets to Policy*, (Washington, Congressional Quarterly Press, p. 8.

4. Commission on Organisation of the Executive Branch of the Government, *Intelligence Activities*, June 1955, p. 25.

5. Commission on the Roles and Capabilities of the United States Intelligence Community, *Preparing for the Twenty-First Century: An Appraisal of US Intelligence*, Washington DC, Government Printing Press, 1996, p. 5.

6. Martin T Bimfort, *A Definition of Intelligence: Intelligence as a Service*, 1958, p. 76.

7. Michael Warner, *A Definition of Intelligence*. Incorporated in Secret Intelligence, A Reader, edited by Christopher Andrew, Richard J Aldrich and Wesley K Wark, p. 9.

Chapter 2

Indian Intelligence and the Handling Officer

Readers may have queries about the functional structure of the Intelligence Bureau and the Research and Analysis Wing. For security reasons in-depth details cannot be disclosed. Broadly speaking, the Intelligence Bureau is headquartered at New Delhi, with Director IB as the head and cascading ranks of senior officers styled as special director, additional director, joint director, deputy director, assistant director, deputy central intelligence officer, and assistant central intelligence officer. The officers of the levels of assistant director to DIB are normally represented by the officers of Indian Police Service. The other ranks are directly recruited by the IB; though at least 40% of direct recruit officers normally reach the level of deputy central intelligence officer (DCIO) and about 5-10 per cent climb up the ladder from assistant director to joint director.

The structural formation of the RAW is almost similar. However, the nomenclatures of the hierarchy are designated as secretary, special secretary, joint secretary, deputy secretary, DFO, AFO, etc.

The Intelligence Bureau works under the Union home ministry, while the RAW is supposed to work under the Cabinet Secretariat. Thus, RAW has more functional freedom than the Intelligence Bureau, which has to obtain approval of the home ministry and other concerned ministries in matters of provisioning its human resources, communication, technical, etc. requirements. Since the ministries are notoriously slow in understanding security and intelligence requirement of the country and the bureaucratic hierarchy are insensitive to the urgency of the requirements, the IB has often to suffer for years together.

Besides its headquarters in Delhi, the Intelligence Bureau has its presence in all states and union territories of the union. These units are called Subsidiary Intelligence Bureau. The SIBs may have sub-units at district, sub-division and tehsil levels depending on sensitivity of the state. In the bordering states the IB had, in the past, rings of Border Check Posts (BCPs). These were later taken over by the RAW. However, some of the sensitive BCPs are still manned by the IB for gathering internal intelligence. The RAW is supposed to concentrate on foreign intelligence, carry out border patrolling on its own and cultivate human assets on either side of the border.

For example, the BCPs in Arunachal, Nagaland, Manipur, Sikkim, Uttar Pradesh, Gujarat, and Rajasthan are supposed to be manned by both the IB and the RAW. When IB exclusively exercised control on the BCPs, it used to carry out summer and winter reconnaissance along the border for tell-tale signs of human movements across the international borders, intrusion by Chinese, Pakistani army and intelligence contingents. The IB raised strings of human assets to patrol and observe the border areas and report to the nearest BCP. It is alleged that after the RAW took over the responsibilities, these aspects of intelligence generation are not diligently attended. Many observers cite the glaring lapse of the RAW in Kargil-Drass sector in Jammu & Kashmir, where the Pakistani Army and jihadis took advantage of casual attitude of the RAW officers and agents and the army units and had established fortified posts on Indian side of the LoC.

The Intelligence Bureau units in the states are, by convention and executive direction, required to maintain liaison with the state intelligence units. The same practice is applicable to lower units as well whenever the information is related to imminent law and order situation, terrorist activities and acts of communal violence. Till 1990 such interactions between the states and the IB were sporadic and lackadaisical. The quality and frequency of exchanges depended on the political colour of the government in Delhi and the states. This is a piquant and embarrassing situation. Political masters are also the policy makers and decision takers. For example, a Congress government in Delhi may like to handle a particular ethnic insurgency, and terrorism in a particular manner. The state government, say a Communist one, may not like the policy of the Centre. This was clearly discernible during the initial Gorkhaland agitation in West Bengal. The state government rather suggested that the ethnic problem in the Darjeeling district was engineered by the Congress. Similarly the Assam Gono Parishad (AGP) managed government alleged that the BODO ethnic insurgency in the State was seeded and watered by the Congress government in Delhi. In a unitary federation such clash of political interest often renders the task of the IB very difficult. Many scholars have, therefore, raised questions that the intelligence agencies should be regulated by Acts of Parliament, made responsible to Parliamentary Overseeing Committee and the Constitution should be amended to prune state's jurisdiction on the police and state intelligence. Some constitutionally approved mechanism should be set up for institutional exchange of intelligence irrespective of political colour of the government. As we walk into the aspects of tradecraft of intelligence an attempt should be made to examine the parameters of intelligence activities in India.

The Intelligence Bureau is solely responsible for internal intelligence relating to internal security. The IB has, therefore, different layers of responsibilities. This may not conform to the Charter of Duty formulated by the ministry of home affairs. The Charter is used more as a defensive armour than a strict rule of business. Many a time the director IB prioritizes the focus, depending what are the hottest demands from the consumers. For example, Maoist turbulence in West Bengal and Chattisgarh may be assigned priority for a few weeks and the focus may shift to Mumbai 26/11 like incident for a few other weeks.

The Charter of Duty is drawn up by the home ministry in consultation with the DIB and with the approval of the prime minister. The Charter had laid, during Pandit Nehru's regime, maximum emphasis on coverage of the Indian communist movement and international communism. During Indira Gandhi's regime it was changed and during her emergency regime all charters were withdrawn and the IB worked as an appendage to the PMO as was the case with the RAW.

Later, around 1988 the Charter was reframed and Punjab disturbances, Kashmir, Assam student upheaval, ULFA movement, etc. received priority. Now the emphasis has shifted to the coverage of subversive thrusts from Pakistan and the Maoist movement. Keeping in view the changing perceptions of threat to national security I would prefer to prioritize the burning issues in the following manner:

1. Insurgency and ethnic terrorism in the northeastern states.

2. Pakistan inspired and subsidized jihadi proxy war in Jammu and Kashmir.

3. Pakistan (often Bangladesh) inspired jihadi violence in the mainland India against selected targets.

4. Maoist turbulence in several states.

5. Sabotage and subversion of loyalty of Indian Muslims by Pakistan jihadists who want further vivisection of India and international Islamic terrorism as promoted by the Taliban and al Qaeda.

6. Muslim and Hindu communalism, coverage of Muslim and Hindu organisations.

7. Hindu, Christian clashes over conversion matters in general.

8. Activities of the political parties (basically opposition).

9. Labour, student, youth affairs, industrial unrest, agrarian unrest.

10. Security, including of government documents, premises, vulnerable places, installations and areas, important, very important and very important person's security.

11. Coastal security, general border security and intelligence regarding induction of terrorists, weapons and drugs.

12. Mafia activities including Hawala transfer of money to and from the country.

13. Regional movements like Gorkhaland movement, Telengana movement, etc.

14. Activities in agricultural sector, market trends, public reaction (introduced by Indira Gandhi).

15. Left and regional political parties.

16. General affairs and developments in the state.

17. Counter-intelligence matters.

This volume would make no effort to discuss each and every item of the Charter of Duty, as serialized above. However, detailed comments would be made about counter-intelligence affairs in a separate chapter. For certain reasons I would refrain from making comments on the Charter of Duty and ways and means of execution of India's External Intelligence.

How does the Intelligence Bureau discharge its duties to the country? Before the tools of the tradecraft are discussed, let us discuss what resources the Intelligence Bureau has been endowed with for giving satisfactory coverage of the vast subjects.

It may be recalled that an intelligence agency is accountable to the consumer and in certain countries to the Congress and the Parliament. In India the intelligence agencies are accountable only to the home minister, prime minister and to some extent the minister for external affairs. Other ministries are tertiary consumers and the agencies are not answerable to them. Nearest accountability of the Intelligence Bureau to the Parliament is answering to certain queries by the Standing Committee of the Parliament in ministry of home affairs. That exercise is more of an eyewash. The RAW does not have to answer about its activities to any standing committee of the Parliament.

As was mentioned earlier the upper echelon of the Intelligence Bureau are drawn from the Indian Police Service, a tradition followed from British days. Certain specialized posts are manned by experts drawn in the concerned field.

The grassroots operatives are the directly recruited officers of the rank of assistant intelligence officer-Grade II, equivalent to a sub-inspector of police. Some police officers are also taken on deputation from different state police forces. A few officers from the armed forces are also taken on deputation for special jobs.

Recruited through open advertisement and competition the crème of the universities normally join the job after several layers of screening. They are made to undergo intensive physical training, arms training, and mountaineering. The IB has a few Everest climbers in its rank, though this aspect like many other laurels of the IB is not advertised. The cadets have to undergo intensive training in computer operations, tradecrafts of intelligence and counter-intelligence and they are encouraged to learn one or more regional languages. To acclimatize with the policing system of the country the cadet officers are exposed to police training for a short duration. Thereafter, they are normally posted out to tougher assignments to borders and checkposts. After normal five years of baking under tougher circumstances and forced living with odds and difficult conditions they are posted out to field assignments according to priority assigned by the establishment.

This small paragraph is not enough to describe the entire training and grooming process. But to make a recruit cadet an intelligence officer it normally takes three years. The Intelligence Bureau can take on maximum 100 cadets for training in a year in its existing facilities. Moreover, recruitment against vacancies cannot be made by the DIB. He has to obtain sanction of the ministry. For example, over 6000 vacancies had occurred a decade ago. The ministerial sanction to fill up the vacancies came in the aftermath of the 26/11. The original proposal by GC Saxena Committee had recommended a working strength of 30,000 personnel in 2001. After eight years, the hardcore working strength of the IB is not more than ten thousand. We propose to discuss the deficiencies in a separate chapter. Here it would be suffice to comment that the present open market recruitment may bring in the best university students; but the best student does not always make the best intelligence officer. Sometime a less educated daredevil person can deliver better results.

In India, especially the officers of the Intelligence Bureau are known as 'Officer' and not as an 'agent' or a 'spy' or operator. The tradition of equating IB ranks with that of the police and the political ethos of equating the IB with a police establishment right from the

British days has led to this officialization of the operative hands of the IB. This historic shackling to babudom may suit the political consumers. But, if the trends in intelligence agencies of the free countries are studied it would be seen that the intelligence services have been delinked from police ethos and bonds and have been uplifted to the strata of intelligence operatives. One has to live with certain historic follies but some observations would be made in later chapters about changing the ethos of the intelligence community from police orientation to superior operational orientations, thus delinking the babu philosophy from the intelligence fraternity.

In Indian intelligence agencies the cutting edge 'officer', 'agent' is the personnel from ACIO (II) to DCIO ranks. In RAW the same practice is followed with changed nomenclature. Often, in rare cases, enterprising IPS officers either in the headquarters or station in charges handle very delicate and top level agents. Here we must state that the officers who generate intelligence, especially HumInt, are designated as 'handling officers.' In CIA and other agencies they are often called 'case officers' and even 'agents.' For Indian scenario we would use the nomenclature 'handling officer'.

These handling officers are required to learn various tradecrafts to discharge their duties. In intelligence gathering field the vista is wide and the canvas is without any horizon. However, there are a few broad classifications of intelligence gathering tools which are practised by the agencies world over. These are:

- Human Intelligence (HumInt)
- Technical Intelligence (TechInt)
- Signals Intelligence (SigInt)
- Satellite Intelligence (SatInt)
- Electronic Intelligence (ElInt)
- Communication Intelligence (ComInt)
- Imagery Intelligence (ImInt)
- Computer Intrusion Intelligence (CominInt)
- Measurement and Signatures Intelligence (MasInt)
- Open-Source Intelligence (OsInt)

As we proceed we would examine each one of these in greater details. It is, however, stated that Technical Intelligence has various components. These would be discussed later.

Ask any veteran of the intelligence community and he would say, 'human intelligence is the toughest of all'. It really is. Human intelligence is gathered by 'officers trained in intelligence tradecraft from human sources, agents and contacts'.

Let us give some emphasis on the 'gatherer-collector' of HumInt. Certain concepts have been developed over thousands of years about the quality of an HumInt gatherer. Even in classical dissertations by Kautilya these characteristics have been detailed. The intelligence gathering system has a cyclic process. It does not work in isolation, on the basis of a single officer's heroic efforts. In modern concept: "The 'intelligence cycle' is a phrase used to capture the idea of a seamless process by which states manage the vast knowledge-intense industries which constitute their intelligence communities. The traditional cycle begins with the targeting of collection assets, be they human spies or satellites. Once raw intelligence has been collected it is processed, validated, analysed and discussed. Thereafter, a much reduced selection of material is passed to the hard-pressed policy maker in order to inform their decisions"*.

The statement appears to be crisp. Indeed it is. However, behind the 'intelligence cycle' is rooted the 'hunter gatherer' — the trained officer of the intelligence agency. It is necessary to understand this creature, often erroneously described as an agent. He is also described as a 'handler' and 'case officer'.

Let us use the phrase 'handling officer' a more honourable phrase to describe the trained officer of the agency. He is required to be well educated, preferably fluent in different languages besides his mother tongue. Suppose the officer is from Hindi speaking area and he is to work in Assam, Nagaland and Manipur, it is a must that the officer has fluent capability to speak and communicate in these languages. During my tenure in Manipur, Nagaland and Assam I had noticed with great alarm that officers from Bengal, Hindi belt, western India and south India were straightaway posted out after their probation period to remote border areas. Manipuri language, known as Meiteilon is a unique language with mixture of Thai-Chinese fragrance and some admixture of Sanskrit and Bengali. Agency officers normally used Hindi for communication — a language hated too much in the northeast. I could convince only a couple of officers to learn Meiteilon. In the hills the Nagas conversed in their own dialect, or Nagamese (mixture of Assamese and local dialect). In Manipur hills they also used Meitei language. Some agency officers managed to learn Nagamese and a few words of Tangkhul or Mao or Zeliang words. Lack of knowledge of local language and culture impeded intelligence gathering enormously. Their success rate was restricted to 40 per cent. Had they known the languages of the local population and learnt basics of their culture and tradition they could have gained minimum 75 per cent success.

My personal experience taught me that lack of knowledge of local language often leads to being trapped by local officers, who collected overt information from open sources (OsInt) and tried to pass on as

*Secret Intelligence: A Reader ibid, p. 21.

'secret intelligence.' After I managed to learn Meitei, Nagamese and Kuki languages within six months my local officers respected me more and I could easily infiltrate the local communities identifying myself with their cultures. I carried this lesson with me when I was posted to a foreign destination with sizable Sikh population. At the height of separatist movement in Punjab, the Gurdwaras and Sikh community congregations became rife with vicious propaganda that turned the ignorant Sikhs against India. It took me four months to learn reading and writing the language and speaking fluently in six months. That made my job easier. I gained easy access to the community alienated from India. This knowledge stood me in good stead when I was entrusted with operations works in Punjab.

Great emphasis is required to be given in language skill. A Hindi speaking 'handling officer' cannot easily operate anywhere in south India or even in a state like Maharashtra.

Let us presume that our 'handling officer' X is a language expert. The next quality he requires is adequate knowledge of the 'target area' from where he is required to pick up an agent, test him, cultivate him and win him over. Suppose the 'handling officer' has been assigned to target a particular human asset from a Naxal (Maoist) organisation in a disturbed area, he should have more than sufficient briefing about the Maoist organisation, its activities and as much as detailed data on the 'targeted person.' Here comes the role of the 'bridging officer.' The 'bridging officer' is the person in the hierarchy who is assigned the target by the desk in charge or the concerned analyst. The 'bridging officer' himself can be a 'handling officer' in certain cases. But in this case he bridges the 'handling officer' to the desk in charge or the analyst. He is required to motivate the 'handling officer', educate him, brief him about probable strategy to be adopted to approach the 'targeted person' and map him further for evaluation of his potential.

The 'unit head' should have adequate knowledge about the Maoist organisation, its structural formation and operational strategy. He should also have adequate knowledge about the 'target' assigned to the 'handling officer'. The 'unit head' cannot one fine morning wake up and decide that it was time to penetrate the Maoist organisation. He must have brainstorming sessions with his 'desk officer' and the 'analyst' and get briefed about the specific requirement. At no time the 'unit head' or the 'handling officer' should raise contacts and agents just to prove that they were competent and had the initiative to enrich the agency's inventory of agents. Organised intelligence does not work on such premises. If such a situation is allowed to grow then the agency would soon be flooded with ghost agents against whom the 'handling officers' draw fat secret service funds.

The 'desk officer' or the 'analyst' is required to brief the 'unit head' about the precise requirement. They also suggest alternative targets if the desired target is not accessible. The 'unit head' in turn has to brief the 'handling officer' and assign him the target with cautionary instructions that the target should be approached after he has completely mapped him.

For the 'handling officer' mapping a target is the most difficult task. He has to survey the uncharted territory around the target, locate him, study his patterns of movements, places he visits, persons he contacts, his family and his personal style of living. These preliminary exercises may take six months before the 'handling officer' can discover a window through which he can establish contact with the target. Such a window may be a journalist friend, a family member, another overground worker, etc.

I would discuss penetration of different kinds of agents through different methodologies of tradecraft. Here we abandon the Maoist target and move on with the 'handling officer'. The 'handling officer', therefore, has to be well conversed with the subject he is tasked to deal with. This requires systematic reading habit and selected studies of areas of operations he is supposed to encounter. I have the tragic experience of handling 'handling officers' posted in Assam, having no knowledge of Assamese language, basic structure of the United Liberation Force of Assam (ULFA) and tragically, having no idea about Assamese ways of life. It took me several weeks to apprise them of the coarse points and teaching them preliminaries of Assamese language and their way of life. Intelligence agencies, especially the Intelligence Bureau and the RAW have not inculcated the time tested doctrine of preparing an officer with regional peculiarities before dumping him in a geographical area. Especially in India, a nation of vast varieties, such mindless dumping can be counterproductive. The headcount of physical strength may be reached, but the cutting edge officers may not emerge from such dumping practice. Unfortunately, this has been the trend of functioning of the two prime agencies.

The 'handling officer' has to bury his ego. At no point of time he should brag about his success in raising an important agent and handling vast number of sensitive agents. The departmental canteens, briefing rooms, and other common places of social contacts provide opportunities to blurt out success stories. Such tendencies are not confined to lower ranks. I had the misfortune of working in Punjab with a senior colleague, who was operationally efficient but his hunger for instant recognition prompted him to pad up his success stories and present the 'controlling officer' or the 'top man' with highly exaggerated version of his achievements. He often misappropriated the success stories of his junior colleagues. Obviously, he had his ways, and was recognized with awards he did not earn or deserve. However, in the process, because of his advertising tendency, the agency lost at least six top level agents to the bullets of the terrorists.

The 'handling officer', be he a junior operative or a senior officer, should bury his ego. His achievements are recorded in the tablets of the department and his reportage justifies the depth and extent of his success. Such an officer is not supposed to disclose his operations even to his wife and children. To live with sac full of secrets is a professional burden that an intelligence officer has to live with.

The 'handling officer' should imbibe humble habits. He should not dress gaudily to be conspicuous, and exhibit amiability even under provocative circumstances. A smile hanging from his face, like a trained actor, may go a long way in making him acceptable in difficult circumstances. If he prefers to have an alcoholic drink he may not do so in a pub. Drinking in private or in the presence of other colleagues may not be that harmful. If he prefers to have a girlfriend, supposing he is not married, he should be careful of the girl he chooses. In the recent past, it came to notice that some senior operatives of the two prime agencies were compromised as a foreign intelligence agency embedded in its embassy in Delhi was successful in planting attractive girls on them. Such forward intelligence operations by embassy based intelligence operatives is an expected phenomenon. Indian counter-intelligence agencies took considerable time to detect such happy-go-lucky flamboyant officers and neutralize them. One of the agency officers, however, succeeded in duping the counter-intelligence sleuths and escaping to the USA.

There should be an in-house periodical 'security vetting' institution which should keep track of officer's personal lives, accretion of wealth by them and their personal lifestyle. There exists such mechanism only in name. This has gone into disuse over three decades ago. Perhaps such 'zebra units' are essential for all intelligence agencies to spy on their own officers.

In real life ground operations it came to my notice that a particular officer, efficient in pleasing superiors by offering personal services, had accumulated considerable wealth. Though a ranker, he had managed to amass huge assets. A discreet enquiry was instituted; it was revealed that he was indulging in real estate business and man-power export activities. Such tendencies of indulging in private business, while being on the ranks of the agency, are rampant. Particularly the Intelligence Bureau of India is highly polluted by such unethical practices by 'unit heads', 'case officers' and innumerable personnel not contributing to intelligence generation.

The 'handling officer' is expected to be a superb actor. He should be able to act naturally to convince his target that he is one of his ilks and he is on the same wavelength with the target as far as his ideological commitment is concerned. The 'handling officer' should be able to elevate or parallel his approach to the level of the ideological orientation of the target to soften his ideological diaphragm. I have experienced this in the case of hardened Naxal, Naga and Meitei separatists. An insurgent or a terrorist believes or is made to believe in certain value system. The 'handling officer' is not required to believe in those values, but he should be able to act so perfectly and keep the cover intact till he is able to convince the target that they both believe in the 'cause', and they can agree to work for mutual benefit. Gradual melting of the ideological or personal diaphragm is a difficult process. But it works if the 'handling officer' is able to act in a sustained manner even to the misunderstanding of his colleagues. Only his 'unit head' or the 'desk officer' should know what part of the script he was acting at what point of cultivation of the target.

Besides being an actor, the 'handling officer' is required to learn the tactics and trade secrets of an excellent marketing manager or a salesman. There are several reasons for a spy to agree to work for an agency. These will be elaborated later. But, whatever the deal is, the 'case officer' has to sell the idea to the targeted spy or agent to purchase the bait out of certain motivation. The cliché that everything has a price is basically a cardinal trick for the intelligence community. The 'handling officer' should be able to sell the idea convincingly, often wrapping up the decoy with gold and silver, and trap the target. Once the bait is accepted the targeted agent in all probability will not walk back. There are tricks that can convince him that his walking back may compromise him in a devastating manner, ruining his life and career inexorably. Only blackmailing tactics are not involved in this process. We shall discuss the elements that create vulnerability in an agent, in a later chapter.

Merging with the background like a chameleon is another sterling qualification of a 'handling officer.' Suppose the 'handling officer' has to visit a mosque or a gurdwara to meet the target, he should be well conversed with the rituals observed inside the mosque or gurdwara and behave as if he was a true Muslim or a Sikh. He may even has to break 'ramadan iftar' with the Muslim target or sit by the side of his target in a gurdwara langar. Religious, social and cultural rituals in India vary significantly. I have often prayed alongside Naga targets inside churches and frequently visited Meitei temples and social rituals to convince them that I want to be a part of their community belief. Some of the 'handling officers' were taught these tricks and they were able to merge satisfactorily in the assigned societal canvas. In a particular case, a junior 'handling officer' even married a Naga lady and lived with the community freely. That operation had given the agency excellent dividend in the manner of surrender of two battalions of underground 'Naga Army.' In another case an officer was given sustained training in Muslim rituals, Urdu language and was made to seek admission in a suspect madrasa. He maintained the cover for over a decade and delivered excellent 'human assets' to the agency.

Finally, I prescribe steely nerves and nonchalant appearance and indomitable courage as the important shields of a 'handling officer.' In the process of pursuing a target in difficult missions, very dangerous situations may crop up unexpectedly. The targets in difficult areas are capable of ascribing any ill-motive on the part of the 'handling officer' and accost him with violent force. Loss of nerve and expression of fear may jeopardise the 'handling officer's life. He should maintain calm and explain the circumstances and convince the target that his interpretation of the situation is not correct. Such situation may often arise while operating in insurgency and terrorism infested areas.

An example would make these attributes of the 'handling officer' clearer. While negotiating with a Mizo underground 'army commander' an important Kuki leader was used as a mediator. A meeting was fixed up in a remote hill village for convincing the Mizo commander to surrender. Things went according to plan and I, accompanied by a junior officer and a driver, reached the village. Accidentally, an Indian army column had passed by that village just before our arrival. The moment we landed in the village armed Mizo 'soldiers' surrounded us. The driver was tied to a tree and someone accosted me with an automatic rifle on my chest. After lot of heated argument he agreed to call the 'commander.' He demanded to know why Indian army was in the area when he was supposed to meet me. I coolly explained that I did not command the Indian army and it was unworthy of him to deploy 50 Mizo 'soldiers' to kill one unarmed Indian official. That shamed him, my driver was unchained and we were treated to a chicken lunch and later talks continued for hours. This finally resulted in the surrender of a full battalion of the underground Mizo army operating in Manipur Mizo areas. In retrospect, I think my cool had unnerved the Mizo 'army commander.' Loss of nerve, even when bullets fly, can be more killing than being hit by a hot bullet.

The 'handling officer' must be truthful and absolutely objective while obtaining the raw intelligence from his agent and debriefing him clinically. He must maintain good humour and must not irritate the agent while debriefing. Once the debriefing is successful the 'handling officer' must task the agent succinctly and explain what is expected of him. Clarity in briefing and debriefing improves the confidence level of the agent and his respect for the 'handling officer' gets augmented. Poor briefing and debriefing inject a tendency in the agent to bluff the handler. The agent is also an intelligent person and he all the time evaluates the capability of his handler. If he gathers an impression that the handler is not honest in money matters, does not keep his promise, does not give him bonus points for excellent performance he starts developing dislike for the 'handling officer' and starts bluffing him. Such devastating situation can only be saved by sharp examination of the raw intelligence by the 'unit head' and the 'desk officer'. They can discern deficiency in the reports and interrogate the 'handling officer'. Over time the 'handling officers' develop a tendency to 'pad up' the raw intelligence with a view to impress the seniors or the higher consumers. Post- 9/11 examination of the performances of the CIA, NSA, and MI6, etc. proved to be highly questionable. The operatives and the 'case officers' had padded up scanty or no information at all to suit the already adopted policy of the policy makers. They all erred on Iraq's WMD issue and padded up intelligence gave initial advantage on the policy makers to declare war on Iraq.

The 'handling officers' should have the moral courage to convey the raw truth as gleaned out from agent operations and information obtained from other sources even if such raw intelligence does not suit the policy or policies already framed up by the policy makers. The policy makers, being political heads have the privilege to take the adverse raw information into consideration to augment success of the policy or ignore such raw adverse intelligence and take eggs in face as happened to President Bush and Prime Minister Tony Blair.

It happened in India also. During the 'emergency regime' of Indira Gandhi, both IB and RAW supplied her with information that only pleased her. She even used these agencies for political vendetta and to arrest and torture her political opponents. All these details were unearthed by the Shah Commission. We need not to go into the details. The subsequent government had appointed a committee for intelligence reform under LP Singh. Unfortunately the report is gathering dust in the archives of the IB and the home ministry.

The 'handling officer' should be able to stand up to his dignity and professional ethics. This criterion is applicable mostly in case of 'honey trap' operations, against himself and against foreign or internal targets. In counter-intelligence cases the 'handling officer' getting hooked by a female mole planted by the counter-counter-intelligence operators is very common. In India three such cases were detected involving three senior officers of the prime Indian agencies. These intelligence operators did immense damage to the country just for casual sexual pleasure followed by blackmail.

The other side of the story is 'honey traps' recruited by Indian agencies to trap internal or external targets. Such 'honies' often 'trap' the 'handling officer'. These officers exploit the recruits for personal pleasure. Such proclivities lead to obfuscation of objectivity of the 'handling officer' and often the targeted subject use the 'honey trap' as a double agent. There are too many such incidents recorded in the CIA and KGB operations. In Indian context it can be mentioned that when I took over charge of a particular counter-intelligence unit, one intermediate level officer whispered in my ears that the unit had several 'honey trap' assets and if I wished I could avail of their 'service.' Obviously I immediately shunted out the officer to an insignificant assignment. I have no regret that I could not lick the honey, reportedly tasted by my predecessor.

These comments make clear that a 'handling officer' or 'operations officer' is required to be totally incorruptible and he should be trained as a Spartan dedicated person. Such qualities are instilled with intensive training, brainwashing, in-service briefing and strict watch on the in-office and out of office life patterns of the officer. Sounds atrocious! The ideal situation is like this. However, in real life the prime agencies can boast of having only 25 per cent of their 'handling officers' made of such spartan staff. The rest are superficial and often peripheral. Therefore, when it is mentioned that an agency has the strength of 30,000, it should be understood that merely 10,000 would be in intelligence production range and only 7000 could have all the qualities counted above. The making of an intelligence officer, is, therefore, a Herculean task. We shall discuss this in the next chapters.

Chapter 3

Making of
an Intelligence Officer

In the previous chapter we have discussed the characteristics of a '
'handling officer.' In this chapter we propose to discuss the making
of an intelligence officer or operative. What goes in making of an
intelligence officer? In India, unlike the USA, Russia and other
countries, the recruitment process is different. Instead of open market
talent scouting from universities, different walks of life, ex-service
men or promising police officers India has opted for recruitment
through service commissions. As stated earlier the crème of the
universities appear in the examinations and are recruited according
to merit lists. The process is democratic and devoid of any corruption.
However, out of the total open market recruitment the agency should
be given the privilege of recruiting through its own talent search in
at least 40 per cent cases. Talent hunting is a crucial task and it is
accomplished by trial and error method. Perhaps this positive aspect
of discretional recruitment is not understood by the controlling
ministry and the administrative bureaucracy. As we commented
earlier the best student may not make a good intelligence operator.
It is heartening to hear that the government is evaluating this request
with sympathy.

The physical training is rigorous. This is meant for toughening
up the raw material and for preparing them to face multifarious
vicissitudes during service career. Aspects of allied trainings include
handling of communication equipment, computers and other technical
gadgets. Thereafter, the recruits are subjected to intensive tradecraft
training. Tradecraft training equips the recruited officers to graduate
to intelligence operators, primarily responsible for gathering
grassroots intelligence from assigned target areas. The main
ingredients of tradecraft training are:

- Political, geopolitical and geostrategic briefing
- Agent creation
- Agent meeting
- Agent communication training
- Agent dropping technique
- Memory training
- Concealment training
- Surveillance
- Secret enquiry
- Operations
- Technical operations
- Security matters
- Preparation of secret reports
- Basics of assessment process, etc.

It is admitted that in the arrays of intelligence terminologies like Human Intelligence (HumInt), Technical Intelligence (TechInt), Electronic Intelligence (ElInt), Satellite Intelligence (SatInt), Communication Intelligence (ComInt), etc., HumInt is treated as the most important and difficult territory.

Human assets are assigned as targets. They are cultivated by the 'handling officers'; rated by the organisation and tried. Once the trial is satisfactory the human talent is recruited as an agent. This can be a tedious process. Human assets are not readily available to work for flimsy motivation. He is often reluctant. To make a target amenable to suggestions to work as a secret agent various spices of tradecraft are applied.

Agents are of different categories:

Casual Agents are low level recruits/assets located in a target organisation with whom 'handling officers' establish clandestine or open contacts for ferreting out information of topical interest through conscious or casual discussions. These categories of assets can be identified and cultivated after assignments are awarded by the analyst or desk officer to the 'handling officer.' These low level assets are located in the media, peripheral locations of targeted organisations, and members of parliament, legislatures and even the mundane static or roving hawkers. Such casual contacts may also be cultivated amongst the relatives and friends of the main target for obtaining basic data, mapping movement pattern, personal habits, family details, friends, acquaintances, etc. Often such contacts, say a media friend, are tasked to ferret out personal information about a government minister or highly placed bureaucrat. Casual contacts are listed assets and they are compensated by lavish entertainment, occasional payment and in certain cases on the basis of quid pro quo. The friend, say the media people, may require some information from the government stores, which are not highly classified. Such minor information exchange always takes place consciously. However, it is not uncommon to ferret out information from the casual contact during informal discussions. The contact may be reserved in nature and may also be garrulous. While ferreting out information through the unconscious or subconscious process it is advisable to gauge the mood of the contact. Such a task can be completed over a cup of coffee or a glass of wine.

Some casual contacts feel proud to establish rapport with a senior government officer. But some such contacts are also in the habit of advertising their connections to other friends and acquaintances. Secrecy often gets jeopardized. Such casual agents are unreliable and some of them tend to innocuously reveal their contacts with an intelligence operator.

Sometimes intelligence operators use such garrulous targets under pressure; demand for immediate 'secret enquiry' results. This practice is resorted to by the 'handling officers' mostly during 'secret enquiry' as a short-cut method of obtaining fast information. It may happen that the consumer wants immediate information about what is cooking up in a group of legislators, rebelling against the government. In such cases the urgency is great and the analyst or top boss may want immediate input. Information about such rebel groups are also collected through line telephone or cell phone monitoring. But the boss may be hungry for HumInt. In such cases the controlling officer should brief the 'handling officer' to be very discreet while activating the casual contact.

A serious fiasco had taken place in 1978. The then ruling faction wanted immediate feedback about certain political moves by the former prime minister. It was not a kid's game to penetrate the inner circle of the leader located at the Willingdon Crescent home. The officer deputed to enquire into the development approached a close aide of the former PM, socially known to him. The aide's loyalty was greater to his leader than to his social friend. The effort turned out to be counter productive. The former PM was alerted and she immediately amended her course of action and a section of the media was briefed about surreptitious efforts of the intelligence agency in penetrating her household. The enquiry soured up and the officer concerned was shunted out to a remote station. Such situations are not uncommon when political fluidity creates brinkmanship and political horse trading—so common to Indian democracy—occur. These are parts of the game. A few exposés create minor blisters and are taken as inevitable parts of the intelligence game. It must be mentioned that secret enquiry, unless done through embedded or high level agents may often misfire. From this point of view casual contacts are both assets and liabilities.

Embedded Agents: Embedded agents are very valued intelligence assets. This category of agents are regular members, functionaries and operators located inside the core areas of targeted organisation, party, institution, insurgent, terrorist and organised bodies about which the controlling authority, desk officers and analysts are keen to have authentic intelligence. It is not a correct perception that political decision makers always task the agency to penetrate a target which is rated important from the point of view of internal and external security threats.

There are soft areas as well as hard and hardest areas which are required to be penetrated for creating an embedded agent. Soft areas include political parties, social organisations, religious bodies, educational institutions, student, youth, trade unions, front organisations of militant underground parties and even NGOs.

Suppose Party X is in power in the central or state government and Party Z is a close contender. Since the intelligence agencies are directly responsible to the executives of the ruling party it has become a regular feature in Indian democracy that the agencies serve the interest of the ruling faction. Decision making in respect of political strategy and likely reaction of the prominent opposition parties are assessed on the basis of intelligence gathered by the tasked intelligence agency from various sources. Embedded agent is the most valuable HumInt asset and his inputs allow the analyst to draw up his final report for which he may have inputs from various other open or secret sources. It is not incumbent on the policy maker to strictly follow the intelligence input drawn from an Embedded agent. Political decision making is a complex affair and is conditioned by several other stark realities.

How to evaluate an Embedded agent material? Preliminary identification is done by the desk officer, analyst or by the research branch (if there is one). Normally, lists of people nearer to the top coterie are maintained by the desk and in some cases dockets on such individuals are regularly updated from open or secret data by the assigned research unit. Once a task is assigned the grassroot officers are directed to examine the existing data and collect penetrating information about each of them. From a presumed number of 12 such coterie members the targets are narrowed down to two or three after thorough study of their vulnerability. Finally, it may so happen that the controlling officer may assign two vulnerable targets to two different 'handling officers' for cultivating them. One officer is not allowed to know that another colleague has also been assigned target in the same area of coverage.

Evaluation of an Embedded agent may take a long period. The handling officer is required to sniff around, evaluate the target's vulnerability and take into stock the softest spot through which the needle of approach can be inserted. In most cases approach is made through a common friend, family member and in some cases certain personal habits and vulnerabilities are exploited. Such targets are slyest fishes; they take time to bite the bait. Inducements are many; offer of money is one of the options. Other options are exploitation of personal requirements, family obligations and blackmailing.

In case of ideologically committed targets, as we have said earlier, the handling officer is required to rise to the level of ideological comprehension of the target, sympathize with his cause and gradually arrange to bring two diaphragms closer to each other so that their psychological nearness converges. These are the toughest categories of assets. However, almost everything has a price. The case officer has to evaluate the price and consult his controlling officer. The price may be money, a suitable job for a dependent, subsidizing children's education, putting money in the kitty of the target during a daughter's marriage, etc.

Initially, the target is not treated as categorized agent, his reports are tried, compared and once the controlling officer is satisfied that the target's productions are real meat and he is reliable then he is upgraded to B grade. Over periods of time, when the flow is regular and production is excellent, then he is elevated to A grade. From a mere contact to reach the top grading, a target may take two to four years.

Let us examine the recent historical event of demolition of the disputed Babri Mosque in Ayodhya. Around 1989 the controlling officer organized a brainstorming session to discuss the growing militancy among the Hindutva organisations and their preparations to heighten the Hindu upsurge by focusing on the Ram Janambhumi a.k.a. Babri Masjid. The conclusion was clear; the Rashtriya Swayamsevak Sangh (RSS) and its Parivar were determined to take advantage of the assassination of two important Congress leaders and utter failure of the coalition government headed by VP Singh. It was emerging as a period of Hindu resurgence as opposed to emergence of acute Islamic jihadism in Pakistan and Bangladesh and their efforts to transplant Islamic jihad amongst the Indian Muslims. The Muslims, in the absence of Congress hegemony lost their political cohesiveness and started shifting loyalty to the regional and caste-based parties.

A few officers from the headquarters and in the states were briefed to target the Hindutva organisations to create high quality HumInt assets. Being soft ideological based entities it was not difficult to penetrate these organisations within three to five months.

Thereafter, avalanches of top grade reports about training the Swayamsevaks in demolition methodologies, propaganda campaigns and other preparations started pouring in. The concerned agency shared all such information with the policy makers.

One particular target in the RSS was very difficult to penetrate. However, this was achieved through a friend who belonged to the same state and was of the same caste. After a period the target was softened and he agreed to meet the top most policy maker in the government. The meeting was organized with utmost secrecy and the two agreed that necessary actions should be taken for preventing demolition of the mosque. The agent agreed to brief his trusted aides to refrain from the final action of demolition. However, the psychological storm built up amongst sections of Hindus was so violent that on the destined day the top leaders either stood as mute witnesses or encouraged the volunteers to demolish the structure. The top policy making authority also suffered from mental debility and failed the nation by not taking a tough stand. His vacillation could not be explained though failure of the top target (agent) in the Hindutva organisation was explained away by the ferocity of the storm that defied his authority. Things were taken over by the politically ambitious leaders, who wanted to ride the crescent waves to capture political power. India is still divided on this issue. As a close observer I felt that both the ruling party and the belligerent opposition were equally responsible for the tragic incident. At the agency level there was no failure. Failure took place at the decision making level and at the level of enforcing the laws of the country. It was a competition between psychological madness and total inability at the decision making level.

Agent creation in the above-mentioned targets was comparatively easier. A tougher illustration is necessary to convey to the readers the onerous task that agent creation is. Way back in 1970–75 it was very difficult to raise a reliable agent from the hardcore areas of the Naga Federal Government (NFG), Naga Nationalist Council (NNC) and underground Naga insurgent army factions. In 1970 it came to notice that in the October session of the Tatar Ho Ho (parliament) the Naga insurgents were to take certain key decisions about sending gangs to China and Pakistan for lifting weapons provided by the Chinese Special Bureau and the Inter Services Intelligence. Instructions were received from the controlling officer that all out efforts should be made to penetrate the Tatar Ho Ho and the top echelons of the NFG and the self-styled Naga Army.

The agency covering the Naga insurgency affairs had no asset at the level that could attend the Tatar meeting and report back. The only way left was to get tidbit information from government officers either related or connected to the important office bearers like the

Kilonsars (ministers), senior self-styled army officer and even an ordinary delegate to the Tatar Ho Ho.

An opportunity walked in. A Naga officer confided to his station chief that a school inspector of Ukhrul district (Manipur) was related to a Naga Kilonsar and he was in urgent need of some amount of money for his son's education abroad. This was an encouraging input. The controlling officer initially did not believe that a Kilonsar could be approached. However, he nodded positively as that was the only window to enter the Naga higher echelon.

For over a month the school inspector was motivated with painstaking efforts and finally he agreed to arrange a discreet meeting with the Kilonsar on condition that the promised amount should be handed over to him once the meeting was organized. The catch was risky. Further bargain resulted in an agreement that he would receive payment only after the Kilonsar attended the meeting lasting three days and personally briefed the operations in charge (local station chief, handling officer).

Discreet meeting with the Kilonsar was organized in a forested area skirting the ravine of Barak River. The place could be reached partly by river raft and partly on foot. The journey itself took 24 hours. The meeting was cordial and during discussions it transpired that the Kilonsar was suffering from chest disease and required immediate medication, including a chest X-Ray. As arranged the needful was done for his medical problem and in bargain he agreed to attend the Tatar meeting and report back as soon as he could explore out a safe place for meeting.

The handling officer was not taken seriously by the controlling officer as the agency had not succeeded in raising an agent at that inner circle of the Naga underground movement. The suspense was over when the Kilonsar contacted the handling officer through his relative and a meeting this time was organised in a jungle camp in Myanmar territory. For crossing the border the officer required permission of the controlling officer and the government. However, exigencies of circumstances prompted him to be a guest of the Kilonsar in jungle camp in Myanmar. After two days of verbal debriefing and collection of over thirty pieces documents the case officer returned to his base. It took five days to prepare a report of epic proportions which perplexed the agency. For the first time the agency made a breakthrough and in one shot two embedded agents were created that paid high dividends during peace negotiations with AZ Phizo faction of the Naga underground movement culminating in Shillong Accord between the NNC and the Government of India in 1975. This case study has been recorded as an important landmark in the sphere of embedded agent creation.

Semi-Converted Agent: Embedded agents are the most precious human assets. The handling officers are called upon to put their best, even at higher risks, to locate identity and cultivate an embedded HumInt asset.

The next lower grade of human assets is the semi-converted agents, which are not completely won over and there exist some psychological gaps between the handling officer and the target. Even after an asset has been located and identified and contacted through a direct contact or contact through a reliable intermediary the target may agree to meet and discuss certain matters bypassing the areas of core interest. Such agents try to ride two boats simultaneously. This tendency cannot be eliminated as some of the semi-converted agents are ideologically very firm, do not want to betray the organisation totally but want to reap some harvest by sharing peripheral information. The officers handling such agents are required to be very circumspect, cunning and should be able to gauge how far the agent is ready to walk with him. The desk officer and the analyst are required to be very discerning in evaluating reports from such human assets. Here is a situation that can be compared with a love affair that meets half the way and refuses to take the final plunge.

Why should the agencies prefer to cultivate partially won over agents? As commented earlier HumInt is not freely available. The Mafia dons, underworld gangs, international terrorists, Maoists, other ideologically inspired separatist groups, insurgents and targets in the higher or highest crust of the system are most difficult areas to cultivate and win over. Looking forward to foreign agencies, about which enormous literature is available, it can be said that the CIA, MI6, Chinese Special Bureau, the KGB, etc. agencies did not and do not pick up agents in modern days either at the point of gun, through blackmail, allurement and ideological pretensions like picking up ripe apples from an abundant orchard. The US failures in Bay of Pigs crisis with Soviet Union, CIA and MI6 failures in Iraq, 9/11 attacks and now in Afghanistan, Somalia, Sudan, etc. countries prove that the agencies mostly suffer from lack of HumInt agents.

An organisation like al Qaeda is very difficult to penetrate. India had often failed with SIMI, Indian Mujahideens, and small organized modules of the HUJI, LeT and other trans-border jihad *tanzeems*. In such cases agencies depend on won over agents also and padded up reports of such agents with SigInt, ElInt, etc. methodologies of gathering intelligence. The incident of killing of Tehrik-e-Taliban Pakistan leader Baitullah Mehsood (August 2009) was achieved by the USA and Pakistan partially through a partially won over agent (Baitullah's father-in-law) and interception of signal intelligence from the phone of Baitullah. The drone that fired the missile was assisted by ImInt (satellite imagery) provided by the spy satellites of the USA.

To achieve such spectacular success inter-agency cooperation and support from SigInt and other modern technical aids are absolutely necessary. Therefore, the semi-converted agents are also valuable assets in intelligence parlance.

Embedding or Infiltrating an Agent: While we propose to talk in details about the tradecraft in a separate chapter, it is necessary to highlight the importance of the technology of embedding or infiltrating an agent from outside to the outer core, and inner core areas of a target organisation. This poses the biggest challenge to the case officer and his pyramidal hierarchy. For intelligence agencies certain areas are grey and certain areas are absolutely dark. Such granite-like organisations are difficult to penetrate and create an agent from existing insiders. In such cases agencies are left with no option but to recruit, convince and win over compatible persons, train them and find out ways and means to infiltrate them in the target organisations. Such agents take longer gestating time, earn confidence of the inner core of the target area and gradually rise up.

In certain cases the process may take years and in certain other cases, depending on efficiency of the infiltrated agent, a couple of months. The handling officer has to be very patient and should not prod every now and then for hardcore intelligence. He must keep in touch, brief him about happenings inside the target area and to look for the real nugget. This training process is continuous and the handling officer is also required to be briefed by his controlling officer.

To illustrate this task we require falling back on certain instances. In case number one, it was noticed that certain madrasas in Uttar Pradesh were imparting training in militancy and egging on the students to take up jihad against *kafir* Hindoostan. Handling officers were summoned and briefed to raise agents in some of these madrasas. The stark truth is that for Indian agencies the area of jihadist militancy is the darkest dead end. HumInt assets are negligible. If there are any, the status of the agents is merely peripheral and limited to certain observation and surveillance utilities. Negative feedback was expected and received in no time.

The agency then opted for embedding some won over assets into some of these madrasas. To avoid suspicion intending students were cultivated from other parts of India. After prolonged briefings they were asked to seek admission as students. Three such hits were successful. After about a year these assets started producing good results. The mission was successful.

In the other case the agency faced total blackout in infiltrating an important Sikh religious seminary which was suspected to be involved in promoting militancy and separatism. No one in Punjab dared to offer services and the handling officers failed to raise any recruit for the mission of infiltrating the seminary.

A study was carried out about some former students of the seminary who were involved in religious activities in states outside Punjab. After deep research two assets were located. They were cultivated and motivated to approach their alma mater again and seek some services in key temples in the highly affected areas. After offering voluntary service to the seminary for three months they were deputed to serve as *granthi* and *pathi* (in charge of the holy book and daily recitation) in two temples in explosive areas of Amritsar district. Gradually, the agents infiltrated certain armed militant groups and brought their leaders closer to the controlling officer. Later, these leaders of the militant groups helped to counter Pakistan's inputs in Punjab turmoil and scuttling the efforts of the separatists. The Punjab insurgency was not won by guns alone. The intelligence agencies played cardinal roles.

In these categories of agents, the handling officer and his controlling officer are required to exercise utmost restraint, patience and adopt all possible tradecraft measures of secret communication and contact. Almost all categories of agents require continuous briefing and debriefing about his tasks and he may also require additional input for sharpening his lookout capability. This teacher-student relationship is required to be maintained at steady pace and the agency officers should maintain delicate balance between suspicion and trust. Nothing should be taken as absolute truth as there is nothing called absolute truth in human behaviour.

Peripheral Agents: It is possible that the agency may not succeed in creating a casual agent, embedded agent and infiltrating an agent. There are certain areas of coverage which look like dark and matter less areas of the cosmos. In such cases the intelligence agencies normally try to encircle the main target area by creating contacts and agents in the front organisations of the main parties, organisations and target areas.

The agency identifies the front organisations of a given party, which may be labour wing, student and youth wing, women's wing and volunteer bodies. Important leaders of the front organisations are studied and analysed, and their degree of closeness to the parent organisation is examined. If it is found that certain leaders in the front organisation have access to the top politbureau leaders, they are won over and tasked to gather information from the top leaders to whom they have easy access. The encirclement process is complicated and may involve several handling officers. All the inputs are collated and the desk officer or the analyst may designate the vulnerable targets. This indirect means of gathering hardcore intelligence is practised by most intelligence agencies of the world.

It has been found that FIS (Foreign Intelligence Service) agents in India often raise peripheral agents to penetrate political parties, top bureaucrats, military leaders and even policy makers. Indian counter-intelligence operators have identified several such human assets raised by the CIA, Russian SVR, Chinese Ist Directorate of the PLA, the ISI and other FIS operators. Detection, identification and neutralization of such peripheral agents is in the domain of the designated counter-intelligence units of India. It was noticed that the CIA had targeted certain front organisation leaders of three major political parties: Congress, BJP and CPM. It is not a part of duty of the Indian counter-intelligence units to notify the concerned parties. They keep the government apprised of the FIS activities.

In a particular instance it was noticed that a senior media person was targeted by the Inter Services Intelligence with a view to penetrate the highest echelon of the bureaucracy in Delhi. The media person was chummy with several top bureaucrats. He even arranged a meeting between a top bureaucrat and an undercover diplomat of Pakistan High Commission. After sustained observation the government was apprised of the efforts of the ISI operative and gullibility of some of the top bureaucrats. Presumably, the government issued fresh conduct rules to be observed by the top bureaucrats (joint secretary and above) while meeting foreign diplomats. Bureaucrats below those ranks are not permitted to maintain contact with open or undercover diplomats and non-diplomatic personnel of any embassy. This also applies to the armed forces.

Indian agencies also recruit this category of agents for triple purposes: Internal security matters, external intelligence interest and counter-intelligence and counter-terrorism tasks. For security reasons we do not want to enter into the operational details of such activities of the Indian agencies.

Volunteer Agents: There are classical examples of persons volunteering services to spy agencies. Volunteer agents are those persons who are primarily motivated by ideology, idiosyncrasy and deep personal conviction on any given issue or clusters of issues. Obviously, some of them are fascinated by the mysterious world of espionage and want to be self-styled soldier of the nation. The third category volunteer spies are motivated by greed and opportunism. Yet, I have come across eminent writers/journalists who are world-wise, understand the style of functioning of the spy agency and convincingly offer services to junior officers, who normally suffer from "hunger" to raise agents and earn credit.

For the ideological, idiosyncratic and personal conviction category let us briefly state the case of Klaus Emil Julius Fuchs (1911-1988) the famous physicist and nuclear scientist who was credited for co-parenting American, British, USSR and Chinese nuclear capabilities. His case is different from Dr AQ Khan of Pakistan, the father of Pakistani nuclear bombs. He traded his knowledge for gain with Libya, North Korea, Iran and other countries.

Klaus Fuchs was born on December 29, 1911, in Rüsselsheim, Germany. Born into a Lutheran family, Fuchs joined the Communist Party of Germany and fled to England following the rise of the Nazis in 1933. A brilliant young scientist, he earned his doctorate in Physics from the University of Bristol in 1937, and was invited to study at Edinburgh University.

In early 1941, Fuchs returned to Edinburgh from Canada where he was exiled, and was approached by Rudolf Peierls to work on the British atomic bomb research project. He became a British citizen in 1942.

In 1943, Fuchs was among the British scientists sent to the US to collaborate on the atom bomb. At first, he was assigned to a team at Columbia University in New York. Later, he was transferred to the weapons laboratory in Los Alamos, New Mexico, where he worked in the theoretical division under Hans Bethe. His chief area of expertise was the problem of imploding the fissionable core of the plutonium bomb. He was present at the Trinity test that preceded bombing of Hiroshima and Nagasaki.

Fuchs later testified to MI5 that he passed detailed information on the project to the Soviet Union through a courier in 1945, and further information about the hydrogen bomb in 1946 and 1947. But it was not until 1948 when it was discovered that the Manhattan Project security had been breached, and not until 1949, when Fuchs had returned to England and the Harwell Atomic Energy Research Establishment, that he was confronted by intelligence officers as a result of the cracking of Soviet ciphers known as the VENONA project. Fuchs confessed in January 1950 and was convicted on March 1, 1950, and sentenced to 14 years in prison. His testimony to British and American intelligence agencies eventually led to the trials of David Greenglass and Julius and Ethel Rosenberg in the US.

Fuchs passed on US achievements to Britain and to the Soviet Union on conviction that there should not be nuclear singularity. The big powers should have equal capability in nuclear warfare. As a communist his loyalty was to the USSR and he supported its nuclear endeavours wholeheartedly. In March 1, 1950 Fuchs was convicted by a British court. On June 23, 1959, Fuchs was released and allowed to immigrate to Dresden, East Germany, where he resumed a scientific career. At Dresden he taught the Chinese scientists about atom and hydrogen bombs. That was the beginning of Chinese nuclear programme. He died in East Berlin on January 28, 1988. Fuchs was an ideological and idiosyncratic agent and espionage thrilled him more than a glass of sparkling wine or company of "Sonia", the cover name of a Russian female military officer who worked as a cutout for the GRU.

On occasions I had the opportunity of coming across "patriotic" enthusiasts who volunteered to work as agents. Adopting a volunteer agent is tricky. The possibility of enemy infiltration in the agency through such volunteers cannot be ruled out. Therefore, it is necessary to make secret enquiries about the volunteer and he can be given tasks after he is found to be "clean".

A youth XX from a particular religious community contacted me in 1992 and offered his services to work as an agent. He was keen to be located in a neighbouring country. Student of a seminary in Uttar Pradesh he claimed he could comfortably locate in the same seminary in the neighbouring country. On enquiry he was found to be "clean." With great difficulty the controlling officer granted permission. The youth XX was infiltrated tactfully after training him in communication devices. The same volunteer agent had sent information through secret writing method about certain groups in the neighbouring country in collaboration with a spy agency which was preparing to dump explosives in the western coast. The readers are aware what happened during Mumbai serial blast in 1993.

The articulate writer/journalist friend had failed to cut grass with me. His offers sounded fishy and highly exaggerated, especially regarding alleged feuds between a mother-in-law and a daughter-in-law in a ruling family. As taught in intelligence tradecraft even a useless agent should not be scorned, even if he is a con artist. However, the same fellow conned a junior officer with a new identity and started planting "intelligence" on the agency. After three sensational reports the junior officer was interrogated and he admitted the real identity of his agent. The officer was "hungry" for creating high level agents for earning quick promotion. Administrative action was taken to remove the officer from the grassroots orbits. The writer/journalist continued to hunt greedy agency officers till he was exposed for conning certain highly placed politicians.

Having discussed these preliminaries about the character and qualification of the handling officer and other pyramidal hierarchy, as well as certain categories of intelligence agents we may now move to the mysterious areas of tradecraft and discuss each item in details.

Chapter 4

Aspects of
Tradecraft Training

Fresh recruits, as mentioned earlier, are required to undergo rigorous physical training and training in communication, ComInt, basics of TechInt, ElInt, SigInt, etc. They are also given basic orientation in tradecraft matters. But the intensive tradecraft training starts after about a year of recruitment. This applies to grassroots level recruits and senior echelon taken on deputation from IPS cadres of different states. The complex tradecraft training consists of:

Political Briefing: Intelligence operatives, irrespective of their service origin, are required to undergo intensive tradecraft training. In India, unfortunately, the senior leadership cadres are given only a limited exposure to tradecraft training. Most of them treat this phase of induction into the agency as a passing phase. They consider themselves as members of the heaven born service. It is taken for granted that because of their educational and professional achievement in police service they are repository of all wisdom and can perform the roles of case officer, desk officer, and analyst and operations expert. This legacy has not been an unmixed boon to the agencies. Some of them continue to retain police attitude and do not graduate to intelligence operators.

Intelligence tradecrafts are age-old polished, tried and continuously updated tools of the intelligence trade. Tradecraft is a living organism. It changes with societal, political, geopolitical and geostrategic changes. The Cold War imperatives of the Free World and the Iron Curtain have vastly changed since 1990. Similarly, the US, the UK, Russian, Pakistani, Chinese and Indian intelligence imperatives have vastly changed since 1979. The scenario is changing very fast, and India is mandated to reorient its external and internal intelligence imperatives to combat the intelligence initiatives of other powers. From this point of view imparting exhaustive tradecraft training to all superior and grassroots level operatives is as essential as water is for the fish. It is, therefore, necessary to discuss the entire gamut of tradecraft training in details.

On completion of post-recruitment physical, preliminary intelligence training and other aspects of communication technology and systemic exposure the cutting edge level officers are required to undergo tradecraft training, which starts with brief orientation about the structural and functional details of the agency. We need not go into the details of this aspect.

The next priority is on orientation discourses on political system and political parties in the country. Detailed talks are delivered by the analysts and desk officers about organizational structures of various parties, their ideological bases and their historical growth. The trainees are made to understand that the agency is required to maintain both closeness and distance from political functionaries. In a democracy with multi-party system the intelligence operatives are required to know as much details as possible of the political personalities in their respective areas of operations. Political intelligence has become, since British days, the daily bread and butter of the ruling parties and the internal intelligence agencies have cultivated the habit of daily updating the consumer with internal political developments inside the ruling as well as major opposition parties.

Internal political intelligence is not the focal point of the agencies like the CIA, FBI, MI5, etc., though several heads of states and premiers have used the intelligence agencies against their political opponents. The Watergate affair in the US is still vivid in memory. The difference is that in other free democracies political intelligence (except subversive groups, cults and saboteurs) is not a part of the charter of duties of the agencies. The intelligence agencies, however, carry out dirty political intelligence at the behest of the consumers, but, if exposed to accountability scrutiny and media exposés the agencies are called upon to explain. Often some heads roll.

In India, and the whole of South Asia, the role is reversed. Though not listed in the charter of duties, the agencies, in the Centre of the Union and in the states, do indulge in political intelligence on daily basis. They maintain dossiers on all the mainstream and subsidiary parties, important leaders including prying on data on their private lives. Why private lives?

There are interesting incidents to illustrate how such private and personal weaknesses are used by the ruling parties to exploit when political fluidity rocks the governments, necessitating horse-trading and besmirching the political opponents. This has become a common practice in Indian democracy since the days of post-Nehru-Shastri era. These political manoeuvres achieved height during the regimes of Indira Gandhi and the unstable regimes those followed her. En masse or group defection by the elected representatives in the State legislatures and the Parliament has become endemic. In the process of buying and selling elected representatives the intelligence agencies are called upon to come to the aid of the ruling factions to provide day-to-day, hour-to-hour developments, personal profiles of the targets for buying and selling. On occasions the agencies are also used to induce the targets to move in the direction desired by the ruling factions. Horse-trading has become an integral part of the limping democracy, which is often marked by physical violence and fraudulent practices.

There are many other sinister aspects of political intelligence. Politicians, not having any connection with any subversive groups, are also periodically subjected to spying operations in their offices, residences, including usual or extra-usual bedrooms. Perhaps the memories of a top political leader's son caught in live sexual action in a private room, sometime during the troubled days of Indira Gandhi, are still alive. The live pictures must be hibernating in the archives. In the age of electronic media proliferation certain media persons are also engaged/motivated to trap the erring politicians. They supplement the intelligence agencies for earning better TRP and for ingrating with certain political leaders. The allegation that media personalities often behave like traders is not frivolous.

The foreknowledge of what is cooking in the opponents' pots is essential for the ruling factions. It is an open knowledge that all the political parties have used/abused the intelligence agencies for survival. The agencies normally impart training on matters related to the Indian National Congress, Communist parties, Bhartiya Janata Party and other caste-based regional parties. We intend to discuss this item along with the need for accountability in the intelligence and security services.

Study of the communist movements and parties and their international linkages formed an important aspect of most of the free world countries. India also followed the British legacy and high priority was assigned to impart training on theory, practice and underground apparatus (tech apparatus) of the communist movement. Priority was continued till collapse of the communist edifices in the USSR. Disintegration of the communist movement in India has tapered off the intensive emphasis on the subject. Study of the Chinese communist movement, Naxal and radical Maoist has, however intensified. Growth of the Naxal movement is, however, not taught in the historical perspective of land related movements that have been plaguing India from 18th and 19th century onwards. More emphasis is given on law and order aspects of the emerging threat to national integrity and national divide between the subnormal poor and the urban and semi-urban privileged groups. This has resulted in myopic understanding of the Naxal and Maoist movement in India, which has deep rooted historical ramification.

Elaborate instructions are imparted on communal parties and organisations. This aspect is divided in two segments: Muslim parties and organisations and Hindu parties and organisations.

Studies on the Muslim parties include sessions on historical growth and present status of the Muslim League (now abandoned), Pan-Islamic movements and impact on India, growth of fundamentalism and radicalism amongst Indian Muslims, Muslim communalism and profiling of Muslim communal organisations, general profiling of Muslim religious institutions and their impact on different segments of the society, international Islamic charities and influence of foreign money on the fundamentalists, etc. Special emphasis is given on Jamait-e-Islami, Ahl-e-Hadith, Muslim Personal Law Board and the Milli Council. Other Muslim entities in public domain like the Deoband and Barelvi seminaries, Jamiat-ul-Ulema-e-Hind, Firangi Mahal (Lucknow), Nadwatul Islam are also included in training courses. Smaller and regional Muslim parties are also studied. This appears to be a vast ocean. The appearance is rather psychogenic. In reality, the agencies have very little access and primed agent level penetration even in public domain organisations least speaking the organisations of the separatist groups and modules of the separatist groups.

Hindu organisations are studied by the trainees as a part of communal movement in India and not exactly as a separate political, social and cultural movement. This tradition was inherited from the British, who treated Hindus, Muslims, Sikhs, Christians and Dalits as different nations. The legacy was continued under the successor Congress government and the agencies were encouraged to study the non-Muslim segments of the nation in segmented compartments.

Among the Hindu organisations the growth of Arya Samaj, Shuddhikaran movement, Rashtriya Swayamsevak Sangh, Hindu Mahasabha, Jan Sangh evolved to Bharatiya Janata Party, Vishwa Hindu Parishad, and other branches of the Sangh Parivar are meticulously studied. The trainees are taught to consider Hindu communalism at par with Muslim communalism and treat the RSS and BJP as enemy of the main ruling party — the Congress.

Regionally, most Hindu organisations like the Shiv Sena, Hindu Munnani, Vivekananda movement, Ramakrishna Ashram, Hindu Pracharini Sabha, etc. are also introduced to the trainees and they are advised to treat these political and religious institutions as parts of the greater Hindu communal movement.

Correspondingly the Sikh, Dalit, Christian desks courses have also been devised to impart training on Sikh and Dalit matters and affairs related to the Christian churches and organisations.

These extensive courses are intended to prepare the trainee intelligence operators with political ground realities in India. However, the course is superficial and most trainees do not take these aspects seriously. Middle class Indian society, from where the most operatives are recruited, are oriented to the idea that an intelligence operative's job is just like any other government job; passing time, climbing the ladder gradually and reach certain level and retire with an honourable pension. Only very few trainees, say 15 per cent take the training seriously as parts of their other identity, the overt and covert intelligence operator. Intelligence job is not an ordinary government job; it requires total metamorphosis of a recruit to a primed and motivated machine, from an officer with middle class social attitude. We propose to discuss this aspect in a later chapter.

Memory Training: The next important item is Memory Training. Why should a trainee be trained in Memory lessons? The science of Memory is an extraordinary subject. In ancient times it was related to philosophy, divinity and even with oracle. Modern science says that it is an integral part of cognitive psychology. It is now treated as a part of neuroscience.

The process of memorization passes through the stages of seeing, hearing, testing certain events, encoding them, storing them and retrieving when required. It is something like an advanced computer being fed with data, audio-visual materials and tasked to code them into categories and store in designed folders. A simple key punching can retrieve the item from the registry hard disk (memory) of the computer.

In human beings the process is more complicated. Nominal memory is a part of neuropsychological process. Memory can be of different types:

Sensory memory is related to spontaneous reaction of the memory cells to audio-visual happening in the immediate vicinity. In less than a second memory cells capture the event. However, in normal human being, vexed with daily life's problems retention power of such memories is very low. Such retention may last for few seconds. Such memories are not photogenic. Unless the mind is trained to retain such memories for a longer period, these get wiped out fast.

Short-term memory can last for 10 to 15 minutes. However, George A. Miller in 1956 propounded his idea that is known as 7±2 items, i.e. retention power is between 7 to 2 minutes, plus and minus. It was also suggested that 'chunking' of words related to an event or nay description improves memory power. For instance, the names of 7 basic colours have been chunked as VIBGYOR. Similarly CBIASIXTER is the chunked form for CBI Arrested Six Terrorists. According to some scholars chunking of 3 words or numerical are most ideal for remembrance. Short-term memory is stored in the frontal and parietal lobes of the brain. Long-term memory is stored in wider areas of the brain in complicated neuronal electronic circuits. These are deeply embedded memories, which can be recalled at the punch of a memory key. However, for this kind of capability in ordinary individuals not trained in memory exercises is rare.

I had a friend, a former *pracharak* of the RSS, who used to fascinate us with his memory power. He could repeat 1 to 1000 in reverse order. A passage read over to him slowly with correct pronunciation for 5 minutes could be repeated by him with correct coma and full stop. He used to tell that besides his original retentive power he used to train himself by mentally grappling with the minutest details of an incident, sound, photogram of an event. If he were an artist he could repaint the whole scenario with original colours and ground details. Unfortunately, he is not alive.

Two scholars of the subject Atkinson and Shiffrin (1968) had presented the following diagram to describe the process of memorization:

Multi-store Model

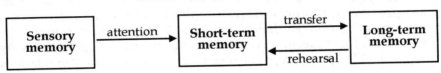

Later Bradley and Hitch worked out a model for working memory in 1974. This model was improved upon in 2000.

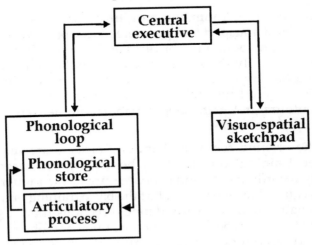

Let us not get lost in the maze of scientific vocabulary and diagrams, because these scientific approaches are not taught in the intelligence agencies. The scientists generally agree that a person requires four aspects to sharpen memory retention process:

Organization of the mind into different compartments, earmarking distinctiveness of each compartment, personal effort and continuous elaboration. This is a difficult process. There are certain minds which can store minutest of events for all along their lives. They never forget.

In intelligence agencies memory training is imparted on the basis of formal police training manual, that lay emphasis on close examination of the scene of crime, frontal, profile descriptions of an arrested person or a suspect, retain in memory full description of a suspected foreign intelligence officer or agent and memorize the lay of the things on the ground. Training is also imparted on training minds to memorize alpha-numerical details of events, file numbers, contents of vital paragraphs, telephone numbers, etc.

A question can be raised about the necessity of memory training in the age of photography, audio recording and other aids to memory. These props can give supportive evidence. However, reproduction from memory of an event or describing a person after having seen him for a while is essential qualifications of an intelligence operative.

Memorization cannot be substituted by technical aids. These are supportive appliances. Depth and exactness of memory, like photographic details, depend on how keenly and consciously the handling officer has observed the details, heard the audio bytes and seen the video pixels. A casual observer with fits of absentmindedness cannot remember all the details. The dedication is of the kind of a devotee praying earnestly for his deity and a lover pining with utmost focus on her object of love.

In the briefing room the handling officer is shown certain photographs of a suspect foreign intelligence operative. He is allowed sometime to photogram the pictures and retain in his memory. It is his duty to identify the suspect even in a milling crowd. Once seen he should be able to identify the suspect even from his silhouette. The officer should remember colour and style of hair, profile and front contours and gait. Such capability immensely helps secret surveillance operations.

In the briefing room the handling officers are required to be imparted training to draw sketc.hes of a given target location, minutely recording each and every feature of the topography. They are not required to be painters. But the basic training of map reading should enable them to clearly define directions (north, south, etc.), location of house, type of construction, open and obstructed spaces, ridges, tree-covers, rivulets, and other physical features. Observation power is an important ingredient of memory. Certain handling officers often miss the details due to lack of concentration and avowed capability of observing the minutest details. Such mistakes result in memory confusion.

Failure of memory or partial memorization can lead to grave tragedies. In 1972 somewhere in the northeast insurgency affected area a handling officer was deputed with a guide to examine the topography of a suspected armed insurgent encampment. They surveyed the location with a powerful binocular, drew a sketc.h of various approaches and presented to the controlling officer. During debriefing they missed out certain vital positions in the topography i.e. location of two high ridges nearby from where the insurgents could locate any advancing police party.

When this information was shared with the security forces and the guide was loaned to them the forces advanced according to the sketc.h drawn by the officer. The tragedy was inevitable. The insurgents could identify the advancing forces from a kilometer distance. They took position on the higher reefs and opened LMG fire on the forces. Located on a lower knoll they could only provide cover to their men and were in no position to mount counter assault. The forces lost three lives and later raided the abandoned camp.

In 1992 a handling officer with the help of his agent identified a house in Anantnag area of Kashmir, where a serving Pakistani officer was supposed to hold a meeting with certain Indian Kashmiri youths. They observed the house from a distance, but failed to notice that four houses in a row were similar in construction and colour. While briefing his controlling officer the handling officer forgot to mention the specific house, though he described the construction details and the surroundings, but not the specific house. In confusion he mentioned the last of the row from the right. In fact, the house was last of the row to the left. The controlling officer, while briefing the security forces mentioned about the house at the right corner of the row. The resultant raid was tragic. Three innocent civilians and four security personnel lost their lives. The Pakistani officer and the militants melted away in the forest. Such failure to memorize the details is against the grains of memory training.

There are innumerable such instances to emphasize the need for imparting memory training to the intelligence officers with better scientific approach, borrowing from the training manual of the CIA and other agencies. It is also necessary for the agencies to consult well-known neuropsychologists and take guidance from them. The present modality of memory training is rudimentary. This only adds to confusion and most of the trainees do not pay attention to this important aspect of tradecraft.

Concealment: In intelligence operations, both forward and counter-intelligence, concealment is a very important trick of the trade. Concealment means to keep some object from being seen, found, observed, or discovered. It also means carrying a super-secret document or information in manner that cannot be detected. The concealment protocol is also observed during agent communication and passing and receiving of clandestine information. The tradecraft of concealment has been refined so amazingly in recent times through constant R&D that various agencies of certain countries have achieved high degree of sophistication. In intelligence game every device can get compromised over time. Once exposed the methodology gets transferred to history book and newer methodologies are devised by the unorthodox operatives and the scientists engaged in the trade.

In normal perception concealment is perceived as ways and means adopted by the drug smugglers. The traffickers adopt various methods to conceal heroin, cocaine and other chemical drugs for international operations. Concealment of such high priced stuff inside undergarment of females, shoe-soles, linings of jackets, inside the anal canal, walking sticks and false suitcase bottoms are common features. In certain cases use of cameras, vanity bags with false compartments, face pack materials, etc. are also used.

However, in the domain of espionage the art and science of concealment and camouflage, derived from French *camoufler* ("to disguise"), a term that came in vogue during clandestine operations by the resistance groups and allied intelligence agencies during the two World Wars.

The term concealment can be related to the art and science of carrying, transmitting, conveying clandestine intelligence from one location to another and from one person to another. It is also a pertinent tradecraft in clandestine communication methodologies. Concealment is an important ingredient in ElInt and TechInt, which demand concealment of miniaturized devices for gathering intelligence. Purveying of such devices by master researchers to the ground operatives for operational uses are considered after detailed study of the location of operation, subject under cover and his preparedness to adopt counter-intelligence measures.

Indian agencies, particularly the internal security agencies depend on age old methodologies of concealment and they have not borrowed from global agencies though hundreds of books are available on the subject. In the famous book 'SPYCRAFT': The Secret History of the CIA's Spytechs from Communism to al Qaeda authored by Robert Wallace and H Keith Melton, with Robert Schlesinger (New York: Dutton, 2008) the authors have elaborated various aspects of concealment and camouflage tradecraft. From Indian point of view we would discuss certain aspects of various types of concealment methodologies applicable to different situational and operational needs. Concealment is an operational aspect used under controlled conditions under supervision of expert performers. Only confident personnel or agent are used in concealment operations.

Concealment of clandestine messages and micromaterials: In intelligence trade the product communication and communication of rendezvous in miniature or micro form is an essential training aspect. The varieties depend on the depth and extent of imagination of the master wizard of R&D section and ingenuity of the handling officers. In fact, the R&D section is expected to come up with newer methodologies of concealment of secret communication materials. In India such innovations enterprises are rare.

Use of Bathing Soap: In certain cases hollow toilet soaps are used to camouflage and communicate clandestine intelligence from one place to the other or from one person to the other person. The trick of precision cutting of the toilet soap, scooping out desired amounts require practice and expertise. Only trained masters can do the job. A thin film, a microdot or a piece of micro-photographed paper can be secured inside the hollow by using water resistant materials. The most important part of the trick is to rejoin the severed pieces of the soap. This can be cleverly done by inserting very thin wooden pins on one side of the soap, insert the other part with gentle pressure. Once the edges merge firmly very gentle brushing with glycerin or purified lard can hide the points of rupture. With some measured heat treatment the cake of soap can be restored to original shape.

In the USA, the UK and other countries the R&D divisions of the agencies are capable of manufacturing such imitation soap with hollow chambers for camouflaging clandestine documents. In India, whenever this kind of camouflage methodology is applied, the laboratory experts do the job manually.

Use of Candle: Fancy decorative candles often used as ornamental pieces in five-star hotels, elegant homes and parlours. French, Belgian, Italian and even certain Indian candles are prized possessions. Normally a five to six inch diameter candle is chosen for case operations. With a long stem scoop the desired amount of candle wax are taken out creating the desired length and depth of hollow. After securing the clandestine document, parts of the hollow section is filled up with liquid wax to restore original appearance. Thereafter, decorative wax work can be carried out with great sense of artistry. In certain cases a felt base is used to deny alien access. To open it, two metal needles are poked through the felt at certain points and an electric current passed through, causing the lid on the bottom to open. Besides this, there are additional tricks to secure clandestine information inside hollowed out candles.

Use of *Bindi*: Most Indian women use various sizes of *bindis* on their forehead. Most *bindis* have two fine layers. The rear portion is sticky and the front portion is attached to it by special glue. Experts can separate the two parts by using very fine blade and heat treatment.

Agencies can secure microdots (prepared through photographic technique) inside the separated layers of the *bindi* and recompose the material to its original look. Use of *bindi* is a novel tradecraft and even used by western agencies.

Hollow Coin: The USA, France, Germany, UK, Russia and even China use this age old tradecraft to conceal documents and clandestine information. The CIA gets some dollar coins manufactured in such a fashion, by weight measuring and edge controlling that once the two halves of the dollar coin are separated and the clandestine document is secured and the coin is re-fixed it becomes very difficult for any agency and counter-intelligence experts to detect the hollow inside the coin. In some cases two parts of two different coins are milled to the desired depth, a micro cavity is created and the two parts are pressed in mint machine to restore the original look. Microdots, thin films and micro-filmed documents can be secured easily and transported as pocket change. An illustrative photo of such US device is produced below.

In India, however, such concealment devices are not taught to the intelligence officers and even the R&D laboratories have not tried using this tradecraft of clandestine communication.

Postal Stamp: Use of postal stamp to send a letter to a cover address inside or outside the country is an age old tradecraft. Normally very thin microdots or chips are hidden on the glued side of the stamp and affixed on the envelope or even a tourist postcard to communicate vital photographs of enemy country's military or super sensitive installations, say locations of radar and missile deployments. The Postal Research Departments of the intelligence agencies normally censor targeted postal communications, but they generally examine the contents of the letters. If the content is desired to be released, permission is taken from the controlling officer. If permission not granted the letter is 'killed.' However, in very few cases Indian agencies pry open the stamps and examine the back side under powerful microscope. In USA and other countries all PRC units are supplied with powerful microscopes and table top X-ray and UV lights to detect smallest microdots or chips without opening it through vapour treatment.

Hollowed butts of Kirpans: A small sword, as a symbol of religious belief, is carried by all Sikhs. These curved swords normally have decorative ivory or wooden butts. In a few cases it was noticed that the ivory and wooden butts were hollowed out by some militant couriers to carry miniature maps, capsule information from one militant hideout to another. In a few cases agents were trained to secure Minox cameras or miniature pinhole video recorders with tiny transmitter inside the Kirpan butt to gather and transmit information of a target location through static transfer or radio communication to a nearby receiving console. This was successful in certain operations in Punjab, especially devised by handling officers under expert guidance. Such camouflage tradecraft paid high dividends in combating the armed terrorists.

Hair Brush Handles: This innocuous self-grooming object has been exploited by the tradecraft experts to carry clandestine messages safely and also to implant automatic micro cameras with noiseless pinions to take photographs of the target suspects, locations, objects and even documents. Similarly, tooth brush handles have also been used to conceal documents and to hide a miniature camera for clandestine photography. Besides Minox, modern miniature cameras have been successfully used in very delicate operations. There are varieties of Minox, Minox B, Minox X and CLX, Minox EC and Riga cameras.

Minox CLX

Later, T-100 was developed as a major improvement over the Minox. Use of Minox and T-100 have played cardinal roles in the USA, German and Russian forward and counter-intelligence activities. A T-100 can take precision photo of about 100 page document. Cameras can be camouflaged in pens, cigarette lighters, and overcoat buttons and even in wrist watches. The CIA introduced a virtual arsenal of miniature cameras. Unfortunately in India use of such tradecraft camouflage gadgets is very rare.

Watch Camera

Goggle Camera

Regarding concealment of cameras we would include details in the part dealing with TechInt. It may be mentioned that the USA, the UK, Germany, France, Russia and China have marketed over two dozen varieties of camouflaged cameras. These are used in forward and counter-intelligence operations. Similarly, cameras and recording devices are concealed in pens. The recorded data can be downloaded in USB and used by operators.

Concealed or Secret Writing: Concealed writing with vanishing ink or prescribed liquids like ordinary milk, onion juices and lime juices, etc. between the lines of a typed or handwritten letter, between the pages of a news magazine is a common practice for clandestine concealment and communication. The secret writing can be deciphered under UV lamp or through chemical treatment. Even moving the paper cautiously over a lighted electric heater often reveals the secret writing. This is a hackneyed process and is easily detectable. In some cases of concealed communication between India and a foreign destination simple milk was used for writing the clandestine messages. On the eve of Mumbai serial bomb blast such information received in apparently invisible communication had revealed the sinister design of dumping explosives in India's western coast. However, the concerned state authorities had not taken seriously the warning disseminated in December 1992. The resultant disaster is now history.

False Tooth or Tooth Cap: The CIA and other agencies used this technique to conceal valuable microdots or microfilms. Using a plastic cap on a tooth filled by an expert dentist is a common practice. In certain cases the carrying agent's tooth is filled to certain measurement and a cap is inserted to give natural look. This cap is removable under expert supervision. A microdot that may contain dozen of pages of clandestine intelligence can be hidden within the cap with special glue that does not tamper the quality. Counter-intelligence experts can hardly detect the insertion. However, in India such advanced technique is not taught and practised.

Use of Female Carriers: The practice of using female carriers to physically carry clandestine documents has been vastly chronicled in western spy-literature. Use of a lady with a plastered leg and on wheel chair is a common practice to carry documents, say from Russia to France. Hems of jeans, trousers, decorative hats are often used as crevices for hiding documents in micro form. In extreme cases the use of sanitary pads has also come to notice. These are not fantasized ideas. These have been experimented by most western, Chinese and Japanese spy agencies. From the realm of strategic spying such tactics are also being adopted by corporate houses to steal secrets of their competitors.

Painting: Valuable secret documents can be concealed inside the hollows of the frame and between the picture and its rear cover materials. A mounted miniature Mughal painting or even a family frame can be used to carry micro documents avoiding detection by counter-intelligence operators.

Food Cans and Jars: Cans and jars containing ostensive foodstuff can be used to hide secret documents. The common practice is to empty the can, clean it, and create a false chamber to secure the document, reload the foodstuff and reseal the can as it is done in a professional packaging machine. The infrastructure required is less expensive and requires usual expertise.

Steganography: It is similar to secret writing. However, a message can be hidden in a painting, like they say in Michael Angelo's Last Supper. It is often symbolic; contains prefixed cryptography, and substitution of phraseology. Only the originator and prefixed recipient can decode it. In one-to-one agent communication the use of steganography is productive. In a classical case of steganography a collage picture using printed images and news items was used to convey the secret missile positions in the USSR to USA by a planted agent. The sender used certain words with similar font and style in between printed matters to convey the vital information.

Books: As is seen in cinema, books are hollowed out to carry small weapon. This is a hackneyed practice and can be easily detected. The most effective process is to conceal a document in a normal page of the book of similar dimension, printing style and font and insert it in the book after removing an original page, preferably from the mid section of the book. This is an effective device and can be easily achieved by the laboratory experts.

There are innumerable concealment devices in spy tradecraft. Depending on imagination, innovative power and circumstances in which the concealment device is required. The experts can innovate devices to conceal vital documents for passing on from the fields to handling officers or from handling officers to controlling officers. Handling officer to agent and *vice versa* is the most important aspect of the art and science of concealment in intelligence tradecraft.

Chapter 5

Agent Operations

The next, perhaps the most important training aspect of intelligence tradecraft is Agent operations. Who is an Agent? Let us avoid the scholarly discourses contained in hundreds of books, some by the former CIA experts. Before any attempt is made to describe the Agent it must be stressed that this valuable commodity is a human being and is the most important ingredient of HumInt. Allen W Dulles had defined an Agent as a man whom a case officer or handler locates, hires, trains and directs to collect information and whose work he judges is the agent. The Agent, who may be of any nationality, may produce the information himself or he may have access to contacts and sources "in place" who supply him with information. His relationship with the intelligence service generally lasts as long as both parties find it satisfactory and rewarding.*

This is an indefinite definition or description of an Agent. The main ingredient of "motivation" is absent. "Hiring" of an Agent is not like American concept of hiring and firing any employee. Intelligence handling officers have to pass through different stages before they are allowed to hire an Agent by his controlling officer. Dulles also adds the ingredient of chain-link like relationship between the handling officer and the Agent, who may also have access to the real source of the information through another human agent. This is contradictory to restrictive security. The link-chain is normally described as a 'cutout', who works between the handling officer and the main Agent. We propose to discuss about the importance of a 'cutout' in intelligence parlance.

The Agent is a covert human asset or source who has been satisfactorily located in a target organisation or body after appropriate

*The Craft of Intelligence, p. 178.

research, contacted directly or through a link-chain or through other method, motivated, won over and has committed to work for an agency on certain considerations.

The Agent must be covert. There cannot be any overt or open Agent. As we have discussed earlier overt sources are contacts, friends and casual sources of information of peripheral value. The word "Source" may be construed as rootage and not merely the place of origin of the information. The root can be a friend, contact, casual source or a hard boiled agent.

An Agent handling has certain golden principles. The diagram should better explain the position:

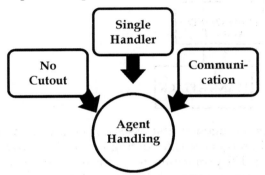

From locating to priming to handling only one case officer is used. Use of cutout is not encouraged except in rare cases. In case the handling officer is promoted or shifted, the controlling officer must choose a competent officer to take over the Agent over a period. This requires gestation period. The situation is like starting the game all over again. For a period the relationship between the Agent and the new handling officer may not run smooth. It is, therefore, prescribed that the departing handling officers prepare a dossier for the benefit of his successor.

A peculiar situation was faced by a new station officer when he took charge of a station in the northeast. His predecessor left 15 days before his arrival. No note, register or agent particular was left in office record. The new station officer had to start from scratch. When the controlling officer was notified about the situation, the departing officer was penalized. The only plausible explanation was that the departing officer was running phony agents and misappropriating secret service fund. This is not an uncommon practice.

HumInt sources and agents are of various types. Separate discussions would be made on various sub-categories in later parts of this chapter. Let us first examine the father tree of different categories of agents or sources of intelligence. Other sub-trees can be illustrated as the discussions proceed.

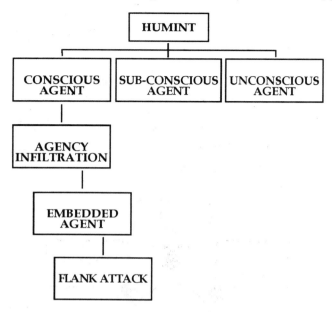

The intelligence agency first assesses the requirement of raising agents in certain target areas following instructions and demands by the policy maker. The prime minister or the home minister may require truthful and cutting edge intelligence about some terrorist and insurgent organisations for operational or political use. They discuss the entire scenario with the intelligence chief and direct him to penetrate certain organisations to gather vital intelligence. On the other hand, the agency through its periodical Intelligence Estimate decide certain target areas requiring penetration and assign the task to ground units or special operational units. Before a decision is arrived at and tasks are awarded, the issues are discussed threadbare and after satisfactory analysis the job is awarded. The job assessment is an intricate process. It involves several data input, analysis of trends and incidents and fixation of the likely targets.

Suppose, after several deadly blasts caused by saboteurs, internal or external, the situation reports are scanned meticulously and some conclusion is reached about the sources that might have caused the blasts. In the Indian context the likely targets could be the Students Islamic Movement of India (SIMI), Indian Mujahideen, Deendar Anjuman, Ahl-e-Hadith or modules of external terrorist organisations like the Harkat-ul-Jihad al Islami (HUJI), Jamait-ul-Mujahideen Bangladesh or Lashkar-e-Taiba (LeT) and Jaish-e-Mohammad.

The immediate reaction of the agency revolves around examination of existing resources and need for additional qualitative resources. The chain reaction is transmitted down the ladder to concerned units who in turn assign the job to most suitable case officers and handlers. Briefing of a case officer and handler is an elaborate affair. The desk officer, analyst or the operations officer brief the handling officer about the target organisation and the likely targets with the help of available data. He is also given security briefing before launching for a hazardous task of penetrating a subversive and militant organisation. The case officers are trained not to charge like a bull before locating a target. The process is arduous and requires intrinsic knowledge about the organisation and personalities suspected to be associated with it. Such knowledge is acquired during in-house training and personal initiative.

As a case study HUJI is selected as the target organisation. HUJI was created jointly by the Inter Services Intelligence (ISI) of Pakistan and al Qaeda at Muzaffarabad, PoK in 1992 from the remnants of Harkat-ul-Ansar and Harkat-ul-Jihad established in 1980 to fight alongside the Afghan mujahideens. The purpose was to infiltrate the activists of the *tanzeem* to Indian Kashmir and other parts of India for carrying out proxy war. The HUJI has three branches—Pakistan, Bangladesh and India.

Identifying HUJI units in Muslim dominated areas of India is considered a near impossible task as the Indian agencies have very insignificant access into the Muslim community, who live in compact areas, ghettos and walled cities. Cultural divergences between the target and the agency officials also create insurmountable walls.

In this particular case direct access is impossible for an Indian agency. It is next to impossible to raise a conscious, subconscious and unconscious insider agent. Such target organisations remain subterranean and function through indoctrinated cells and modules inspired by religious zeal. With the virtual rupture of Hindu-Muslim trust during the process of partition of the country, the psychological barriers are nearly insurmountable. It may be possible for a Christian or a Jew operative to penetrate an Islamist organisation in the Middle East. In the context of South East Asia it is nearly impossible for an Indian case officer (Hindu, Christian or Sikh, etc.) to penetrate the hardcore areas of Islamist organisations. History stands as the barrier.

In such cases the handling officers are instructed to either try to infiltrate the target organisation or attack from the flanks. To locate, cultivate and win over a target for infiltration is as tough as penetrating main target organisation. The primary requisitions are: compatibility in religion, culture and language. The infiltration target must be from near about the areas of locations of suspected modules, should know the contours of the modules and organisation and be acquainted with some insider. He cannot just walk in and offer services. HUJI like organisations are drawn from compatible madrasas, root *tanzeem* like the Ahl-e-Hadith, religious seminary, etc. To better his acceptability some criminal tinge is more appropriate. Since violence is the main tool of proxy war, people with criminal tinge are welcome by the insiders for certain specific purposes. It must be added that certain other layers, say ideological fronts, are kept afar from criminal activities. They are the master planners; may be a computer engineer and holding a respectable job in a multinational company.

A case study of effort to infiltrate an outsider into the suspected proxy-war organisation was tried in 1994. After elaborate research an infiltration target was selected from somewhere near western Uttar Pradesh. He was cultivated, and motivated. To earn credibility he was encouraged to get involved in a minor communal brawl and spend few weeks in police custody. After release he disappeared from the village and surfaced at a place nearer to the suspected location of the proxy-war module. He succeeded in contacting a "recruiter" who guided him to a madrasa for orientation training by an *alem* (accomplished teacher). After completion of the training he was deputed to a neighbouring country to undergo advanced courses in a camp of the master organisation. On return he was elevated to the rank of deputy chief of a module. In about two years the "infiltration agent" became an important functionary of the target organisation. It was a slow, painstaking but successful effort of infiltration from outside.

Luck is unpridictable. She does not favour even the bravest. However, luck is an important ingredient in making flank attack on a hardcore target. Here comes the concept of "cutout." A cutout is a human asset who enjoys confidence of the handling officer as well as of the main target. A cutout is also used to establish contact with a "conscious agent" whenever vis-a-vis with him is hazardous and impossible or it is not safe to use "brush", "dead letter box" or "live letter box" for communicating with the agent. We would define these technical tradecraft terms in later chapters.

A flank asset may be a family friend of the target, his family member, a professional colleague or even a religious teacher. The range is vast. Success in flank operations depends on resourcefulness of the handling officer.

A particular target in a Left extremist organisation, an over ground activist, was a regular member in a sports club. Besides working as an ideologue, he developed passion for tennis. After studying the flank asset considerably the handling officer approached his controlling officer to arrange for his admission in the sports club, a respectable institution. Little string pulling helped the handling officer to don tennis gears and warm up relations with the ideologue. Over a short period they developed ideological affinity (feigned on the part of the handling officer). This affinity later gave access to the handling officer to important intelligence inputs about the organisation and the particular main target in the core of the Left extremist body.

Having discussed these two categories let us proceed to elaborate the process of agent breeding. Agent making involve different stages:

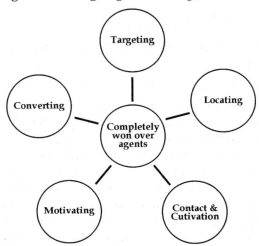

Reading clockwise the diagram illustrates different stages of cultivation of a target and converting him to an agent. The initial aspect is targeting an organisation, establishment or person for accessing clandestine information on the basis of situation and task requirement. The task requirement is decided by the top operations officer, analyst, desk officer or the head of the agency depending on situational developments having bearing on national security. Often political decision makers also task the agency bosses to target certain suspected organisations and individuals. It, however, must be stated that at the grassroots level regional and local station chiefs may also do targeting as they are the main producers of intelligence. In fact, the chain travels from the top to the lowest in the hierarchy. The only difference is that at the highest level top grade penetration is targeted and at the grassroots level the target may be of middle or lower order.

There are some exceptions to the rule. The operation officers, operating in a disturbed or violence infested area may decide himself who to target and for what purpose. However, he has to keep the higher formation informed including security measures adopted in targeting and the process of cultivation.

Once the target is decided, one or more handling officers are selected to take on the job. The handling officers are selected after studying their background and performance record in difficult job areas. They are briefed by the station in charge or the analyst-desk officer with as much details available in the data bank of the agency. Personality of the target is also explained. The handling officer is tasked to gather more details about the target and mull over his vulnerabilities. It is imperative on the part of the superior command to brief the handling officer with security matters prescribed for the game. The case officer has to keep in mind his personal safety, safety of the target and safety of the agency. All targets are not won over, some misfire and some 'blow back', compromising the case officer and the agency. This may often involve physical harm to the case officer.

After being tasked and briefed, the case officer is left to his ingenuity. He has to locate the particular individual or make a list of individuals in the target area and gathers all personal data involving personal life, family, friends, acquaintances, temperament, propensity, personal habits and lifestyle and his position in the target area. The gleaned data are discussed with the desk officer, station chief or analyst and a progressive advancement chart is made. After the process of analysis of the data is completed the case officer is allowed to approach the target stealthily. This can be through a common media friend, a person sympathizing with the activities of the organisation and working philosophy of the individual, or a known friend or family member and any such needle hole through which he can pass and get nearer to the main target. The via media used in the process is not the classical cutout in intelligence terminology. These are mere access cards. The cases of direct approach or walk in are different categories.

After the locating task is complete, the handling officer starts priming the target through a warming up process. He has to understand the mental caliber, psychological make-up and personal philosophy of life and his loyalty to the organisation. These data are also analysed by the desk officer or analyst or the station chief. This is a kind of psychoanalysis which acts as a window to peep into his psychosomatic make-up.

Besides his psychoanalysis the involved officers also carry out study of his intellectual, personal and family lives. His needs are assessed. The questions to ask: Does he like to consume alcoholic drinks? What kind of entertainment he prefers? What is his food and eating habit? Does he believe in personal ostentations? What are his family commitments? Does he love his wife and children? What is his economic status? Has he got any shoulder to cry up on? Does he mind brushing with a beauty outside marital status?

The handling officer is required to shadow his target and peep into his personal life discreetly crossing the boundaries of social nicety. This process can be very tedious and requires full application of intellect. No animal approach would do. The entire process involves research, isolation and zeroing on the appropriate needle-hole to enter the personal life of the target. Unless the handling officer is endowed with such intellectual characterstics he may not succeed in merging his balloon of personality with the balloon of the target. Once they are synchronized then only the priming task is completed. This target priming stage is most painstaking and requires adduction of physical proximity alongside merging of the psychological parameters. However, in spite of apparent merging the handling officer should maintain his strong personality and never allow the target to swallow his personality as a black hole does. Instead, the handling officer is required to engulf the personality of the target with his subtle, suave but superior personality and gain inches of superiority and command position. Attainment of the command position takes place during cultivation process.

The entire process can be illustrated in the following flow chart:

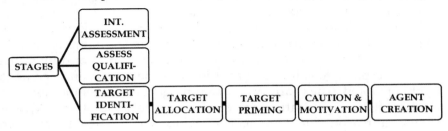

Target priming requires three other ingredients besides equilibration personalities and penetration of the psychological diaphragm and gaining superiority in subtle degrees. These are: blending of personal habits of the handling officer with that of the target. What does it mean? Suppose a target is a hardcore vegetarian and the handling officer has invited him for a dinner. The foreknowledge that the target is vegetarian can help the case officer arrange vegetarian food for his target.

This requires illustration. When in the northeast of India a station deputy was allotted to target a top Naga underground office bearer. He belonged to Sema tribe that played vital role in the insurgency movement. His main food items included roasted pork and beef cooked with ginger, garlic and some other local herbs. He was in the habit of munching his food with Naga Jalopino, probably the hottest chilli in the world. Since Nagaland did not have worthwhile hotel in early eighties, the target was invited to the home of the handling officer. The problem arose about cooking pork and beef, both banned items in his wife's kitchen. The lady of the house was persuaded to allow a Naga assistant to cook the items in local style leaving the service to the hostess. The hostess discharged her duty smilingly and received an application from the target that he had not eaten such delicious pork and beef even in his own kitchen. The day was won. The target was softened. Even after conversation with an agent he never hesitated to visit the handling officer's home for his favourite dish. This agent had later played a vital role in Shillong Peace Accord in 1974-75.

Besides blending or pretending to blend personal habits, the handling officer is required to explore opportunities to push in material benefit to the target. A high statured person of dignity would be offended if a packet of currency note is pushed into his palm. It is necessary to understand the material needs of the target. Suppose a target was required to foot the bills of higher studies of the children in prestigious institutions. The handling officer can subtly gauge the mood of the target and assess his reactions during talks about his children's education. As a normal human being, he will disclose the seriousness of his burden. He may have expensive habit of drinking and maintaining extramarital relations. Through these gaps the handling officer can step in cautiously and start extending material benefits. This is a part of the game of introducing moral erosion in the target. Espionage is moral as it is an integral part of duty to the nation; espionage is immoral as it induces the targets and agents to get corrupted. There are very few top agents who would agree to betray their organisation or country just because of some queer personal reason. The dilemma of morality and immorality has been excised from the dictionary of espionage profession. Spying is a process of war engagement. In a war like situation minor hiccups of morality and immorality are overlookd. Obviously, violation of human rights is not tolerated.

The next point is to hit the pin straight; on the motivation factor. Mere pseudozideological identification and personal relationship cannot induce anyone to agree to spy. Human beings, besides being made of bone and flesh and neuronal facilities, consider the gain factor as the most motivating firmament to take to uncertain flights. People get addicted to share market on the hopes of quick gain, growing greed and fatter pockets. In the case of Cold War affected top military officers and nuclear scientists some USSR assets offered services to the USA on the ground of honourably settling their families in a free country. On the reverse side of this some western talents offered services to the USSR on ideological ground and also for material benefits. If a Mohajir Pakistani agrees to work for India, he may bargain for a return ticket to India and honourable settlement in his home province with better facilities of life for himself and his family.

The handling officer must be able to ascertain the gain factor of the target and in a subtle manner offer him an attractive compensation process. Once the bait is bitten, the handling officer wins 50 per cent of the war of wits. His wit, humour and his acting capability should tempt the target to bite the bait, rod and wheel. The following diagram should be useful to illustrate the motivational and other factors that go in creation of agents.

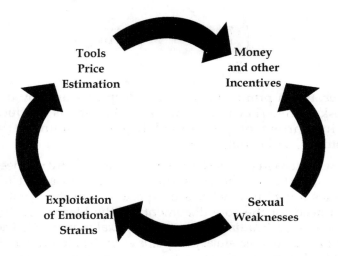

The most important aspect is to pretend to give in more than taking out anything from the target. In case the target belongs to a terrorist outfit the handling officer should be briefed by the desk officer or operations in charge to deliberately "leak" to the target certain innocuous information regarding government preparation against his organisation and movement. These need not be real secret information. However, it must be realized that such targets live in capsulated world of ideas. They are always eager to know more about the government agencies and their preparedness. Skilfully concocted deception material should be fed to the target in a credible manner, which be neither false nor wholly correct. This pseudo-exchange of information allows the target to come out with "real" information about his organisation. This subtle deception is an important part of priming the target.

Ultimately, the process of target priming requires subversion process. This includes study of the personality, understand his needs, financial status, family problems, personal problems, study likings and dislikings, degree of ideological commitment, exploitation of emotions and finally penetrate his personality as per the procedure discussed above. In fact, the handling officer is required to be a psychoanalyst and some kind of exploiter, actor and warrior of wits.

Cultivation stage is practically an on-the-job training process. The target is by now semi-converted. He requires education about what to look for and take order from the handling officer with basic understanding of the task.

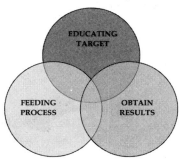

Educating a primed target needs deep reasearch by the analyst and desk officer. They have to work on the aspects of educating the taget in matters of pinpointed tasking, document security, concealment, and commnication.

How to zero in on a task? The task is defined by the needs of the agency and that of the consumer. The top boss and his senior colleagues must know what are expected from the agent. Suppose there is need for the core documents of the Plenary Session of the CPI Maoist spearheading the so-called Naxal movement. The Central Committee adopts certain action plans after detailed discussions with the political, ideological and military commanders of the movement. In case the agent is tasked to obtain the valuable documents, he should have access to the material. If it is ascertained that he has access then he should be taught finer aspects of clandestine manners through which he can smuggle out the material. How to secure the documents? The agent requires training in concealment and communication methhdologies. All these aspects are explained to the handling officer by the departmental experts. The handling officer in turn teaches the tradecrafts to the agent. All these complicated tradecraft aspects require repeated practice. There is no scope for hit and run methodology.

The planning officers must know what they want from the primed target. Asking him for omnibus information would end in futile exercise. In case the primed target is located in the Central Committee of a subversive and terrorist organisation, the agency obviously would be interested to know the structural formation, functioning methodology, training, weapons, battle plans, etc. He would require education what to look for and what to deliver.

Once won over, the target has to be given security briefing continuously about his personal security, secured measured to obtain, copy and conceal documents. During this feeding process he would require some training in using concealed camera, sound recording system and document copying pens, which can copy at least 50 A4 size pages. The case officer would be required to supply the target with such equipment with approval of his controlling officer and to brief the target how to use these with precaution.

Whenever a person is subverted, his personality changes vastly. He often develops hesitancy, slight stammering and inadequacy in his expression and usual demeanour. He becomes a victim of stress. The target would require periodical briefing to behave normally even under stress. Stress management by an agent as well as a handling officer is an important element of behavioural requirement. Even if the agent is not suspected, he develops a trait to suspect that he is under observation. Every criminal knows he is committing a crime. However, over time he develops a cautious and conscious effort to don a normal façade on his personality. The abnormality gradually turns to a normal character trait. The target has to be fed with such psychological training that he learns to put up a normal show without betraying his new compromised personality. Some Abwher officers of Nazi Germany got in touch with British intelligence and they nonchalantly put on normal behavioural pattern even while working in close proximity of the Fuehrer and his principal aides. They did so either willingly to sabotage the oppressive regime of Hitler or they were won over by the western agencies. Most of them remained undetected till the fall of Hitler.

Communication security is very important. The taget is taught to contact his handling officer with utmost precaution meeting places Dead Letter and Live Letter Boxes, Brush meetings, etc. changed everytime. These terminologies would be explained later in the description of tradecrafts.

The initial reports by the converted target are examined with great attention and care to ascertain if he is not playing a phony spooky game. Each and every aspect of the reports have to be checked and cross-checked with existing and reports supplied by other agents to evaluate the veracity and accuracy. Whenever any discrepancy is noticed, the handling officer has to go back to the agent to brief and debrief him and direct him on the correct course. This process may take couple of months to steady the working habits and methodologies and truthfulness of the agent. At the initial stage even if the agent gives very authentic intelligence, this has to be vetted and analysed before the matter is conveyed to the consumer. Evaluation of reports is the main responsibility of the desk officer, analyst and the hierarchical upper ladders. Even if the agent earns confidence, his reports are required to be vetted and analysed everytime. Unassessed and unvetted inputs, if conveyed to the consumer in raw form may cause serious consequences.

In a sensational alleged espionage case by a foreign agency involving India's space agency innumerable reports from secret sources and interrogations pointed fingers at the existence of a transborder international spy ring trying to penetrate and steal secrets from the space agency. The station incharge, however, truthfully pointed out that there were inconsistencies and the reports would need verification. The desk incharge also pointed out this to the controlling officer. However, the controlling authority was in a hurry to convey summary of reports to the top policy maker with a view to preempt other agencies from reporting to the top boss ahead of his reports. The result was devastating for several officers of the agency, involving premature retirement, sacking and criminal cases. Perhaps, in India's intelligence history that was the greatest goof up. Communication to the policy maker cannot be decided upon by the controlling officer himself. He must consult his station officer, desk officer and analysts and only the final result is required to be passed on after considered evaluation.

In another incident emanating from the northeast, one single report that 700 members of uderground Naga army were on way to China for lifting weapons and training was conveyed to the upper command structure by the desk officer/analyst in a raw form. The Military Intelligence disputed the information and they asserted that there was no supportive evidence. The dispute dragged on for about a year. Ultimately the station officer convinced the analyst that only 70 volunteers had gone to China and not 700. The analyst did not like the idea of withdrawing his earlier report. With great difficulty an understanding was reached with the Directorate of MI to convey that only 70 persons were sent and they were likely to return to India. The hasty action had compelled the army to make saturated deployment on Indo-Burma border for nearly three months. That was an expensive but futile exercise.

An agent can be trusted after his initial reports pass the touchstone test of verification and conform to the known parameters of the organisation he works for. Even after reliability of the agent is established the handling officer, desk officer and the analyst are required to vet every segment of the report. This is not distrust. This amounts to trust by trial and faith on intrinsic quality and loyalty of the agent to the intelligence agency. If appropriate evaluation and judgment are not applied the agent may turn complacent and even start acting as a double-agent. A reliable agent turning double is not new to intelligence agencies. The probability of his detection by the organisation he belongs to or an enemy agency is very high. If he can sell himself to one agency he may not demur working for another agency at a better price. In such cases the agent is required to be either given a golden handshake or straightaway discarded.

The handling officer faces couple of more problems. He is trained to be a successful deceit master and superb actor. He is required to decoy several falsehoods under the garb of tons of positive promises and act so naturally that the prospective agent is compelled to buy his story. An agent is more concerned with his security. Besides gain motive, his main concern is his personal security. In a conflict zone like Kashmir or even in the hinterland amidst thickly populated Muslim areas, the agent is always under threat from his peers and *tanzeem* members whom he is betraying. The handling officer is required to teach all security precautions to his agent and take abundant precaution during his movement and contact establishment.

In a sensitive area of Kashmir a habitual border-crosser, a kind of smuggler was cultivated as an agent. By nature a desperate wanderer and smuggler he had contacts with the mujahideen groups based in Pakistan. Obviously, for his survival he was compelled to feed intelligence to the militants, carry their messages and suggest safe infiltration routes. The higher management was weary of using him as an agent. However, double agent is a double edged saw. If used adroitly he can cause more damage to the enemy than to own officers and organisational structure. In this instance the handling officer promised to relocate the agent in Goa to set up a carpet business. He was convinced by the sincere deception used by the officer. Despite higher management's reservations, the handling officer promised haven to the agent. He acted well but had not taken into consideration the facts that the agent was being deputed in an area where skirmishes were going on between the army and a group of militants in which five infiltrators had died. The mujahideen zeroed in on the agent for betrayal and he along with his family was exterminated.

Such desperate action by case officers even in the face of higher management's reservations ended in another tragedy in Punjab. An agent was successfully used to nab the killer of General Vaidya. The handling officer was advised to deactivate the agent for some time as the militants might suspect him. Instead, the overambitious officer stationed the agent in Amritsar in a rented accommodation with false promise that one more job done and he would be rehabilitated in his home state with a grant of land. In no time the militants detected the agent and killed him by cutting his limbs and questioning about the organisation and the handling officer. Such acts of desperation are vastly harmful.

Here comes the question of moral obligation. Intelligence is a part of statecraft and it is often immoral in the true sense of morality. No intelligence operation can be accomplished within the bounds of moral considerations and strict interpretation of the laws of the land. Often the handling officers are allowed to step out of the bounds of legal parameters. For illustration let us presume that an agency is required to use false number plates in surveillance cars. There are ways and means to paste sticky number plates on the original and keep on changing numbers as demanded by the situation. This is punishable under Motor Vehicles Act. But such violations are often resorted to.

The handling officer often suffers from moral inhibition and develops psychological affinity with the agent. There cannot be more dangerous development in agent running than the handling officer developing tenderness for the agent. As a human being he is bound to feel moral pangs that he cannot share with anybody. Intelligence is not hopping in and out of bed. The case officer has to be remorseless, unless he has willfully or by mistake pushed the agent to the mouth of a tiger. In such cases the higher management is required to debrief the handling officer, reprimand him and if necessary withdraw him from agent running operations.

The higher management or the controlling officers review performance of the handling officer and the agent constantly. Their job is to doubt both the officer and the agent and accept the report after it is vetted. Unless such vigilant watch is exercised some handling officers submit "padded" reports interpolating personal knowledge, in the report submitted by the agent. Once padding is detected the controlling officer is duty bound to grill the handling officer and reach the bottom of the fraud. They cannot afford to be sympathetic to the handling officer. He should be under scrutiny all the times and regular evaluation alone can keep him from harming himself and the agency.

In a disastrous case in Assam during Operation Bajrang a handling officer submitted the sketc.h of location of a suspected ULFA camp. Repeated debriefing of the officer pointed out that his agent was correct about the location in a deep forest near the banks of Brahmaputra. Accordingly, the security forces were briefed and a plan was chalked out to raid the camp where ULFA top leaders were reportedly hiding. The high profile raid was launched but after eight hours of marching, the camp could not be located. Later, it was discovered that the handling officer had charted a route based on his knowledge of the topography with a view to make the agent report more convincing. By the time the exact camp was hit the ULFA leaders had vacated the camp and escaped by boat. The handling officer who "padded" the report was grilled and removed from the operational area.

There is one more problem in agent operations. The forward intelligence handling officers like to trust their agents. The trust in this case is a fine diaphragm of deception. No handling officer should trust his agent as he would like to trust his girlfriend. On the other hand, the counter-intelligence officers are taught to distrust most agents. In case the agent of a forward intelligence unit happens to be a suspect of the counter-intelligence unit the later should not advance recklessly to neutralize him. This should be brought to the notice of the controlling officer and a balanced view should be taken. Under no circumstances the counter-intelligence unit should neutralize the forward intelligence agent till the issue is considered at the highest level.

The process of intelligence generation and processing can be depicted in a pyramid form:

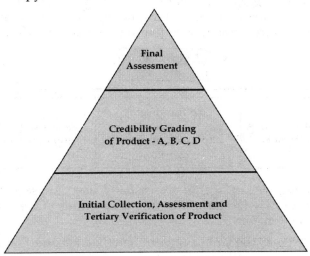

Earlier we have discussed about subconscious and unconscious agents.

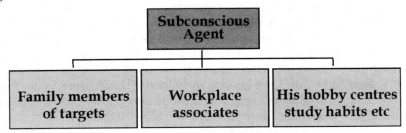

Subconscious agents are those who are gradually drawn into the network of the handling officer through constant efforts, cultivation and association. The facade of innocence is maintained. The agent is dragged into conversation on the targeted topic and during discussions vital intelligence are gleaned out. Often a topic is brought up and during discussions a subtle tasking is made in the ruse of discussing the issue again to resolve the disputed points. Such intelligence help the handling officer to compare veracity of the reports submitted by his main agent. Moreover, such subconscious agents often get enamoured with the world of cloak-and-dagger gets fascinated by the prospect of his being a part of the shadow world. These propensities are required to be exploited to the desired level. The subconscious agent can be a university professor, journalist, scientist, strategist and even an important government employee.

Unconscious agents are those who have either access to the targeted information or have the facility for static and mobile watching capability to collect seemingly innocuous intelligence or find out what was being planned in the headline banners of the newspapers next morning or to look for information inside the house of a suspect. They are not "khabris" in police terminology. They are unconscious informants who are exploited by the ingeneous case officers.

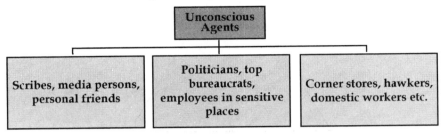

These categories of agents are casually used for secret enquiry and insider knowledge tasked by the controlling officer on orders from the policy maker.

During 1986-89 the Union Government had become controversial and haunted by several scandals. Some newspapers had penetrated certain layers of the Government and accessed inner information about couple of controversial deals. Every morning the headlines cried foul and blamed the Government of thievery, corruption, kickback scandals, etc. An important task assigned was to find out next morning's banner and lead editorials. The task was difficult. The concerned handling officer was supposed to deliver the information by 2 am. In certain cases the newspapers were restricted by incentive, bulk purchase and by influencing the dealers to destroy the day's supply. This job was not a pleasant one but to satisfy the consumer the concerned newspapers were infiltrated by the agency and it managed to deliver 50 per cent satisfactory results. The scandals did not stop, the media did not resile but the handling officer and the agency were spared the rod. They could at least place on the table of the decision maker most of the news dailies by 3 am. The situation was like having a preview of the writing on the wall.

The successor government was also burdened by inner contradiction and instability. Powerful ambitious factional leaders dreamt of a last chance to capture the prime ministerial chair. Their conspiracies in cahoot with the main opposition have become a legend in political chickenary in India. The hallmark of political infamy almost destroyed the fabrics of democracy. However, the handling officers were tasked to glean out inner working of each faction and their action plans. The intelligence was collected from friendly politicians and some leading bureaucrats who still maintained loyalty to the earlier regime. Such information was speedily analysed and passed on to the consumer. Political leaders are a commodity who yearn for information about his other camp followers or adversaries. Informal give and take policy achieved the desired result. However, what can be given as compensation package to such unconscious agents are decided by the controlling officer. This is called measured doctoring.

In smaller but sensitive operations domestic workers play an important role. A high profile political target's house can be penetrated by winning over a domestic servant. In a given case direction was received to plant a bug in the house of a target. After proper situation analysis the domestic servant, a Nepali, was cultivated by a Nepali knowing officer, by posing as another domestic hand in another house. Through this process access to the house was obtained and the bug planted. There are several such incidents.

We propose to discuss counter-intelligence agents and contacts in separate chapters.

Interrogation: However, before exiting from this highly complicated issues of tradecraft some grounds should be covered to examine one of the most important source of information gathering. This is the art and science of interrogation. Interrogation is an important source of intelligence and information and aid to investigation.

Interrogation is carried out by police, armed forces and the intelligence community from a criminal, a security suspect and a suspected spy while the person is either in protective or legal custody for extracting information about the detainee's own culpability, culpability of his associates, his leaders and future plan of the group he belongs to.

There exist legal frameworks in the USA and UK about interrogation, limits of torture, human rights. The US army field handbook as well as manual issued by the Indian armed forces have laid down interrogation procedure. After Guantanomo Bay infamous interrogation process during Bush regime several changes have taken place in the US legal framework. New rules have also been laid down for the CIA and the FBI. In December 2005, the United States eliminated use of fearsome techniques by passing the Detainee Treatment Act, and limiting interrogation methods to those explicitly authorized by the *United States Army Field Manual*. Obama administration has completed the procedure of high value interrogation group for interrogating high value terrorist suspects.

The US Department of Defense normally uses the following interrogation methodology:

- Yelling
- Loud music, and light control

- Environmental manipulation
- Sleep deprivation
- Stress positions
- 20-hour interrogations
- Controlled fear (by using ferocious looking dogs)

The CIA is known to use the following tactics:

- The interrogator forcefully grabs the shirt front of the prisoner and shakes him

- An open-handed slap to the face aimed at causing pain and triggering fear

- A hard open-handed slap to the abdomen. The aim is to cause pain, but not internal injury. Doctors advised against using a punch, which could cause lasting internal damage

- Long time standing is described as among the most effective. Prisoners are forced to stand, handcuffed and with their feet shackled to an eye bolt in the floor, for more than 40 hours

- **Cold Cell:** The prisoner is left to stand naked in a cell kept near 50/10 degrees Celsius, while being regularly doused with cold water.

- **Waterboarding:** The prisoner is bound to an inclined board, feet raised and head slightly below the feet. Material is wrapped over the prisoner's face and water is poured over them. Unavoidably, the gag reflex kicks in and a terrifying fear of drowning leads to almost instant pleas to bring the treatment to a halt.

It is not necessary to enter into the labyrinthine Laws and Acts available in the West to protect human rights, prevent torture and provide custodial security as the existing Acts and Laws in India are more observed in violation.

Police interrogation in India is often associated with torture and third degree treatment. In vast number of cases there is no designated interrogation room equipped with concealed cameras, one-way glass wall, lights that can be dimmed and brightened as and when necessary. Some of the military outfits have prescribed interrogation facilities. The intelligence agencies are also known to have such special facilities at certain locations. Basic needs are: a remote isolated place; an inconspicuous accommodation properly secured physically and scientifically; civilized detention rooms; enough space for some physical exercise; kitchen facilities; soundproof interrogation rooms fitted with light that can be dimmed and brightened like arch lamps, noise creating machines; facility to pump out and pump in oxygen, one way glass wall that facilitates viewing the suspects from outside but the suspect cannot see anything happening outside the room;

stiff back chair-reclining chair; hanging ropes to lift the suspect by hand if necessary.

The officers interrogating a suspect or a group of suspects must be well trained in the art and science of the technology. They are given some basic training on the subject, but, in real terms, they are not trained like psychoanalysts, refined actors, cruel intimidators, sympathetic souls and taciturn tacticians who can enter the inner minds of the suspect. Only seasoned officers with varieties of field operation experience should be picked up for further training in interrogation methodology. For interrogating female suspects some lady officers are also required to be trained as members of the central interrogation team.

Interrogation training includes the arts of studying complete background of a suspect from available dossiers; locating his weak point; locating personal disabilities; details of his family and friends; his physique; endurance power; picking up threads of penetration from the suspect's disclosures; contradicting him with facts that he cannot deny and his power to tolerate thirst and hunger and sleeplessness.

An interrogator should possess superior personality and should physically look more impressive than the subject under interrogation. He should be an expert in understanding the psychological situation of the suspect. A hardened criminal may not give in under normal technique of interrogation and police officers may often have to use threat of physical violence. In intelligence agencies use of physical violence is not permitted, but posturing by a seemingly tough person is not ruled out.

Another important aspect of interrogation is clandestine videotaping of the entire interrogation, especially by the intelligence agencies. In the famous or infamous ISRO counter-intelligence case certain videotapes were produced before the Kerala High Court to prove that no third degree was used on the Maldivian suspects. Moreover, from the videotapes detailed transcripts are made for maintaining record, further investigation, neutralize associate suspects and unearth the spy network.

When a person is detained and isolated in informal custody, his position as a human being melts down by several notches. His self-esteem crumbles down. Isolation opens up windows through which fear and apprehension enter his cranial process. A defenceless person starts building new defences; fabricating stories, inventing alibis and insulating himself. The interrogator has to discover what new defences he has built up. After analyzing those he has to demolish the new defences ruthlessly, making the suspect psychologically naked.

In a case a long term resident agent of a hostile country was detected and picked up. He was informally incarcerated in the isolation centre, which also doubled for interrogation centre. He was not tackled for three days and was allowed to have normal food and other facilities. Through one way mirror it was noticed he was talking to himself, moving his head in affirmation or negation, clinching his fist and often patting his head. That was the time he was inventing his new defences. In the meantime most details of his espionage activities and his sub-agents were unearthed and separately tackled. The top LTRA was in India for 8 years and had established a network of 10 sub-agents, mostly located near military installations. The LTRA was given the cover of a Northern Bihar Brahmin.

On the fourth day his interrogation was started and within a day his defences that he belonged to a village near Bhagalpur and he was a practising priest were busted by contradicting him with evidences collected from his sub-agents. Several other tradecraft methodologies were applied to finally break him and elicit information about other LTRAs planted in India by his agency. Crafty application of interrogation tradecraft is mostly awarded with rich dividends.

Interrogation tradecrafts include:

- Making suggestions to the suspect and watch his reaction.
- Breaking down invented defences with exclusive evidence.
- Sleep deprivation
- Noise creation
- Focusing bright light on eyes
- Use total darkness
- Use deception
- Use intimidation
- Plant false information about family welfare
- Hit his pride
- Down his ego
- Use simultaneous rough and kind approaches by two different officers
- Use drugs like Sodium Amytal, Ethanol, Scopolamine, 3-quinceclidinyl Benzilate, Tempazepan and Sodium Thiopental, etc.

These are also known a truth serum. These medicines are injected under specialist supervision and the suspect is pushed to dream zone where he cannot hold back the truth.

In the USA and the UK certain Acts have been promulgated regulating use of truth serum. India does not have any specific law. The so-called Narco test is nothing but controlled use of truth serum. This weapon is used by police and CBI in routine manner. A time has come for providing Acts of the Parliament regulating and protecting the procedure of interrogation as a part of intelligence gathering and investigation. At the same time the elements of human rights of a suspect or a criminal or a spy have to be blended with such Act, so that the agencies do not indulge in Iraq and Guantanamo Bay type interrogations permitted by the Bush administration.

Chapter 6

Agent Meeting and Communication

Agent communication is an important aspect of tradecraft. **Communication includes:** personal meeting by the handling officer, Dead Letter Box (DLB), Live Letter Box (LLB), drop, electronic communication, brush and concealment.

Agent meeting is an absolute clandestine affair. To achieve this objective both the handling officer and the Agent require security training. Communication security is an elaborate subject. On the part of the handling officer the trainers teach him all the tricks of the trade. A demonstrative flow chart is given below:

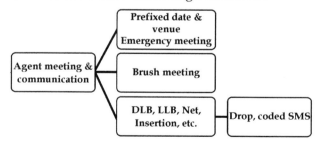

How to set up a meeting? Agent meeting requires elaborate planning. There cannot be any fixed routine, say every Thursday at the Sai Temple on Lodhi Road or behind the Neela Gumbad (blue dome) at Nizamuddin. The meetings are pre-fixed for which variable time and venue are pre-decided. The details for the next meeting are fixed before breaking the current meeting. In the alternative a concealed message can be left under the soil of the agent's flower tub in front of his house, or a prefixed hollow of a tree, in Lodhi Garden or in a hole behind the loose brick of a monument at Sarai

Julena, behind Maharani Bagh. In some handlings some coded marks can be left on a monument wall (though against rule) saying something like: "Love, shall we meet next Friday at our favorite place X?" Even three small circles with a digit showing the day of the week can be chalk marked on an unfrequented monument wall indicating the desired date of meeting. Sometime more than one rendezvous are pre-fixed. In handling one RV is busted by the presence of suspected counter-intelligence agents or curious watchers the next pre-fixed RV can be selected automatically.

A curious handling of insertion of newspaper advertisements had attracted the attention of a station officer. The simple advertisement read — *dear, remember you on 5th next month on our anniversary day; you are invited to attend our son's birthday on 14th of July; Chautha of late Parmeshwar on 7th January at Ram temple, Karol Bagh.* The station officer verified the ads and tried to connect these with suspected events. The final picture emerged after six months: a visa agent of a particular High Commission had inserted the ads on behalf of his foreign handler for fixing meeting between the undercover diplomat and the Indian agent belonging to a sensitive service. After eight month's study and surveillance of suspected movements of the diplomat the espionage racket was busted with careful planning and both the diplomat and the Indian agent were picked up.

In another incident a retired officer of Indian army, self-employed as a weapons supplier, was seen in a particular five star hotel on 7, 21 and 31 of every month for dinner. He came under cloud for passing on Indian military secrets to a western embassy based diplomat. That pattern continued unbroken for five months. Since it was not possible for a grassroots level field officer to enter the posh area and maintain surveillance, the handling officer hired a hotel employee to plant a miniature recording and radio relaying device under his table. The effort turned out to be a dud. The target and his guest talked about politics, current affairs, weather and even women. Nothing suspicious was recorded and relayed by the audio transmitter. To eliminate any mistake and misjudgment the hotel employee was given a button video camera that could transmit to a distance of 100 meters. On third trial the device transmitted a live picture of the retired officer passing on a *Debonair* magazine to his western handler. After three concrete studies the duo were whisked away from the hotel and interrogation revealed that a single page of the magazine was substituted by a paper of same quality and size to convey military secrets of India and plans of the government to procure new weapons system. The diplomat was declared PNG and the retired officer was prosecuted under Official Secrets Act.

Communication methodologies can be varied and diverse. However, before a handling officer is deputed to contact his agent he is subjected to security briefing. Preserving his own identity,

identity of the agent and that of the agency are supreme considerations. Under no circumstances these parameters can be violated, even if the urgency of gathering a piece of intelligence is great. The controlling officer should have the courage to stand up to the policy maker and say that a particular intelligence cannot be produced off the hat.

Security briefing includes foreknowledge of the rendezvous and its surroundings, apparently genuine ruse to visit the location and being there for some time, cover for the visit, and circumstantial dress code. A handling officer cannot afford to be in a posh restaurant in ruffled clothes. He should be properly dressed and should carry the appropriate air in his demeanor. If he chooses to visit a busy place like the zoo, a monument, a cinema hall or a jogging track he should be properly dressed, look like a tourist or cinema visitor. If a meeting is fixed in a crowded cinema hall the handling officer may purchase two tickets, instruct the agent to enter little late and take seat beside him and get out after the business is transacted.

There are instances of pre-surveillance of the RV by a trusted team to ensure absence of counter-intelligence by any enemy agency. However, the surveillance team is withdrawn after they study the situation and convey all clear messages. They are not allowed to see or identify the agent.

Similarly, the agent is trained by the handling officer to adopt security measures. If he happens to travel in a vehicle he is advised to park it at a common parking slot and casually walk down to the RV. Suppose a meeting is fixed at India Gate lawns the agent should be briefed to stand by the side of an ice cream vend, enjoy the delicacy and choose a family gathering to sit and wait for the handling officer. Taking seat near a family gathering gives good cover to pass as a family member without evoking suspicion. Certain agents are in the habit of frequenting libraries. That is an excellent RV. The handling officer should brief him to seat with a pile of book and dog-ear a particular book to indicate the hiding place of the document. The handling officer seated in the library can leisurely walk up and pick up the document.

Setting up personal meeting is an important aspect of tradecraft. The meetings are prefixed. However, no RV is chosen for more than once. Next meeting is fixed after mutual discussion. Frequency of meeting should be infrequent, not more than one in a month. If urgent meeting is necessary the same may be conveyed by using a DLB or LLB. Appearance in the meeting place should be conscious but an air of informality should be exhibited. Both the parties have to be conscious about the surroundings but feign indifference. Preferably an indistinct location should be chosen, where countersurveillance is difficult. The meeting should be brief, walk in and walk out. No open socialisation should be exhibited if not required by the situation.

If a lonely and unfrequented location is not available, a busy location can be selected only for a Brush meeting and crafty passing of document. Busy locations are often chosen to fox the counter-intelligence observers. Avoiding counter-intelligence is very important.

It happened in a northeastern state where the handling officer assigned to an agent of an underground outfit delivered excellent and pinpointed information about plans of violent actions by the underground outfit. The state police chief was foxed by the accuracy of the information, and he summoned the station chief to disclose his source. He politely denied. Despite briefing by the station officer the handling officer was excited by his success. He started meeting him frequently. The police chief mounted surveillance on the agency's handling officer and zeroed in on a meeting in a paddy field. They were nabbed. It was an unethical kick, but the police chief scored his point by neutralizing the agent and implicating the handling officer in a criminal case. The matter was sorted out at higher level, but damage was inestimable.

This leads to the point that the handling officer should not get hyperactive and exhibit his performance. The success goes to his credit and he is silently rewarded. Moreover, local police chiefs should also never try to know the source of information catered by the station officer. It happened again in Sikkim, where a bumbling police commissioner tried to force the situation on the station officer and created an unprecedented row by demanding that the agency should report to him. He deployed a surveillance team to watch movements of the station chief. The funny incident lead to a tragedy. One of the surveillance team tried to cope with anti-surveillance maneuvers of the station chief. Negotiating a sharp curve on hill road the police vehicle rolled down a gorge and three officers lost lives. The foolish exercise was later withdrawn.

Very rarely a cutout should be used to set up agent meeting. Such cut-outs should enjoy mutual trust, preferably a family member. Cut-out or a go-between is a double-edged weapon. This easy process of setting up agent meeting should be chosen after mutual consultation and verifying the strings that might impede the operation. In intelligence trade no one is a friend unless that friendship passes the test of tradecraft applications.

A delicate agent had suggested use of a media person as cutout to establish contact with him. On verification it was unearthed that the media person was a habitual hawker of information to police, other agencies and even to politicians. He would peddle the same information either for Scotch or money packets. A test was set up to trap him. A junior officer was given a piece of disinformation and directed to verify from the same media person. Within two days a police formation shared the same information with the station chief.

The game was unfolded by a single operation. The proposed cutout was never used.

Postal communication with an agent is not a safe device. The postal research cells (PRC) of intelligence agencies have a stop list which they use to intercept domestic and foreign letters. These are opened read, photocopied and sometimes allowed to pass or killed on instruction of the officer in charge. Agent of one unit of the agency may figure in the stop list of another unit. A bitter lesson was learnt from such an incident. The agent belonging to an Islamist organisation lived in a northeastern state. Often he used postal communication to address his remote handling officer. His letters were intercepted and destroyed. Enquiries with the PRC revealed that the agent was in stop list. After great endeavor the name was delisted and the agent was advised to insert steganographic advertisements in a vernacular newspaper on varying dates whenever a meeting was necessary. The camouflage trick worked and lasted for years.

Should the handling officer use disguise during agent meeting? This possibility has been engaging the agencies for a long time. This is not generally encouraged. But, under certain circumstances disguise and changed identity is allowed after elaborate preparation. In strife torn areas the handling officer may require assuming the identity of a utility engineer, salesman, doctor and even a newspaper representative. For such operations the handling officers are trained in the presumed vocation. Suppose he is camouflaged as a journalist the department has to manufacture fake identity card of a national or international news agency, equip him with cameras and a transport with fake number with PRESS inscribed on windshields. His driver and assistant are also given cover and training not to betray the agency.

During Punjab turmoil a senior operations officer often used the camouflage of a reputed western news agency. A van was designed adequately with the trappings of a news agency and it became a normal sight in troubled areas of Punjab. The "journalist" easily accessed his agents and as bonus interviewed several militant leaders. He even succeeded in accessing the hostile premises of the Golden Temple, snapped vital locations, which helped in later operations. In a curious situation a handling officer acted as a taxi driver (belonging to the agency) and met sensitive agents who hopped in as passengers.

Certain busy and often frequented places where milling crowd mingle can also be selected as suitable for brief meeting with agents. This application depends on the considerations of the personal habit of the agent. He may be a regular visitor to a mall, shopping complex, art gallery, book fair, etc. He merges in this background easily. The handling officer may also survey these areas meticulously and select safe RV in such places. Walking together and pretending to shop or appreciate a painting gives enough time to brief and debrief. A particular agent was fond of visiting Sunday book bazaar in Daryaganj. Fond of rare books he was a normal feature in that crowded market. Very suspicious in nature he declined to meet at other RVs. The handling officer was compelled to visit the book bazaar at least once in a month and shop from Jain Pustak Bhandar. This offered unique opportunity for debriefing, briefing and fixing the next meeting.

If an agent meeting is fixed in a hotel room or dining table the handling officer should be equipped with an electronic device, bug sensor. It can be a miniature hand held sensor, cable scanner or portable spectrum analyser. The model shown below is compact and can be used to examine if the room or the table is bugged. This applies more in handling counter-intelligence agent, who may be an intelligence officer of an adversary country. In industrial intelligence such devices are usually used to scan conference halls and all furniture. Even windowpanes are treated chemically to bar implantation of micro-bugs that can pick up sound and transmit to a receiver at safe distance.

SuperPru 3000 hand held scanner

Brush agent meeting is a novel way of agent communication. Whenever personal meeting is not feasible brush contacts are set up through secret communication process. Such process may include a concealed SMS message, internet mail with digits, pre-determined marking in a common agreeable place and any other means of safe communication. Since telephone lines and fax facilities are more vulnerable these means of communication should be avoided.

According to Norman Polmar and Thomas B Allen, Brush agent meeting is "A brief, public, but discreet meeting of an Agent and his handler or another intelligence officer in which information, documents, or funds are exchanged. There is no conversation between the two. To the untrained observer, such a meeting (also called a brief encounter or meeting) would appear accidental, between two persons who are unknown to each other."*

Brush meetings have to be planned meticulously. The Agent may be a known personality and the handling officer may also be known

---

*Spy Book, Encyclopedia of Espionage

in certain areas. Therefore, it is necessary to select a location where both are not frequenters and known eyes are less. If the agent lives in the diplomatic area the brush meeting may be fixed at a place like the INA market, where many foreigners visit usually for shopping. There is the facility of a metro station, busy shopping mall and even a crowded temple where people congregate in large numbers on a given day of the week. The dress code should not be classical spy movie like long coat with a hat to match. Depending on the season the agent and the handling officer should dress normally and accomplish the task silently.

The agent and the handling officer should preferably have radio contact facility, in absence some other pre-signaling device. It is necessary to pick an innocuous site, and keep several sites ready so that one site is not used repeatedly. Before DLB is used the agent or the handling officer must let know each other that they are ready for the task. The agent should wait for a signal that the handling officer is ready to pick up the Dead Drop. They should have some signaling device to convey that the coast is clear. Maintaining DLB security is very important. These should be located in such places where common people may not suspect. In a case a loose bolt on a footbridge was used. After opening the bolt the message was inserted and the bolt refitted. The handling officer/agent unscrewed the bolt and recovered the message.

In a city like Mumbai a brush meeting can take place at the racecourse, busy market and even a temple. The agent and the handling officer may walk in the same direction and one can walk past the other, facilitating transfer of a document without being noticed by other passers-by. Similarly the agent and the handling officer may walk from opposite directions and complete the transaction while brushing past each other.

Brush contact can be transacted with novel innovation. While walking in same direction the agent may feign to drop his handkerchief inadvertently. The agent may walk up with the object and pass on the object uttering a few vital words. In the process they can exchange document or money. In another trick the agent may pass on a book or a magazine to the handling officer. However, it is desirable that the object to be passed on should be small so that it can be fitted inside the palm.

Use of Dead Letter Box is a common communication practice. DLB or Dead Drop is pre-fixed between the agent and the handling officer. Pre-fixation can be done by hanging a particular coloured cloth out of the window, keeping potted plant of a particular flower, making chalk mark on a lamp post, pasting chewing gum on the underside of a garden bench and an agreed newspaper left in a garden.

DLBs must be indistinct. These should not raise curiosity of common people. A potted plant can be used to shuffle a document under pebbles. It can be a loose brick on a monument, a hollow stone like object can be left at a predetermined location. For library goers concealing a document inside a predetermined book is an easy way of secret communication. Often a wayside boulder or hole of a tree works as efficient means of agent communication.

Certain gadgets are now in vogue to conceal messages and leave for the agent or the handling officer to pick up. These can be a waterproof pen like device in which document and money can be concealed and left in a shrub or a shallow stream. In a curious handling the outer cover of a matchbox was ripped open and a microfilm was concealed. The agent, while walking in a garden lighted a cigarette and abandoned the empty match. After he disappeared the handling officer visited the same spot, tried to light a cigarette and looked around for a lighter. He lazily picked up the abandoned matchbox, lighted his cigarette and pocketed the box.

In another curious case a Russian agent used to leave an irregular shaped stone like object at place near the pre-fixed RV of the DLB. The hollow inside contained a miniature wireless signaling device. The Federal Security Bureau (FSB) detected the device through signal interception and lodged protest with Britain in 2006. Obviously a denial was forwarded. Therefore, using radio device is not a prudent device.

There are other ingenious ways to device DLB kits. In certain handlings a standard bolt and nut used in a fence or railing can be chosen. The spymasters take help from laboratory experts to drill out the spike to desired extent and place the waterproof material inside. The spike and the nut can thereafter be replaced in such a manner that can be taken out and inserted back by the recipient of the DLB.

In certain handlings a redundant looking wallet can be used by creating a waterproof chamber where the document can be tucked in and the wallet left in a garden spring or a shallow water channel or water discharge pipe. The user can retrieve the wallet at a pre-determined time.

The below portrayed pen alike is a treated DLB device that is waterproof. This can be easily dropped at a mutually agreed rendezvous.

An innocuous waterproof DLB device

Live Letter Box (LLB) means transfer of clandestine document between the handling officer and the agent that may involve another human asset or other means. In this handling also the agent and the handling officer are not required to meet personally. However, they have to exchange prior signaling to indicate time of delivering and picking up of the LLB. The timing should be precise – say on a given date and time.

Some unique cases of using LLB may require the handling officer to position his own departmental person as a laundry shop aid. This cut-out should be thoroughly trained and should be able to merge with the milieu of a laundry vend. He should be humble, smiling in nature and have the capability of befriending all and sundry customers. However, the handling officer should never expose his agent to the stationed laundry boy. The agent may get an agreed logo sticker stitched in his coat or trouser and insert the document in an inside pocket. After delivery of the document he is required to communicate about the drop to his handler, who can visit the laundry at a safe margin and pick up the document from the planted laundry aid.

Another ingenious way is to position a waiter or bar attendant at a chosen restaurant with appropriate training to discharge his job flawlessly. This person, if positioned in bar should have proper knowledge of different brands of spirits, cocktail mixing and even preparing a nice glass of mixed punch. Ready wit is an important asset.

The restaurant waiter should be able to recognize the agent or the handling officer from the color and shade of his tie, a cap and even from accepting an order for a particular drink. After eating the food the agent or the handling officer may leave a message along with some tips or attach the material with chewing gum to the underside of the plate. Someone later identifying himself with a code word can collect the document from the waiter or bar attendant.

A funny method was adopted in communicating documents with an agent. The handling officer and the agent used identical walking stick, which was hollowed to contain small documents. Either of them would leave his stick inadvertently. The restaurant attendant removed the stick and kept in his personal custody. Later the handling officer or the agent conveniently returned to pick up the favorite walking stick. This novel method was successful in an operation involving a foreign embassy based agent.

Other means of LLB operation include setting up more than one valid post box in addresses considered and vetted as safe. In case the handling officer uses three post boxes the agent can send communication by post in coded version or by personal delivery after taking precautions.

The use of SMS or email in coded language is a common practice. However, such operations should be undertaken under very special circumstances. Intelligence agencies normally undertake monitoring of suspect cell phones and emails. However, use of burst transmission in HF wireless in frequencies mutually decided is a practice for communicating with long term resident agents in foreign countries. All radio transmissions create radiation. Once detected, the location of the transmitter can be zeroed in by triangulation method. Instances of only one-sided voice transmission from the handling officer to the agent are not uncommon. In modern times miniature walkie-talkies are marketed by foreign companies. Some hand-held VHF sets look like cell phones using special frequency. There is facility of modulation of frequencies. Certain VHF sets are of the size of miniature USB type music storing and playing back equipment.

PMR 446 VHF walkie-talkie.

However, use of VHF sets should be avoided where security agencies normally monitor the airwaves. Conversation should be brief and only for the purpose of communicating signals regarding readiness of both the parties to consummate or call off a meeting. Fixation of RV should not be communicated on the air.

Agents are not permanent assets. Over period occasions may arise requiring dropping of an agent. The disengagement process is delicate and often tricky. An agent may turn rogue and try to blackmail the handling officer. If he possesses superior intellectual capability he may start influencing the thinking process of his handler. Often an agent may turn "Double" and "Cross" the agency by collecting intelligence from a weak and emotionally attached handling officer. He may dry up: meaning his access to the targeted area or object may diminish and he may be shifted to another non-productive work area. In that case he cannot have access and may for some time fabricate a few reports to continue the show. This can easily be verified by the analyst and station officer. He may refuse to work with a new handling officer in the event of promotion or transfer of the existing handling officer. "Handing over" of an asset means smooth transfer of agent to a new handler. This may materialize but may not click. Finally, the agent's need dries up and the agency wants to get rid of him.

In rare handlings involving fear of expose if abruptly discarded the senior formation assess the damage potential. If it is perceived that the discarded agent may compromise identity of the handler and the agency, some kind of parting gift is offered to him against written commitment that he would never open his mouth or push his pen. The quantum of golden handshake depends on the quality of the agent and his placement. A nuclear scientist or a very senior party official may require final compensation package of about rupees 5 to 10 lakhs. This kind of buying silence is applicable to higher grade agents. This practice is applicable to counter-intelligence agents and agents belonging to targeted intelligence agency of a foreign country or defence officer of a country that works for the Indian agency. There are hundreds of books on such episodes involving the USA, the UK, Germany, France, Russia and China.

In Indian context certain top level agents were either given "golden handshake" or rewarded in some other manner. In Assam a top ULFA leader was given handsome monetary reward for identifying underground camps of his outfit. Unfortunately, he was later compromised and fell to the bullets of his former rebel colleagues.

In Nagaland the fissure in the NNC was initiated by self-styled General Kaito in 1972. After he was killed by the NNC faction, Scato Swu and 'General' Zuheto spearheaded the split on tribal lines. Several Revolutionary Government of Nagaland (RGN) leaders were helped to settle down nicely in life. Scato Swu was nominated to the Parliament and Zuheto headed a brigade of Border Security Force with the rank badges of a serving brigadier. There are several such instances in Punjab and Kashmir. Since some of the involved persons are alive and active in public and religious life, it is not prudent to disclose their identity. It should suffice to mention that in Punjab election in 1989-90 the political policy maker funded former militants to contest from Parliamentary seats and at least 9 militant leaders were elected to the august house. This had enhanced normalization of the situation in the state. One of the agents who rebelled against the Panthik Committee (committee of the congregation) and helped in splitting the terrorist movement was rewarded to build a big house in a prominent city in Punjab. There are several such incidents of "golden handshake." In a peculiar handling a Pakistani intelligence officer housed in its Delhi embassy was rewarded handsomely in 1993 by transferring an agreed amount to an offshore bank.

"Golden handshake" is awarded as a rare policy. In normal handlings important agents are dropped after some prolonged briefing with some compensation. A dry agent may be discarded after his compromising presence with the handling officer has been recorded on celluloid and his voice recorded to advise him that misdemeanor might lead to his expose. In other cases also the agent is not dropped like a pin. He is persuaded to disengage by engaged argument that his personal safety is involved and the agency has decided to play safe by disengaging. In some rare cases family members of an agent dying in action (DIA) are compensated handsomely to avoid adverse publicity. However, in India the culture has not been truly imbibed. In a peculiar incident when I happened to write a novel on the case study of an Indian agent compromised and sentenced to death in a neighbouring country, the family members, after popular acceptance of the novel, kicked up a row that the agency had not taken any step to protect their agent. The family was silenced by offering a big amount.

The handling officers are required to be trained in the finer aspects of 'agent dropping' and 'handing over.' India has not developed the culture of physically eliminating its rogue agents. Such illustrations are plenty in Pakistan, the USA and Russia , etc. countries. Agent recruitment and agent discarding are equally tough assignments.

Before this chapter is concluded a few words should be added to rogue handling officers and false agents. In secret services certain field officers try to inflate the numbers of low grade agents with dual objectives — to inflate his agent statistics and to misappropriate the secret service fund. Most reports are based on personal knowledge. This abuse can be checked during periodical evaluation of the reports and examination of the suspected officer.

In a rare incident a senior officer working as handling handler in a sensitive case used to produce sensational letters from the top leader in exile to his followers in a northeast Indian state. This lucrative business continued for nearly 6 years. After certain doubts the letters were examined in the backdrop of available local ground information. The fraud was clear. The agent did not exist and the letters were typed with sign and signature of the exiled leader. The bluff was called and the officer was taken to task. Such dangers lurk as the lure for easy money is very tempting.

In recent times a senior officer of an Indian agency was allegedly won over by a US intelligence agency. Taking advantage of his access to top secret material he leaked out secrets to a female operative of the US agency. The counter-intelligence unit detected the clandestine nature of meeting between the Indian officer and the US intelligence operative. The officer was retired from service without any other penal action, because of fear of greater scandal compromising the office of the top boss of the agency. In another recent handling a senior officer of another agency was detected working for a US agency. He was spirited out of India, probably to the US by his handlers. These aspects will be discussed in chapters related to counter-intelligence.

Chapter 7

Special Operations

There exists a misperception that Special Intelligence Operations (SIO) is in the domain of warfare. Intelligence operations also belong to the category of warfare, mostly bloodless and seldom gory. Every intelligence agency, in a democratic country, has to undertake special operations to meet the challenges of severe contingencies. This methodology of intelligence production is not confined to collection, collation, and analysis and sharing with the policy makers. Operations require application of all the ingredients of intelligence tradecraft—HumInt, TechInt, ElInt, SigInt, etc. to achieve the desired result targeted by the policy makers. This is different from task oriented military operations aimed at external enemies. In this category, in vast majority of handlings, internal security matters prompt the government to fall back on the agencies to take up operation to supplement administrative, police and political actions.

Operations are conceived by the top boss of the agency after brainstorming with concerned senior analysts and coordinators after obtaining general approval from the government. The Operation schemes are confined to specific situational developments which pose threat to national security. Such operations may be directed at external and internal threats.

Intelligence Operations are clandestine in nature. According to *Dictionary of Military and Associated Terms*, US Department of Defense 2005, "An operation sponsored or conducted by governmental departments or agencies in such a way as to assure secrecy or concealment. A clandestine operation differs from a covert operation in that emphasis is placed on concealment of the operation rather than on concealment of the identity of the sponsor. In special operations, an activity may be both covert and clandestine and may focus equally on operational considerations and intelligence-related activities."

The definition is complex. An operation is an action oriented intelligence venture taken up under cover both in war and peace times. It has to be more than covert and include elements of deception, singular purpose oriented, adopting maximum clandestine tradecraft to reach the target, destroy or neutralize or isolate and inactivate it. In normal intelligence tasks use of force is absent. In clandestine operations force may be involved and law of the land may be bypassed. So, this kind of intelligence operations differ from normal overt and covert intelligence, though elements of covertness may dominate certain aspects of the operation.

Such operations may relate to internal situations, external security ramifications. These can be aggressive and defensive in nature with the objective of assessing the threat quantum, locate the cores and peripheries, and mount operational attacks from different angles to destroy or neutralize or isolate the threat.

Intelligence clandestine operations may include tradecraft tools of generating several agents, contacts and tertiary friends, may require application of concealment devices, technical and signal intelligence assistance, deception technology and propaganda warfare.

Before proceeding with the discussion it is necessary to understand various steps required for launching a clandestine operation of higher magnitude. There should be defined structure consisting of the policy maker, controlling authority of the agency, director operations, operation chief, support unit and the end product.

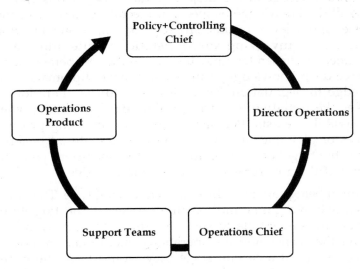

There must be a political sanction to conceive an operation project with clear-cut defined objective. Often multi-directional operations end in fiasco and internal noncooperation, backbiting and rivalry may destroy the operation project from inside. It is necessary to have a Directorate of Operations with several Directors commanding different operation projects simultaneously. Operational areas, targets and personnel involved should not overlap.

For instance the Directorate of Operations may have four separate directors having their separate operations chiefs, with respective support teams. Each operations chief should separately report to the Directorate of operations, having separate cells to handle different types of operations. In Indian context there may be separate directors of operations to combat Islamist Jihad exported from Pakistan and Bangladesh, Kashmir related matters, Maoist movements and insurgency movements in the northeast, etc. In a state like Manipur where there is plethora of terrorist outfits, special operations are required in addition to normal intelligence generation mechanism.

The Operations Chief is backed up by support teams of intelligence handling officers, agent handlers, foot soldiers, surveillance teams, technical support group and if necessary a compact trained commando group. The last item of provisioning is exclusively meant for operations where the direction is to destroy the target. In India, the practice of attaching commando group to Operation Units has been very sparse and operations chief is allowed to use force only as a last resort and mainly in self-defence.

The Director Operations and the Operations Chief are required to qualify in tough physical requirement, grave determination, and thorough knowledge of the subject, terrain and persons and should possess all the knowledge of special tradecraft required to penetrate the target and achieve results. His support staff teams are assigned specific duties involving survey, static, mobile and electronic surveillance. A chosen few may be used in the real penetration job if they have deep knowledge of the subject, have diplomatic skill and knowledge in negotiation. They all report to the operations chief. He takes the initiative to start the diplomatic dialogue, wherever such possibility exists. Persuasion, gradual softening process and promises of give and take and some visible material benefit may convince the target of the operation that the operations chief has the authority of the government and can build a bridge.

Human beings are by nature not renouncing type. They desire to possess, achieve gains and assume power. If the targets of the operation are susceptible to such overtures, the government must empower the agency and the operations chief to talk in those terms and assure that at a certain stage they would have the benefit of talking to someone top in the governance system. Once this wick is fired the power of ambition can be stoked and a fire of desire can be created. The raging fire requires more fat to blaze. The Operations Chief is required to assess the heat of the fire and then hit the hammer. Normally, at such heat and psychological condition the targets yield and agree to negotiate with the representative of the policy maker. That is not the end of the operation. Post-operation responsibilities are enormous. Most promises have to be fulfilled. Some overlooked promises may be vital from the points of view of the targets. Frustrated parties often get stuck like herringbones causing immense problems for the state. We shall illustrate these in later parts of the chapter.

In the USA, the UK, Israel and some other countries the Special Operation Groups are basically war oriented and directed against large bodies of organised terrorists and insurgents. The Israeli Operations are basically oriented against the Palestinians. The US policy was basically directed against the USSR. But after cooling of the Cold War the operations are mainly directed against the Islamist terrorist groups, jihadis, war theatres like Iraq, Iran, Afghanistan, Somalia, Sudan, Kenya, North Korea, etc. The other area of operations that engage US attention is the drug lords of South America.

In the United States Special Operations Command (SOCOM) is the Unified Combatant Command charged with overseeing the various Special Operations Command (SOC or SOCOM) of the Army, Air Force, Navy and Marine Corps of the United States Armed Forces. The command is part of the Department of Defense. The United States Army Special Forces, also known as Green Berets, is a Special Operations Force (SOF) of the United States Army tasked with five primary missions: unconventional warfare, foreign internal defense, special reconnaissance, direct action, and counter-terrorism. Besides this there is the Special Operations Group (SOG). It is a specially trained and highly disciplined tactical unit. It is a self-supporting response team capable of responding to emergencies anywhere in the United States or its territories. Most of the deputy marshals who have volunteered to be SOG members serve as full-time deputies in Marshals Service offices throughout the nation, and they remain on call 24 hours a day for SOG missions.

The Special Activities Division (SAD) is the Central Intelligence Agency's (CIA) covert paramilitary operations unit. They are one of America's most secretive and lowest profile special operations organisations. The Special Activities Division, sometimes referred to as the 'Special Operations Group', is made up of Paramilitary Operations Officers. CIA paramilitaries are typically ex-military personnel and veterans of military special operations units such as the Green Berets or Marine Force Recon. SAD also recruits from within the Agency. The SAD operators undergo extensive specialized training.

The CIA has been credited with huge clandestine operations in Chile, Venezuela, Panama, Colombia, Guatemala and Mexico. Russian involvement (post 1990) includes countries like Georgia, Ossetia, Dagestan, Chechnya and other countries in the region. In limited scale Russians operations spread to the Balkans, Turkey, Syria and Egypt, etc. However, such large scale operations involve Marines, Special Operations Forces, and Special Air Service (SAS) of the UK, etc. Special Operations of the CIA are often gun totting.

Russia also runs special operations groups. Spetsnaz (Spetsialnoye nazranie = troops of special purpose) were raised as the troops of the Glavnoe razvedyvatel'noe upravlenie (GRU) (= main intelligence directorate of the General Staff). In the 1980s the Spetsnaz numbered some 30,000. One Spetsnaz company is earmarked for per Army formation. Spetsnaz brigade are deployed in most military districts of Russia. Besides this special force, the reorganized FSB and KGB usually undertake operation inside the country and abroad.

Pakistan's Inter Services Intelligence is reputed for Special Operations. The Afghan Bureau of the ISI had played cardinal roles to train, fund and direct the mujahideen wars inside Afghanistan. It worked in collaboration with the CIA and the Saudi Royal Intelligence. The CIA had also used the ISI to supply weapons to the Muslim rebels in Bosnia, Herzegovina and Kosovo. At some point the ISI was used to supply weapons to the Chechen rebels.

Inside India the special operations in Kashmir are directed by the Joint Intelligence North (JIN) and in other parts of India the operational directions are with the Joint Intelligence Miscellaneous (JIM). The jihadist activities in India are basically executed under ISI guidance by the jihadi *tanzeem* recruited by it or formed under encouragement of Pakistan army.

The Joint Intelligence X (JIX) of the ISI handles operations related to support systems to al Qaeda, Afghan and Pakistan Taliban, Jamat-ud-Dawa, Lashkar-e-Taiba, Jaish-e-Mohammad, etc. organisations. Pakistan Army and ISI maintain labyrinthine linkages with terrorist and jihadi groups. It is known to most agencies that Tehrik-e-Taliban Pakistan was created to extend support to al Qaeda and Afghan Taliban. Later, the operation boomeranged and under US pressure Pakistan was forced to take some military action in FATA and NWFP. The Talibans have now entered the interiors of Punjab and Sind.

As far as India is concerned, we propose to exclude the domains of Operation Groups of the Indian Armed Forces and operations in the domain of external intelligence agencies. However, some instances of India's Special Operations in the neighbourhood will be cited to explain the basic mechanism.

In India the two main intelligence agencies conceive special operations to combat internal disharmonies and armed groups, especially in terrorist affected areas of the country where foreign countries' proxy-war operations are directed and implemented in sustained manner. No special operations have so far been launched by the internal intelligence agencies against any democratic institutions, legal bodies and groups of people engaged in civil rights domains. However, often special operations are conceived against Mafia, Maoist bodies, drug rings and underworld having connection with groups of saboteurs.

Concept of Special Operations is formulated to tackle special security situations that cannot be solved through normal policing and intelligence inputs. Some operations are short term and others are long term. Normal police intelligence and intelligence agencies may lead to locating a gang of narcotics peddlers, criminal gangs and mafia network. These operations are conducted in normal policing process by using informers, insiders and violent raids. Intelligence special operations are of different types.

Special Operations, short term or long term has a defined action plan.

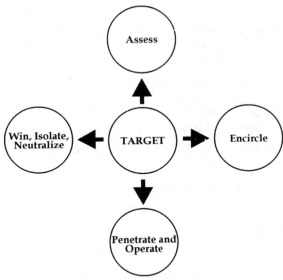

The basic task of identifying the target is under supervision of the Operations Directorate in consultation with the station chief and Director Operations and Operations Chief. The process is tedious. Personality and all the tradecraft qualifications of the target are evaluated and if found that the balance is in favour, then alone the Director Operations is given green signal. Assessment is done by the Operations Chief with inputs from his field staff and other HumInt and TechInt inputs.

After the assessment stage is satisfactorily completed a process is started to encircle the target both physically and psychologically. Encirclement does not mean confinement. It means cultivating institutions and individuals with whom the target may have umbilical, spiritual or ideological ties. He will not be normally in a position to take a vital decision all by himself. He may have to take into consideration the views of his comrades, fellow travellers and groups affiliated to him or he is affiliated to. This is a lengthy process and requires patience. The gestation period may take a few months.

Once this stage is satisfactorily and convincingly crossed the next bridge is to penetrate the target, apply all tradecraft techniques, including deception, lies appearing to be truth, and obviously the elements of igniting the fire of personal ambition in the target must be thrown in at regular intervals. His reactions are judged by his physical demeanor and clandestinely recorded words. All the recorded tapes are analyzed and the transcripts are examined by the top bosses before coming to any conclusion about proper priming of the target. If any lacuna is noticed fresh attempts are made to remove most vacillating irritants. Once the penetration is complete and the target is ready to take a plunge, the operations chief takes permission to activate him for achieving the desired result. The end result may be removal of an impasse in prolonged civil or armed conflict, divide the feuding groups and initiate the process of normalization through the process of negotiation, confrontation and if necessary limited use of auxiliary forces.

Special Operations do not have fixed constant subjects and areas. The targets suddenly pop up and the operations are required to be oriented to cope with the developments. However, certain broad areas are defined for better understanding of the mechanics.

In the context of India, Special Operations can be classified under the following heads:

- Geopolitical and strategic operations
- Politically motivated operations
- Operations related to ethnic insurgent groups
- Operations directed at terrorist organisations
- Operations against ideological guerrilla groups
- Operations related to religious fanatics and jihadists
- Operations against civil society organisations
- Operations against subversive groups nestling in neighbouring countries
- Disinformation operations
- Deception operations

Geo-political and strategic operations are mainly in the domain of the external intelligence agency and the Directorate of Military Operations. The USA excels in conceiving and implementing such operations through CIA's Special Operations Units and units related to the agency. Directorate of Operations of the CIA has a vast operational force under it. These units carry out geopolitical and geostrategic clandestine operations almost all over the globe as extension of US foreign and military policies.

The US has a Special Operations (PM) Group and Special Activities Staff (SAS), otherwise known as Military Special Projects. CIA contingents are always supplemented by the Marines and other special units of the armed forces.

After the 9/11 the US constituted on October 13, 2005 the National Clandestine Service (NCS), which includes CIA's Directorate of Operations. The NCS coordinates HumInt matters with the CIA, FBI, Naval Intelligence, Marine Corps and other intelligence generating units like the Army Intelligence and Activity Command (INSCOM). Some of the clandestine operations are also coordinated by the NCS.

In the UK besides the Special Air Service (SAS), the Secret Service (MI5) and Secret Intelligence Service (MI6) carry out geopolitical and geostrategic operations whenever the government decides to apply these tools of extended diplomacy and foreign policy.

Indian internal intelligence agency does not have separate Directorate of Operations under a senior controlling officer. There is no institutional arrangement in which the internal and external agencies, Military Intelligence and other intelligence and security apparatuses of the country can jointly operate. The structure is bureaucratic and hierarchical and follows the old British pattern. Special Operations, if any are assigned to an officer (with a complement of staff) who normally handles the territorial and subject desk. This archaic system allows the traditional practices to continue unhindered, though this fails to address many burning issues, that require special operations to quarantine, neutralize, or pacify the protagonists of the problematic issues.

There may exist a couple of operation in charges dealing with different targets. But these operation desks operate as isolated islands. Interrelationship between one or more operations is not openly shared. Each sacred cow grazes in own turf. Lack of a controlling and central Directorate of Operations present a disheartening canvas. In the face of threat from neighbouring countries, Maoist guerrilla threats and other internal security perceptions the government may consider establishing a multi-discipline Directorate of Operations (DOP) in addition to in-house DOPs maintained by each agency.

Two instances of geopolitical and geostrategic operations can be cited from recent history.

Majority of Pakistani population was located in its eastern wing — East Bengal or East Pakistan. Ethnic, linguistic and cultural differences between the two wings of Pakistan were contrasted by imposition of a non-ethnic language called Urdu, hegemony of the bureaucrats and politicians from the west and economic exploitation of the eastern wing. Since 1958 these issues agitated the people of East Bengal and by 1965 the agitation gathered momentum leading to balkanization of Pakistan and creation of the new country of Bangladesh.

Pakistan alleged that Indian intelligence agencies had played vital roles in subverting the leading figures of the movement and providing them with financial and military assistance. India never admitted and its agencies were never compromised even if they were assigned with Special Operation to assist the people of East Pakistan seeking freedom. Indian clandestine effort, if any, were followed by open military involvement as Pakistan opened front against India in the west and its armed forces had started chasing the Bengali freedom fighters into Indian territory. Millions of refugees escaping genocide by Pakistan army also forced India to militarily intervene. This was a most successful geopolitical and geostrategic operation that created a new nation for the first time after World War II.

The global intelligence community and especially the former king of Sikkim and his followers alleged that India had initiated intelligence operation in the Himalayan kingdom by inciting the pro-democracy forces. Allegations of use of the office of the Political Officer and his team of Indian officers for subverting loyalty of the elected representatives, monetary incentive to Nepali legislators and arms twisting by the Indian intelligence officers had emboldened the course of the movement for democracy. The Indian manipulators had allegedly forced the merger of Sikkim with India by rigging the referendum. They alleged that India had earlier intervened in Nepal in support of the pro-democratic political party. Whatever the truth be, the democracy movement gathered momentum after 1971 leading to minor show of force and final merger of Sikkim with India through popular support by the elected representatives and a referendum. This was hailed as a huge success of Indian statesmanship and covert intelligence operation. Whether the allegations are correct or not, it is recorded in the annals of Indian history as the hallmark of achievement by its towering Prime Minister Indira Gandhi.

Politically motivated intelligence operations are limited to internal manipulation of political, ethnic and other forces. The classic example of such operational effort was exhibited during 1988-94, when All Assam Students Union (AASU) movement turned violent and later the United Liberation Front of Assam (ULFA) initiated armed struggle. The state police agency was more or less defunct and the central intelligence agency also limped as its functionaries were unable to penetrate the movements. One senior officer, conversant with the area and a leading politician of Assam basically formed an Operations Group. When inducted to help implementation of the operation I noticed with horror that the agency had no or very little local talent and most of the resources were provided by a leading politician. This was an incorrect situation and violated all norms of intelligence tradecraft. Some efforts were made to generate HumInt assets, but in the absence of SigInt and TechInt inputs it turned out to be a nightmare.

The Ahomiya Hindu populace was pitted against policies of the Congress party and the Central Government on the issue of "bahiragoto", illegal Muslim immigrants from Pakistan/ Bangladesh. Attack on local police and intelligence personnel was common. It was rather impossible to generate HumInt assets. However, patient implementation of tradecraft formulae with local innovations helped in generating intelligence from those segments of the populace who were not active participants in the often violent civil disobedience movement. With some lucky breakthroughs a few leaders of the AASU were softened and persuaded to accept the ballot box as their political expression instead of the bullet. Rest of the developments are parts of Assam's ongoing political history.

The United Liberation Front of Assam (ULFA) had already established strong roots in Assam. They had set up training camps in several places and obtained sophisticated weapons from the Naga insurgents, Myanmar based arms peddlers and Bangladesh. Reign of terror pervaded the political scenario. Two major flush out operations conducted by the Army with intelligence input were marginally successful. With limited intelligence assets some excellent scouting of the ULFA camps was carried out and on some occasions photographs were obtained. The Eastern Command of Indian army was briefed with as much intelligence as was available with the Operations Group.

Operation Bajrang and Operation RHINO were not flawless successes, but these yielded some tangible results. The ULFA cadres were dispersed; some escaped to Myanmar, some to Bangladesh while elements continued to operate in Assam.

Even after this no effort was made to constitute a Special Operations Group to handle the insurgency situation. The situation was mainly left to the army, paramilitary and police forces with whatever intelligence inputs were available. Assam operation was basically a politicized exercise for the benefit of a particular party and a few individuals. If the operations were taken up as intelligence surge the end result could have been different. By world standard the Assam political problem was not successfully addressed by the intelligence agency, because it depended on the "genius" of one officer and interest of a particular political leader. These aspects of flaw in Assam operations were never made public, which is not uncommon in supra-secretive Indian intelligence system.

The concept of Special Operations directed against the ethnic restive and insurgent groups was experimented in the handling of the Gorkhaland Movement and the Bodo Movement. The policy makers believed that by launching special intelligence operations they can manipulate large groups of people and direct their political destiny. This is a wrong perception. Such operations mostly backfire.

The low-key Gorkha self-rule and autonomy movement apparently gained momentum during 1985-87. The Gorkhas of Darjeeling district of West Bengal were unhappy with the power sharing system and the state of governance. In this handling the intelligence agency and certain individual troubleshooters were used to fork-lift the low key agitation at shrill pitch by a ruling party in Delhi with a view to destabilise the ruling party (Left Front) in West Bengal. Patna, capital of Bihar was used as the base for handling the disgruntled Gorkha leaders under supervision of a senior intelligence operative. Another centre was started at Varansi for similar exercises for tackling the Gorkha National Liberation Front movement (GNLF). The end result was visible in an accord with the GNLF and the government of West Bengal conceding greater autonomy to the political and administrative matters of the district. This special intelligence was rather directed at exploiting an existing movement to gain political benefit. Regrettably, the Gorkha movement has again surfaced with greater demands and concessions. The Indian political class is yet to learn that such political special operations often create Frankensteins.

The other dirty political special operation was initially directed at the agitating Bodo people of Assam who demanded separate statehood for the Bodo-Kachari-Mech inhabitants of Assam. The Bodo movement for separate political identity was an old demand. It gathered momentum in and around 1980, when Assam was also rocked by AASU sponsored agitations. An intelligence agency was used to launch special operations to "channelize" the movement with a view to dwarfing the AASU movement. Initially an agency of the government had also imparted arms training to the Bodo agitationists. This special operation also went weary and the Bodos adopted the ways of the ULFA and started obtaining arms from Pakistani and Bangladeshi sources. Rest of the violent phase of the movement and a fractured peace agreement is part of the developing history of the Bodo people. It is not possible to disclose more in the interest of national cohesion and security.

Special Operations against insurgent and terrorist groups were experimented in the troubled northeast states. The classic example is exploitation of the fissure between Sema and Angami factions of the Naga underground and emergence of the 'Revolutionary Government of Nagaland'. In Manipur special operations were conceived on the efforts of infiltrating trusted individuals inside the movement and helping them to climb up to positions of prominence. The efforts were successful, and the original RGM (Revolutionary Government of Manipur) was splintered and the movement suffered irreparable damages.

However, these special operations were conceived and executed by individual intelligence station chiefs; there was no special operations directorate in the agency. The concept of Special Operations Group was first initiated in 1987 to handle the troubled situation in Punjab. Two senior officers were placed to conduct operations involving the Pakistan supported terrorist groups. There was a gaping lacuna. Operational jurisdiction was not defined and often the two groups headed by two different officers acted as rivals and crossed paths creating immense problems. One operations officer was action oriented and believed in physically neutralizing the terrorists in tandem with police forces and the other adopted the process of infiltration, dialogue and feigned negotiation with the aim of fragmenting the terrorist groups and neutralizing the fountainhead of ideological base of the separatist movement. The other Operations Officer adopted the approach of infiltrating the militant groups, split them from inside and infiltrate trusted agents to penetrate the Pakistani nexus.

In a war zone killing and getting killed are the natural principles of frontal warfare. However, in a war zone splintering the enemy to position of weakness, exposing foreign machinations and influence the populace are equally important. The later often produce lasting results. This approach had succeeded enormously. A group belonging to the family of Jarnail Singh Bhindranwale, the high priest of Sikh separatism, was cultivated and through whom a number of underground armed groups were contacted and were gradually drafted closer to the idea of peaceful dialogue and solution.

Some fifth column elements were infiltrated in some of the militant groups and were sent to Pakistan. On return they propagated the stories of inhuman treatment to the Sikh partisans, forcing them to eat beef and praying in Islamic way. Such propaganda and disinformation campaign helped antagonizing the populace against the underground formations and their fountainhead the Dam Dami Taksal, etc. Gradually the populace started distancing from the violent movement. Coupled with pressure from police, these operational approaches paid lasting dividend. Within ten years the mainstream terrorists lost ground and the movement died a natural death. Some hardcore elements took shelter in Pakistan with ISI support. Now Punjab is one of the most peaceful states today.

With the demolition of the Ayodhya mosque, Mumbai serial bomb blasts and communal riots Muslim militancy surfaced with ugly manifestations. To approach the problem in a systematic manner the agency was persuaded in 1993 to start a Special Operations Group to tackle the problem of jihadist militancy which received active support from the mafia groups of Dawood Ibrahim and from the Inter Services Intelligence in Pakistan and the Directorate General of Forces Intelligence, Bangladesh. This group and another group addressing the troubled area of Kashmir are still in existence.

It is necessary to mention something about special operations against the civil society organisations and groups. The most important example was utilization of the intelligence and investigation agencies against the leaders of the Nav Nirman Movement headed by Jaiprakash Narain. Groups of intelligence sleuths were tasked to influence, intimidate, threaten and even detain several leaders to weaken the movement. This was the first example of utilization of the intelligence agencies against a civil disobedience movement in independent India. Similar exercises were carried out during the British Raj in 1942 movement. Several disinformation and deception operations were carried out during this period by the intelligence agencies under pressure from the political policy makers. These are not the only instances of using intelligence operations against the civil society.

Unfortunately, the Union and State intelligence agencies have so far not formed any special operation groups for tackling the Maoist insurgents. Frontal police action has limitations; often beset with serious reverses. Delicate intelligence operations inside the populace and the target areas of the Maoist groups by special intelligence operation units can prepare better grounds for regaining "mass control" on the people and hurting the movement from within. Any number of special armed commando groups cannot win back the territory and minds of the people. In an insurgency infested area the ruling government is required to prove that it can provide security and fight the enemies of the people effectively. In this cardinal space the governments are losing ground. It is high time for them to conceive the idea of special operations, disinformation and deception operations coupled with operations-infiltration and breaking the movement from within. Once the enemy is weakened, strong military intervention can shrink the operational and functional bases of the Maoists.

Chapter 8

Surveillance

Surveillance is one of the most important branches of intelligence tradecraft. It is a top priority technique both in forward and counter-intelligence operations and exercises. There is a misperception about surveillance and countersurveillance tradecraft. Many intelligence operators believe this tradecraft in classical intelligence game is applicable to counter-intelligence only.

One cannot escape from quoting the master spymaster Allen W Dulles. According to him: "Surveillance is the professional word for shadowing or tailing. Like every act of counterespionage, it must be executed with maximum care lest its target become aware of it."* While agreeing with this basic definition we would try to survey the contours of surveillance in different perspectives and usages.

In modern era the definition and application of surveillance in classical espionage activity has undergone some welcome changes keeping pace with technological advances. Besides classical professional intelligence controlled by the state players, the private players have also come into the field. They play important roles in detection, enquiry, static and mobile security works on behalf of their clients, both individuals and corporate houses. Besides manual surveillance technical surveillance measures are also applied to achieve the objective. Technical surveillance has several dimensions, which may include hidden and remote controlled cameras, satellite imagery, computer scanning of signals traffic and radio and signals monitoring. However, here we would exclude the private players and concentrate on surveillance methodologies adopted by the state players.

---

*The Craft of Intelligence, p. 124.

India does not have Integrated Intelligence, Surveillance and Reconnaissance (IISR) system. Major western countries, Russian Federation and China have adopted the integrated system without discarding the classical concept of surveillance in intelligence generation and counter-intelligence. The USA can be examined as a model.

With the advent of total and all-comprehensive need for integrated intelligence the USA, in addition to concepts enunciated by Dulles and Hoover, has adopted several measures both for civilian intelligence/counter-intelligence and defence requirements. Total surveillance is no more in the domain of the DCIA (Director CIA). Under Communications Assistance for Law Enforcement Act the government has assumed vast command on total surveillance, intelligence and reconnaissance even in "social control" matters; meaning snooping on private lives of its citizen. Programmes like ADVISE, High Speed Surveillance Computer, Biometrix, etc. have added new arsenals to US intelligence agencies. Computer surveillance includes software based high-speed monitoring of data and traffic that pass through Internet. To implement these parameters of surveillance the CIA, FBI, NSA, etc. organisations use software based programmes like Carnivore, NarusInsight, and ECHELON to intercept and analyse all of this data, and extract only the information which is useful to law enforcement and intelligence agencies.

Since personal documentation and information collation about individuals is highly inclusive in the US, computer programme like FBI's Magic Lantern is used to process and collate personal information about any suspect. The TEMPEST programme involves reading electromagnetic emanations from computing devices in order to extract data from them at distances of hundreds of meters. The NSA uses Pinwale programme to process, collate and store data passing through Internet of all suspected US and foreign nationals of countries outside the USA. Such information can be retrieved by just pushing a computer key. For instance, a Chinese national in Shanghai exchanging emails with a US national is logged under key "frequent visitor" and all such mails are analysed by the experts. If both the numbers use Skype like programme for computer telecommunication those are also monitored and voice spectrum analysed.

It is necessary to briefly discuss some of the advanced features of IIRC system in the USA. ADVISE (Analysis, Dissemination, Visualization, Insight, and Semantic Enhancement) is an important wing of the US Department of Homeland Security. This comprehensive programme has the capability of storing ability to store one quadrillion data item. Such data may include everything from financial records, phone records, emails, blog entries, website searches, and any other electronic information that can be scanned by surveillance expert to determine whether a person is engaged in stealing national secrets or is a potential terrorist. Privacy watchers vehemently objected to this programme and it was officially abandoned in 2007. But there are inputs to indicate that the system is alive and kicking; though unofficially.

The CARNIVORE computer software system was adopted by the FBI to monitor emails and all electronic communications. This comprehensive system adopted during Clinton regime was later modified by the Federal Court only to be applied in respect of listed suspects and earmarked terrorist suspects.

The Magic Lantern software was invented by the Federal Bureau of Investigation and is now used by the CIA as well. This system is sent as an attachment to an email to selected suspect computers used by foreign intelligence operatives and internal counterespionage suspects and even suspected persons living in other countries. Once the attachment is opened it roots down in the computer as a Trojan virus, not easily detectable, and helps the agency to gather all data from key-strokes used by the suspect computer.

The NARUS system was invented by a private company. This high speed computer based system has mass surveillance capability once connected to the Internet server gateways and telecommunication as well as sat-phone gateways. Trillions of data can be stored with the following derivative advantages:

1. Quantifiability to support surveillance of large, complex IP networks

2. High-speed Packet processing performance, which enables it to sift through the vast quantities of information that travel over the Internet.

3. Normalization, Correlation, Aggregation and Analysis provide a model of user, element, protocol, application and network behaviours, in real-time. It can track individual users, monitor which applications they are using like web browsers, instant messaging applications, email, etc. and what they are doing with those applications, i.e. which websites they have visited, what they have written in their emails/IM conversations, and see how users' activities are connected to each other.

4. High reliability from data collection to data processing and analysis.

5. NarusInsight's functionality can be configured to feed a particular activity or IP service such as security, lawful intercept or even Skype detection and blocking.

CONTELPRO (Counter-intelligence Programme) was designed by the FBI in 1956 and was officially terminated in 1971. This programme included infiltration, harassment and false propaganda and illegal surveillance of civil action bodies, communist entities and persons and even radical intellectuals and suspected Church organisations. There are reports that Presidents Roosevelt, Truman,

Kennedy and Johnson used this counter-intelligence programme against their political opponents, suspected White House aides and entities suspected for having links with communist countries. Though officially abandoned under public pressure this CONTELPRO system is still in operation against suspected foreign agents and terrorist suspects and persons having sympathy with Islamic terrorist causes.

CTS or Combat Zones That See is a project of the United States Defense Advanced Research Projects Agency (DARPA) whose goal is to track everything that moves in a city by linking up a massive network of surveillance cameras to a centralized computer system. Artificial intelligence software later identifies and tracks all movement throughout the city of any suspect individual and vehicle.

Since Reconnaissance is a part of the integrated intelligence and surveillance system in the USA it is necessary to mention about advanced reconnaissance mechanism. Micro Air Vehicle (MAV) is used to fly over an area designated for area surveillance or vulnerable installation surveillance, take real time still and video pictures and transmit to a designated receiver. Modern MAVs are incredibly miniature, less noisy and are more precise. If a suspect terrorist or an undercover diplomat travels in a car the same can be followed by the MAV, provided the counter-intelligence operatives can break the GPS frequency of the user car or plant a radio-transmitting bug. In Netherlands developments have been made to utilize dragonfly sized MAV. The data recovered are fed to the integrated intelligence and surveillance system programming for comprehensive surveillance of a given target. Researchers are engaged in developing Nano Aerial Vehicle (NAV). As satellite mapping and remote sensing facilities are used in strategic military purposes these aspects have been excluded from the present discussions.

India is yet to adopt such integrated intelligence, surveillance and reconnaissance system in counter-intelligence system and even in counterinsurgency warfare. The thrust is on classical surveillance methodologies with recent addition of computerized data scanning system, limited telephone, cellular phone and satphone monitoring capabilities. Postal interception is another branch of the surveillance system that has been in practice since British days.

Even though a multi-agency cooperation body has been in position and the Joint Intelligence Committee, a part of the National Security Agency is supposed to coordinate all intelligence activities, in reality, each agency tries to stick to its sovereignty. The National Technical Research Organisation (NTRO), a specialized body for integrated electronic surveillance is yet to measure up to the needs of the nation. In fact, there is no integrated intelligence, surveillance and reconnaissance system in India. An organisation like the NTRO has very little direct communication with other internal and external intelligence agencies. Often the other agencies resort to their exclusive electronic surveillance system. India's homeland security is further disadvantaged due to strict demarcation of areas of responsibility between the Union agencies and state police and intelligence agencies. Even the political policy makers in the Union and the states, where coalition governments are in position the partners in governance pull and push in different directions giving priority to vote bank compulsions rather than total national security. The prime intelligence agencies have to function under all such constraints.

Broadly speaking, the following graphic offers a bird's-eye view of the broad contours of surveillance methodologies adopted by the state players.

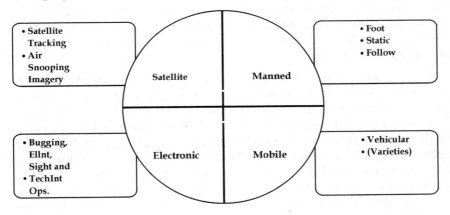

There are several stages of preparations before Human Surveillance can be launched. A surveillance operation is launched against a confirmed undercover intelligence officer of a target country operating from within his diplomatic premises. The supposed intelligence officer (IO) or suspected undercover intelligence officers (SIO) are required to be investigated thoroughly before a surveillance order is obtained from the controlling authority of the agency. Such verifications are based on data input obtained from India's diplomatic missions abroad where the IO or the SIO might have worked earlier. The civil list of the Foreign Service officers of the target country is also scanned and his personal data are collated. To such knowledge additions are made from local surveillance to ascertain movement patterns, local contacts, places frequented, personal habits, etc. The data record was earlier manually handled, now computerization has started and regular updates are entered to obtain a discernible pattern. After all such exercises the target is selected by the forward or counter-intelligence authority. The procedure is more or less same in cases of terrorist and insurgent targets.

The next important aspect is selection of a surveillance team. No member of the team should have been burnt on any earlier occasion. The term Burnt means exposed to the target or the target agency.

Quality of the surveillance team cannot be quantified. However, they must not be conspicuous looking, strikingly dressed, should not have tell-tale habits like frequent hair combing, chewing beetle leaf and nut, smoking cigarettes, not have unsteady eyes and nervous looks, distinguished gait, etc. Each member of the team should have the capability of merging with the background, take credible cover, carry cover-supporting ID cards, and not betray nervousness or panic in the vent of being challenged by any curious neighbourhood watch team or individual.

The team members are briefed in the briefing section by a competent officer about the personal habits, traits and proclivities of the target, shown his photograph from all conceivable positions and the field operators are directed to memorise the profile and even the silhouette of the target.

Static surveillance is mounted at the residence or workplace of the target. As far as the residence is concerned, in possible cases, a safe house is rented opposite to the target house and discreet watch is maintained through high-powered binoculars. All suspicious movements, arrival and departures are logged. In possible cases certain category of sensory or planted bugs are used to monitor room conversations. There are several ways and means in monitoring room conversation. Some of the technical aids are: use of Phone-007, a specially treated phone that can be substituted for the original phone used by the target. Some collaboration with the telephone authorities is required. Similarly, if opportunity is available, the existing phone can be bugged that would radio-transmit room conversation that can be recorded in an auto bug-phone conversation recorder. Such a recorder can record room conversations for 2,600 hours. Sometimes the rooms are also bugged with audio/video bugs. Recent developments have added to the sleuth's arsenal a new weapon for bugging-Bluetooth Mobile Phone Spy.

In case it is not possible to rent a place agencies often post their own men as utility hawkers vending vegetables, fruits and even ice cream. He should have mobility, should be regular and trained in the trade of a hawker. His duty is to watch the house of the suspect, record his movements and communicate the same to the nearby mobile surveillance unit by using a VHF set concealed in his cart. Often the miniature VHF set comes in cell phone size which is convenient to use. The static watcher should be able to pose, at times, as another domestic hand working in the area, or a telephone lineman, plumber, etc. Under that garb he should be able to strike acquaintance with the domestic helps in the target house.

Before mobile-foot surveillance is launched the surveillance team must pre-survey the suspected area which the target frequently visits. Such surveillance is more necessary in an area like the walled city of Delhi where lanes, by-lanes, and intricate mazes of exit and entry points seem labyrinthine. Even a crowded market area like Karol Bagh or Paharganj is very tricky locations for the surveillance team. It is more difficult where a single watcher is deployed for shadowing a suspect. In western countries low flying MAVs are used for pre-survey of areas frequented by the suspect. Since such facilities are not available in India, personal knowledge of the terrain is essential.

A major case-study will illustrate the risk involved where the surveillance officer or team is not acquainted with the intricate areas frequented by the SIO for contacting his Indian contact. A surveillance officer claiming to have very good knowledge of certain areas in the walled city around Suiwalan, Delhi, was tasked to shadow a suspected intelligence officer of a foreign intelligence agency based in a diplomatic mission. On the third day the officer was rescued by a police team on the request of the Indian intelligence agency. The surveillance officer was interrogated and information was gleaned out about the faux pas committed by him. He followed the target in a narrow lane. The suspect exited the lane and reemerged from opposite direction by using an ally-path and recognized the officer following him. After three days the suspect followed the same tactics and arranged to get the surveillance roughed up by using three local toughies on the ruse that the officer was ogling at young Muslim women in the lanes. The surveillance officer, due to ignorance of the topography had shown his face to the suspect and committed the major cardinal mistake. The surveillance officer and team should abandon surveillance if the terrain is hostile and under no circumstances come face to face with the suspect. Remote invisibility and safe distance is one of the cardinal principles of surveillance.

If the pattern of movement of the IO or SIO is well established the surveillance team may deploy a team of three or five. One officer should peel off after half an hour and a new face should take over. Such relay surveillance denies opportunity to the suspect to identify the shadowing faces. Positioning of the relay team is normally decided after studying the pattern of movement of the suspect over a period. The team personnel should be shuffled and substituted at intervals of three days to ensure new faces following the suspect.

Another cardinal rule of foot surveillance is "never lose the trail and never allow the suspect to go out of sight." This is a difficult process. Safe distance from the suspect must be maintained without losing sight of the target. In case the target takes unexpected turns the shadow should alert the nearest team member to take over. The original shadow should reposition him at another location point to pick up the trail when radio-directed by his colleague.

The surveillance teams must carry camouflaged still and video cameras to document sensitive movements of the suspect and his meeting with Indian contact. Often night vision binoculars, video and still cameras are deployed to monitor movement of the IO and SIO contacting his Indian contact well after the sunset, in shadowy and dark alleys and spots.

Micro Video Camera   Thumbnail sized Micro Camera

Some such cameras, including pen camera, buttonhole camera and cameras concealed in handbags are in use in India. These are handy tools of recording "suspect movement" and his meetings with Indian contacts.

Once an Indian contact is identified another branch of the surveillance unit takes up secret enquiry about him. The purpose is to determine the Indian contact's motivation behind meeting an IO or SIO of a foreign country or an Indian linkman working on behalf of any foreign intelligence agency. This phase of surveillance requires illustration.

Individual X, an employee of an Indian defence establishment was noticed by a static watch coming out during lunch break and walking down to the India Gate lawns for having lunch and playing cards. An Indian linkman, who feigned to be working in another ministry and carried an identity card also joined the card games and often lost money. It is a common practice amongst the ministry officials to lengthen their lunch break, play cards and gossip even long after the lunch break time. Watchers of a surveillance unit noticed a pattern in the movements of the Indian linkman. He feigned to return to nearby Vayu Bhavan (Air Force office). However, he managed to slip away and straightaway drove down in his scooter to a kebab shop in nearby Khan Market purportedly to enjoy delicate kebabs. He would brush past another customer and pass on some papers in his hand and disappear. After the pattern was established enquiries revealed that the linkman was a white-collar employee of defence production establishment and was cashiered for embezzlement of funds. This linkman was contacted by an embassy based visa officer when he went there to get a visa for visiting his relatives in a neighbouring country. He was gradually tasked by the IO of the enemy agency to contact serving personnel and obtain information from them about the affairs of the armed forces. The linkman also identified potential agents by cultivating acquaintance with such defence related employees who were in dire financial need, or were habitual alcoholic and did not mind some extra income by whatsoever means possible.

Regular enquiries and surveillance established existence of a network of six defence related serving personnel who were recruited by the Indian linkman to work for the undercover intelligence officer of a foreign intelligence agency. The IO was intercepted when receiving a strategic war room map from a defence employee and simultaneously the rest of the network was also picked up, interrogated and prosecuted. The foreign undercover IO was declared persona non grata and was expelled from India.

Real-life illustrations are titillating and exciting. But real foot surveillance has moments of nightmares. When following a suspect in a sparsely populated area and fewer crowds the Footman is required to maintain respectable distance. In such cases more than one Footman watcher may be necessary to avoid the suspect's suspicion that may arise out of often turning back by him and seeing the same face following him constantly. Some clever IOs adopt the time tested counter-counter-intelligence measure by suddenly stopping, fishing out a packet for cigarette and lighting with lazy motions. During this act he surveys his vicinity and often scares away foot watchers.

However, in a crowded place, like a mall or shopping complex or a cinema hall the watcher may have to move at safe proximity pretending to window-shopping or surfing. The motto is not to lose sight of the suspect. If the suspect enters a crowded restaurant the watcher should use ready wit and take a seat from where he can continue to watch.

Some IO and SIO prefer meeting Indian contacts in wooded parks which are not crowded during noon times. Such parks have more than one entry and exit points. In such cases the Footman must summon extra help over the radio (even cellphone) and arrange to man all the entry and exit points. The watcher is trained to take cover of a bush and keep watching and alerting his colleagues to pick up trail of the IO or SIO and the Indian contact. In a peculiar case a foot watcher was paired with a lady officer to pose as lovers idling in the park and moonshining. In this process they succeeded in making a video film of the IO-Indian contact meeting lasting for about twenty minutes. This video was later used to blackmail the Indian contact inducing him to play double agent for the Indian agency. Such practices are not uncommon.

The foreign IO may prefer to meet his contact in a guest house or a hotel. In cities like Delhi guest houses are plenty but such suspect meeting places are difficult for surveillance team. A particular guest house in Delhi's Sundar Nagar was used by the IO of a foreign agency almost twice in a month. It was not possible for the Footman to go beyond the reception area and spy on the movements inside the guest house. In such cases it may become mandatory to win over some employees of the guest house to keep watch and report back about the identity of the IO and that of the Indian contact.

There are certain special entertainment tenements in the walled city of Delhi. These are managed by organized cartel for entertaining customers who visited the nearby historic Red Fort, the mosque and Meena Bazar. Along with sight seeing some visitors preferred to spend some time with prostitutes brought in by the host madam or the cartel owner. Flesh trade is not a part of intelligence tradecraft. But, non-diplomatic intelligence officers of certain countries were in the habit of visiting these pleasure spots after Friday prayer. Besides enjoying sex they often met their outstation clandestine contacts inside the tenements. It was not possible for surveillance teams to penetrate the vigilant bouncers and other protectors for gaining entry into the tenement areas. After sustained observations a lady talent was spotted, who supplied food items to a few tenements. She was targeted and persuaded to gather information about specific tenements visited by the intelligence staff of certain embassies. Gradually three pleasure holes were identified and penetrated. Sustained watch also established that a person from Rajasthan frequented one of the tenements twice a month on Fridays. His movement was followed to Jodhpur. He worked as a mason in a cantonment location. On a visit to Delhi he was intercepted and interrogated. Few valuable documents about deployment of Indian armed forces were recovered. He disclosed the identity of the foreign IO. Later, through counter-intelligence operations the IO and his Indian network in Rajasthan and Punjab neutralized.

In case a five star hotel is used by the suspect the Footman should be adequately dressed to merge with the guests and visitors. He should be trained to take the same lift used by the IO. However, on such occasions some theatrical changes are necessary to decoy the watcher. He may wear a moustache, a wig and a costly looking suit. He must carry a miniature camera clicking silently and capturing the IO's movements. If he takes the same lift he must get down on the same floor and walk in opposite direction and casually look back to ascertain the room used by the IO. More than one Footman may be necessary to follow the Indian contact separately on foot or vehicle. It may or may not be possible to snap the Indian contact in hidden camera. But physical following may ascertain his residence and other identity details.

Mr. YYY was an important arms dealer of India who was earlier occupying a high position in Indian army. A room in a five star hotel was reserved for him for meeting foreign vendors and arms bazaar captains. Mr. YYY was allured by an embassy based foreign agency undercover intelligence officer by planting on him an Indian socialite famous for her lack of inhibition from going to the beds on hefty payments. A few such adventures were filmed by the foreign agency and the Indian ex-army weapons dealer was trapped. It took over a year to gather sufficient evidence to nail the Indian contact and book him under Official Secrets Act. The foreign diplomat was given 24 hours to leave India. The defence ministry blacklisted certain arms bazaar captains after this incident. However, the controlling authority of certain surveillance operations must ensure that five star hotel savvy watchers are used in such high profile operations where posh hotels and high quality ambience are involved. A bull in china shop is more dangerous than a charging lion.

There are varieties of situation that may arise during foot surveillance. A diplomat (not undercover) of a foreign country stationed in Delhi was found to be fond of Indian beauties, married ladies not excluded. Some such socialites are fond to be seen in embassy parties and certain social gathering of cluster of diplomats, i.e. diplomats of Asian countries, Americas, European, etc. One such lady, estranged from her husband, a supplier to the Indian armed forces, was picked up by a foreign diplomat. They met regularly for biological needs and needs of the diplomat to find out from his lady friend about key supplies her husband made to the armed forces. He even blackmailed her to steal papers of her husband. Once detected and established beyond doubt that the clandestine contact was not limited to biological needs and the relationship was Solomon's mine for the foreign diplomat, a policy decision was taken to contact the lady and explain to her the dangers of her liaison with the diplomat. She vehemently protested. But production of certain photographs convinced her that she had walked into a trap. A mother of two, she understood the gravity of the situation. She ceased to attend such rev parties. The external affairs ministry was advised to politely request the concerned foreign country to withdraw the diplomat quietly. Sex weakness of certain foreign agency operators were successfully exploited by an Indian agency by planting some "honey trap" talents. We shall discuss the "honey trap" tradecraft in a separate chapter.

Foot surveillance can be combined with two- or four-wheeler vehicle surveillance. In such cases, where the person under surveillance, may deploy convoy (a person employed) to detect foot surveillance) or a decoy (a person engaged to divert attention of the surveillance team); the Footman may abandon shadowing and summon the vehicular associate to shadow the target. Often, when a convoy or decoy is identified, separate footmen are deployed to distract their attention. On one occasion a decoy was obstructed by directing a two-wheeler borne watcher to hit the decoy mildly in a busy street and pick up a raucous fight. The decoy could thus be diverted and the main Footman continued his task uninterruptedly. Often a conscious target may jump into a taxi or three-wheeler vehicle. In such cases the adjunct vehicular support is summoned to take up the surveillance task.

Peeling off from a surveillance operation is an important part of intelligence operation. Peeling off means planned withdrawal under circumstances that are not expected by the Footmen. Often stray dogs can take fancy at the watcher and start barking exposing the operation. Sometimes curious neighbours and street urchins may intercept the watchers in a congested locality suspecting them as potential law breakers. Often, a very conscious target may use the ruse of entering a dead-end lane and suddenly turn back. Under such circumstances the watchers should automatically peel off posing as genuine neighbourhood person, may enter a shop to pretend purchasing some personal or family items. Crossing the target for three times means the watcher's identity has been exposed. This should be ascertained during debriefing and the watcher should be withdrawn from the team for at least six months.

Mobile Surveillance means following a target by motor vehicle. Vehicular surveillance is more difficult than foot surveillance. In this book we are dealing with classical intelligence and counter-intelligence matters. Hence we would avoid discussing vehicular surveillance methodologies and philosophy and technique adopted by professional detectives and corporate bodies.

Professional forward or counter-intelligence requires vehicular surveillance to detect, record and log movements and activities of the intelligence operatives of foreign intelligence agencies and their Indian contacts.

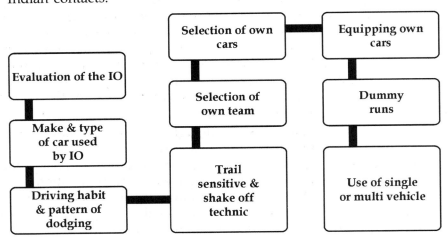

The above flow chart enumerates some of the cardinal principles to be followed by intelligence agencies. First of all a chart is maintained about digital identification of the cars used by the foreign embassies: 75 CD may belong to the USA, 77 CD to the Russian Federation and 89 CD may belong to Pakistan. Normally CD 1 and 1A is used by the head of the Mission and his spouse. Rest of the cars used by an embassy are required to be listed along with specific user name and designation. There are some cars meant for general duty and certain other cars are used by Indian staff members. This identification and enumeration process may take painstaking efforts over a period of time. Normal tenure of a diplomatic staff or undercover diplomatic staff is between 3 and 5 years.

Identification of foreign intelligence officer embedded in embassies is a time consuming process. The counter-intelligence units painstakingly verify antecedents of all diplomats and some non-diplomat staff by collection of data through own embassies in different countries, from civil list of foreign service officers, phone books of the embassies, with help from India based staff (drivers, domestic helps included). Identification is also made by closely following movements of some of the open and undercover diplomats. Wherever possible, photographs of the suspected IO and SIO are displayed in the gallery of the briefing rooms. Normally diplomats use their own cars with distinct diplomatic number plates. Often the IOs and SIOs use miscellaneous cars and even taxis to hoodwink the intelligence sleuths. Logging of IO, SIO and cars used by them are logged over periods and after identity of the suspect is ascertained technical surveillance is mounted on them. This exercise may include telephone, cell phone, fax, and Internet communications. Often teleprinter machines are also intercepted to locate clues. To mount such technical operation for aiding the surveillance units prior government approval is necessary. If necessary, similar technical operations are mounted on the suspected Indian contacts of the foreign intelligence officers. They are also brought under foot, static and vehicular surveillance. The "rogues' gallery" is updated whenever a suspect IO and SIO is brought under surveillance exercises and data about them are logged regularly.

Once a decision is taken to mount vehicular surveillance on an IO/SIO the controlling officer considers all the details about the suspect as indicated in the flow chart on the last page. Personality evaluation of a foreign intelligence agent is very important. Comprehensive information is logged and analysed about personal proclivities, habits and the degree of aggressiveness and tradecraft used by him. The controlling officer picks his team along with the cars to be used and the drivers to be deployed. The role of the driver is very important. He is required to memorize the physical features, movement patterns and diversionary tactics adopted by the IO/SIO. He is required to anticipate movements of the suspect. In open countryside he is required to maintain longer distance to avoid detection. But the surveillance operative and the driver should not lose sight of the suspect. If negotiating a sharp curve, the surveillance car should fall back and gain desired proximity after negotiating the curve.

In a congested city tailgating is permitted but it is not desirable to tailgate. At least less than a standard car distance should be maintained to deny possibility to another car to intrude in between. Some suspects are in the habit of jumping the red lights assuming that diplomatic cars are not penalized. In that event the surveillance car may also jump red light. Tickets issued by police are tackled at a higher level. In congested city traffic, if any other car manages to stray in between the suspect car and the surveillance car the later should manoeuver to jump other cars and pick up the trail as quickly as possible. Intersections and roundabouts are very tricky areas. Often the conscious suspected IO prefers to take a few rounds of the roundabouts to detect if the surveillance car is following him doggedly. In such cases the surveillance car should abandon the operation and request another car to pick up the trail. This calls for multi-vehicular surveillance.

The surveillance cars should always be fitted with two-way VHF/UHF radio facility for communication with other vehicular surveillance teams. Often-radio-fitted two-wheelers are used to aid the main surveillance car to pick up trail in difficult situation. After the situation eases the four-wheeler can replace the two-wheeler. The surveillance cars should be fitted with a special rear view mirror to be used by the surveillance operative to detect if the foreign agency has deployed any counter-countersurveillance. He should be equipped with a powerful binocular, night vision binocular and an audio recording device. He should verbally record all developments in the recorder for later transcription and perusal by the controlling officer. It is always possible to mount a micro-mini cordless video camera on top of the car to record and transmit all images of the suspected IO/SIO. These data are later analysed by the operations incharge to learn lessons of tradecraft used by the foreign agency operative. An example of a micro-mini camera is displayed below. This is a 1 inch square camera with 3 lux (quantity of illumination) in colour version/it has 411.888 pixel resolutions. With 3.7 mm lens the camera is only .80 inches deep. Regrettably such cameras are not in use in India. Some experiment was made with small crude pinhole cameras, but the results were not encouraging.

Vehicular Surveillance can be of different formats. Single vehicle shadowing is applicable in less complicated operations where the IO/SIO are not tail conscious and do not adopt anti-surveillance measures. Anti-surveillance measures may include installation of a special mirror to locate and identify the vehicle constantly following the target car. Certain cars used by IO/SIO have facilities to tune in the frequency used by the surveillance teams. Simple research, trial and error methodology can identify the VHF frequency used by surveillance cars. It is necessary, therefore, for the surveillance team to use digitalized scrambling VHF/UHF radio for car to car and car to control room. Unfortunately Indian surveillance cars mostly use analog system which can be broken into by foreign intelligence agencies. The best way of communication can be the use of cellphones, ear-hole mercury battery operated receivers, and colour mounted wired concealed radio microphones. The ear-hole receivers are best suited for two-wheeler borne surveillance operatives.

Two or multi-vehicle surveillance are mounted in special cases where the suspect IO/SIO are known to experts in anti-surveillance measures, dodging techniques and harassing the surveillance team. In multi-vehicle system more than two four-wheelers or two four-wheelers and two scooters or motorbikes can be used.

A sample exercise is narrated to explain such an operation. The V-I can take up the surveillance and fall back after half an hour. V-II car can go advance and fall back handing over the shadowing task to a motorbike. In this way the relay system keeps the target under constant watch till the operation is complete when the target returns to his den.

The other format is Sandwich Surveillance. The Sandwich concept consists of deployment of two or more cars and motorbikes. Car V-I may tail while car V-II may remain ahead of the target car. The motorbikes can be used for brush passing and observing from tangent angles and notify V-I or V-II as and when the suspect car tries to take unexpected turns to shake off the trail. Such Sandwich Surveillance foxes even veteran foreign agency operators. However, in Sandwich or any other Vehicular Surveillance operation vehicles should be rotated at regular intervals, if necessary, with fake number plates pasted on the originals. Make and brand of the cars should also be rotated. Earlier Surveillance units used to maintain Jurassic brands of foreign cars to match the foreign cars used by the foreign agencies. These white elephants have now been phased out, so also the government-branded Ambassador cars. Even a common person on the streets knows that Ambassador cars are mostly supplied to government agencies. It took a long time to convince the clerks and babus in the ministry that Ambassador cars are identified with the government departments and these were not suitable for secret surveillance proposes. Some modern cars of different makes have now been introduced.

Some surveillance units use black-yellow taxi cars (genuine taxis licensed in the name of some fictitious persons) for highly sensitive surveillance purposes. Often such taxis are parked in taxi stands near the target embassies and passengers coming out from the visa section of the embassy are induced to use agency owned taxis. Out of ten such persons at least 5 are visa agents, who are cultivated by the undercover visa officers as agents or talent spotters. Gradually, when sufficient proofs are available the visa agents are blackmailed to work as double agents, catering information about other visa agents and touts.

Some agents recruited by the foreign agencies are summoned inside the diplomatic premises in the wee hours and they are kept in the safe house inside the diplomatic premises and dropped out late in the night or very early in the morning. In one such operation an unknown person was noticed entering the diplomatic premises through the family gate late in the night. He was snapped by a night vision video camera. One of the taxis owned by the agency followed an embassy drop-car around 4 am. The two taxi surveillance team located the embassy car dropping the person near a railway station in Delhi. A radio clearance was taken from the controlling officer and two members of the surveillance team boarded the same compartment and detrained along with the suspect at Ambala station. The team followed the person to a grocery shop cum residence in the cantonment area.

After prolonged enquiry it was established that Mr ZZZ was a wet ration supplier to the Cantonment Officer's Mess. After logging three visits to the embassy by the Indian suspect the Indian agency picked him up. His interrogation identified the IO of a foreign country enjoying status of a Counsellor. He admitted being recruited by a Long Term Resident Agent of a foreign agency. He was paid Rs 20,000 per month for supplying all details of the Indian Army locations in the cantonment city and all movements they made to outside destinations for deployment. The Counsellor of the foreign mission was later neutralized when made a trip to a popular Dargah shrine in Jalandhar, Punjab in the act of receiving document from the Ambala based agent against payment of remuneration. Such success stories are quite a few.

Some foreign agency operators are well trained in shaking off trails. They move about aimlessly for hours together, enter eateries, cul-de-sac and turn around confounding the surveillance vehicles. Even Sandwich formations cannot follow aggressively. The best way out of such situation is to abandon the surveillance temporarily. Every moment in surveillance operation cannot be golden moments. Frustrations, compromise and abandonment are parts of greater war strategic retreat, only to remount renewed surveillance with changed strategy.

Three technical devices that are in use in advanced countries are: GPS tagging of a suspected car used by foreign agency target, mobile phone tracking of the driver and bugging of the cars of the intelligence agents under observation.

These objectives can be achieved in cases where the embassy based operator use host country based drivers. The Indian agency can have the manoeuvrability to win over the host-country driver to plant a miniature GPS device or a bug that transmits location-position of the car. This makes the job of the vehicular surveillance team easier. Examination of the mobile phone of the driver in the technical laboratory can decipher the routes and places taken and visited by the user. This data is fed to the data bank and in-depth enquiries can ascertain location of the suspected Indian contacts.

Another important tradecraft of surveillance operation is related to postal interception. The Postal Research Centres are authorized by the government to monitor suspected postal mails of suspects against a Black List maintained by the agency. The list is updated at regular intervals. Equipment required are ultraviolet lamps, long and narrow nozzle cattle for steady steam generation, thin bladed knives, etc. for safe examining and opening of suspect postal communications. In case of very serious security threat contained in any postal communication the letter is impounded and the addressee is investigated. In other suspected cases photocopies are kept and the letters are resealed and released.

Some unscrupulous operators often misuse the technical operation. Many foreign Church bodies and Muslim charities often send currency notes along with letters. There were instances where the operators misappropriated the currency notes. However, such illegal infringements are easily detectable and the violators are punished by the controlling authority. Postal surveillance should not pry into personal lives of common citizen. This operation is done against a stop-list (Black List) approved by the government. Some private agencies, however, carry out postal surveillance by bribing the area postman. Such activities are illegal and punishable under the laws of the land.

It must be understood that surveillance operations are strictly meant for counter-intelligence, forward intelligence, mafia and criminal gang identification, detecting drug cartels and in counterinsurgency operations. This tradecraft should not be used for jeopardizing privacy of the citizens by the government agencies under any circumstances. Individuals and corporate bodies using surveillance through private bodies are covered by the laws of the land. If they are compromised the aggrieved party can move the higher courts and even people's vigilante groups and conscious individuals can use countersurveillance measures to bring charges against the violators. Clandestine surveillance against foreign intelligence agency operators are not strictly covered by the penal codes but certain other acts and laws empower the Indian agencies to apply such tradecrafts for protecting secrets of the nation. Such practices are covered under specific Acts in the USA and the UK. Perhaps India should also consider empowering the designated agencies as it is done in the USA and the UK to undertake protective and penetrative surveillance operations. Such provisions can be included in empowering Acts passed by the Parliament.

Chapter 9

The Strange World of Technical
Intelligence (TechInt)

Technical Intelligence is a vast subject. It encompasses Technical Intelligence (TechInt), Electronic Intelligence (ElInt), Communication Intelligence (ComInt), Signals Intelligence (SigInt), Human Intelligence (HumInt) and Computer Intrusion Intelligence (CominInt), etc. In popular perception TechInt means use of technical gadgets in collection and production of Intelligence. This is only a part of the complicated game. However, according to US Department of Defense (12 July 2007) (PDF), *Joint Publication 1-02 Department of Defense Dictionary of Military and Associated Terms*, accessed on 01.10.2007, "technical intelligence — Intelligence derived from the collection, processing, analysis, and exploitation of data and information pertaining to foreign equipment and material for the purpose of preventing technological surprise, assessing foreign scientific and technical capabilities, and developing countermeasures designed to neutralize an adversary's technological advantages."

Scientific and Technical Intelligence include collection process through all conceivable means of tradecraft, evaluation, assessment, precise conclusion about military, defence production facilities, industrial infrastructure used in defence related industry and research and development activities of potential and real enemy countries and sharing the final product of Technical Intelligence with the policy makers at political level and the various branches of Defence wings. Technical Intelligence also includes Economic Intelligence.

The production of technical intelligence includes collection through open and clandestine sources, reports from own embassy about military hardware and preparation of reports and documents for the Military command and the national defence policy makers.

TechInt documents include a wide range of materials prepared by scholars appointed to study defence preparedness of a target country, preparing military inventory of that country and preparation of manuals on military equipment of the target country. For example, the Indian defence establishment prepares exhaustive scientific data based reports on new fighters, bombers and air to earth missiles acquired by China and Pakistan. Most of the data about Pakistani acquisitions from the US sources are known. But subsequent modification by Pakistan, specific to Indian targets are difficult to obtain. In such cases clandestine procedures are adopted as per tradecraft prescribed by the concerned agency, i.e. the Directorate of Air Intelligence.

India does not have elaborate establishments in the armed forces and civil intelligence establishments for gathering strategic Technical Intelligence. Very little efforts were made to appoint bodies of researchers to study technical data and formulate manual about weapons holding by deemed enemy countries, especially nuclear warheads, delivery mechanism and China's latest air power acquisitions and establishment of new bases from where China can target important Indian targets.

Compared to India the USA has elaborate Technical Intelligence gathering mechanism. These are:

- The Missile and Space Intelligence Center is a unit of the Defence Intelligence Agency.

- The Armed Forces Medical Intelligence Center is a unit of the Defence Intelligence Agency. AFMIC is the only organization in the world with this comprehensive medical intelligence mission.

- The National Ground Intelligence Center is a subordinate branch to the US Army Intelligence and Security Command. The NGIC provides scientific and technical intelligence (S & TI) and general military intelligence (GMI) on foreign ground forces in support of military commanders, force and material developers, Department of the Army, Department of Defense, and National-level decision makers.

- The National Air and Space Intelligence Center is subordinate to the US Air Force, Air Intelligence Agency.

- A section in the Office of Naval Intelligence handles technical intelligence activities for the US Navy. Those activities were formerly carried out by the Naval Intelligence Service and by its successor the Naval Technical Intelligence Center.

- Besides these military units the National Security Agency takes up scientific and technical analysis on foreign communications and communications security equipment, as well as foreign research in these areas.

- The CIA is also authorized to collect Technical Intelligence and Economic Intelligence, which is considered as a part of Technical Intelligence.

In addition to the above, according to the US National Counter-intelligence Executive (NCIX), 108 countries tried to obtain US technology during the fiscal year 2005. Most of the efforts, however, centered on a small number of countries like China, Russia Japan, etc. In the USA systematic collection of intelligence about theft of technical data by foreign countries was systematically started in 1997. Some methodologies adopted for such intelligence collection may include:

- Stealing of economic and technical data is rather common operation that exploit business relationships, marketing and sales phase. There are also efforts targeted at individuals with sensitive knowledge.

- Such intelligence is generated often by asking companies for classified, sensitive, or export-controlled information. In some cases, a single would-be foreign buyer sent out multiple requests to a variety of US companies, searching for a seller willing to ignore or bend export-licensing requirements.

- Joint ventures are often used to bring intelligence collectors in contact with people or facilities with sensitive information.

- Offering support services to facilities established with foreign collaboration can camouflage intelligence operators to gather clues about all sorts of manufacturing details.

- Conventions and trade shows offer scopes for gathering economic intelligence. It can be quite easy to enter a show for the industry only. It is not difficult to fake documents to access entrance and examinations of the wares displayed.

- Use of spyware or other malicious hacking techniques to penetrate information systems of foreign governments and sensitive industries are normal practices of the western countries and the Russian federation. In case the USA succeeds in hacking the website of China's missile system the Chinese may not know about the operation for a long time.

Most industrially advanced countries like Russia, China, Japan, Korea, Vietnam, Germany, France, etc. are involved in collection of economic intelligence as a part of Technical Intelligence. The famous case of Dr AQ Khan of Pakistan stealing nuclear technology data, sharing it with China and manufacturing uranium enriching plants and making nuclear bombs for Pakistan is a recent classical case. The storm over "open nuclear marketing" by Pakistan to North Korea, Iran and Libya is still raging the world. The events are even endangering global security with the distinct possibility of the jihadi terrorists accessing the nuclear arsenal of instable Pakistan.

India has taken steps to set up the Central Economic Intelligence Bureau of India, an apex body to coordinate gathering of economic intelligence, detecting economic offenders in collaboration with different economic intelligence and enforcement bodies and with the Central Bureau of Investigation and Intelligence Bureau. It also acts as a Secretariat of the Economic Intelligence Council which acts as the apex body to ensure full co-ordination among the various agencies.

The Economic Intelligence Council of India was formed to facilitate coordination amongst the enforcement agencies dealing with economic offences and ensure operational coordination amongst them, a two-tier system has been established by the Government of India with an Economic Intelligence Council at the Centre under the chairmanship of union minister of Finance, and 18 Regional Economic Intelligence Committees at different places in India.

Among the non-government bodies two agencies are worth mentioning. International Market Assessment (IMA) India provides business enterprises with strategic research, business intelligence and market insights together with sound independent advice on various aspects of the operating environment. Established in 1994, the firm offers four broad service lines built around the objective of delivering authentic, analytical and practical insights to country managers and other senior executives.

The Economic Intelligence Service is designed to present an analytical macroeconomic view of the Indian economy. It brings out a *Monthly Review of the Indian Economy*. This approximately 100-page document provides CMIE's view on the Indian economy. It contains forecasts on Indian economy and presents the most regularly updated statistics along with descriptive analysis for a range of lead economic indicators.

For Technical Intelligence management the National Defense Intelligence College of the USA offers courses in Master of Science in Technical Intelligence. This programme enables the students to know the global context that shapes the world system and understand the complexity, velocity, and interdependency of world issues and events. The core curriculum is designed to have students develop global awareness, and understand how historical, economic, cultural, political and social contexts affect intelligence and national security. Such understanding is essential for a programme founded on the premise that world events can only be understood by employing a variety of disciplinary perspectives, and that they must be understood in a global, regional, and local context. The students are required to be graduates. All prospective NDIC students must be US citizens who are members of the US Armed Forces or federal government employees. Additionally, the students must possess security clearance.

The Indian Army also recruits soldiers (10+2 qualification) for technical cadres. The other major direct recruitment is Indian Army Technical Graduate Course for which an engineering degree in different disciplines can only qualify to be recruited. This cadre of officers is assigned to the Corps of Engineers. These officers are not designed after the Master of Science in Technical Intelligence of the USA.

Among the civil intelligence agencies the Intelligence Bureau and the RAW recruit officers equivalent to the ranks of Sub-Inspector of Police, styled as Assistant Central Intelligence Officer (Grade II), Technical. Rarely some recruitment is also made to higher ranks. However, these officers do not perform the duties of aggressive gathering of Technical Intelligence, as the terminology has been defined by the global intelligence agencies. They are assigned to certain areas of EIInt, SigInt, ComInt and other branches of TechInt. They are generally designed to assist the general duty intelligence officers in running operations where electronic and similar gadgets are involved and also in Signal Intelligence management.

In the beginning of this chapter it was mentioned that TechInt is heavily dependent on HumInt, EIInt, ImInt, SigInt, ComInt, MasInt and CominInt (computer intrusion intelligence), etc. branches of tradecraft. TechInt, as the subject is commonly understood in India is a part of the intelligence cycle, the process through which intelligence is obtained, produced, and made available to users. We propose not to discuss the military aspects of the TechInt, but incorporate in this discussion the interrelations of EIInt and HumInt. In its proper implication an EIInt expert is an intelligence operator who operates electronic monitoring and related equipment to detect electronic emissions: conducts continuous search and monitoring of assigned portions of radio frequency spectrum, using special search or monitoring equipment. He observes video presentations or listens to signal to determine primary characteristics of monitored signals. The expert operates cameras to photograph signals, operates recorders to record signals, determines azimuth from which the signal originated, using direction finder procedures. He determines accurately and rapidly parameters, directional bearing, and point of origin of electronic data recorded on photographic film and magnetic tape through operation of technical laboratory analysis equipment, such as electronic parameter display consoles, oscilloscope, electronic counters and sorters, X-Y plotters, sonographs, visographs, brush recorders, video and audio playback units, complex viewers, visual projectors, and associated analog and digital equipment.

The description given above cannot be found in one person. Several expert operators work in assigned fields and the data obtained are processed and assessed by the hierarchical experts and the final product is shared with the HumInt analyst and controlling authority. Utilization of the data procured and processed is subject to directions of the hierarchical chief. Very sensitive informations are immediately shared with the political policy maker, as in the case of satellite phone talks between General Musharraf and General Ziauddin Butt, the ISI chief, intercepted by an Indian intelligence agency, which clarified amply to India and international community that General Musharraf had plotted the surprise attack on India in Kargil sector of Jammu and Kashmir.

ElInt has a broader connectivity with SigInt. However, in regular intelligence collection and collation through HumInt certain electronic gadgets are used. In normal intelligence vocabulary in India use of such gadgets is described as ElInt, in aid to HumInt. In specialized application these electronic equipment aid to general information and data collection for supplementing HumInt efforts. Some of the electronic gadgets used in daily intelligence operations are: still and video camera, miniature-micro cameras with built-in radio transmission, miniature radio signal emitting bugs, hand held micro document copiers, bug detectors, miniature GPS, miniature voice recording devices, etc.

Use of still cameras, normal, miniature and special resolution lens cameras and infrared cameras for night shooting capability are usually used to take close up, long focus and night-time photographs of suspects. Conventional cameras have several disadvantages. The shutter noise even in a SLR digital camera can be heard by people standing nearby; often flash is used in case the subject is located in dim light area. However, India's hope for silent cameras eluded the intelligence community for a long time. Certain research organisations in India were tasked (DRDO and IIT included) to produce noiseless cameras. However, in global market quite cameras like Rollie 35, Leica M7 and Hexar-AF are available and are popular. Certain cellphone cameras are also noiseless. However, the US Congress has deliberated on a Bill to ban silent cellphones. The Mobile Phone Predator Act (Bill HR 414) was introduced in the Congress on 01.09.2009 sought to ban noiseless cellphone cameras.

Standard cameras are used to photograph a static subject or a counter intelligence subject with a camouflaged camera. Camouflaging devices are adopted to suit the location and occasion. The standard practice is to camouflage a miniature camera in a briefcase, lady's purse with automatic switching facility. Once pressed, the camera can take photograph every 3 to 5 minutes, as per predetermined timing set by the technicians. Certain miniature digital cameras can be concealed in pens. Few illustrations are given below. These equipment can be still or radio transmitting video cameras. In private detection work some such fancy miniature cameras are in use. Use of such cameras by the intelligence agencies is rather infrequent due to paucity of the gadgets and lack of training of the intelligence generating general duty officers. The problem of Indian agencies lay in the policy of watertight compartmentalization between the general duty and technical officers. The two cadres normally do not trust each other and very few general duty intelligence-generating cadres are adequately exposed to the use of such electronic equipment. Even most of the senior level officers coming from the police ranks (RAW cadre in case of the external intelligence) are not intensively exposed to the use of sophisticated electronic equipment. Such gaps between the two cadres often create difficulties in the application of EIInt equipment by the general duty officers.

Watch Camera

Keychain Camera

Pen Camera

However, a few successful experiments by some senior controlling officers using some such video cameras had immensely helped in concluding certain counterespionage operations. Individual XX was a serving technologist in a defence related research project developing and manufacturing certain kinds of ground-to-air indigenous missiles. A static surveillance near the work premises of XX noticed his habit of leaving office late in the evening between 8 and 9 pm, while most other employees left latest by 6.30 pm. Mr XX was in the habit of taking a private bus to his residence in a South Delhi location. One late evening he was noticed taking lift from a Delhi registered car. This was repeated on five occasions. The controlling officer ordered mobile surveillance of Mr XX taking lift in the same car. After dropping XX near his residence the car generally moved around in different parts of the city. On a lucky day a static surveillance team noticed the car entering an embassy through the rear side family gate. This pattern was confirmed after 6 sightings. The operations desk decided to use an infrared still camera with night vision facility to take photographs of Mr XX while entering and exiting the car. The car driver was also snapped on three occasions. After analyzing the data it was decided that a senior officer would accost Mr XX and record the conversation. Mr XX was approached during lunch break when he visited a nearby eatery. He was shown the photographs of his entry and exit from the questioned car and the photos of the driver, who was identified as a non-diplomat employee of the embassy in question. Mr XX caved in. He was taken to a safe house and interrogated. A wristwatch video camera was used that radio transmitted the interrogation sessions to a nearby video recorder placed in an adjacent room.

During interrogation Mr XX broke down and admitted on video recorder that he was trapped by the foreign spy on the lure of money which he badly needed to marry off his three daughters. Over three years he had earned about half million rupees. He was allowed to go under advice that he should not betray any emotion and continue to take ride from the foreign agent. In the meantime, the seniors of Mr XX were taken into confidence and he was shifted to some non-critical area. He was given option to cooperate by feeding doctored information to the foreign spy for sometime. It must me mentioned that the "playback" operation was planned after the issue was discussed between the two ministers of the government handling internal security and defence matters.

After adequate "playback" it was decided to terminate the operation by apprehending the foreign spy in action. On another winter late evening Mr YY in the foreign spy's car, was intercepted in a South Delhi location along with Mr XX. The later was whisked away and the foreign spy was taken over by police for appropriate action. Since he did not enjoy diplomatic immunity, the concerned ambassador was summoned to the foreign ministry and advised to send back the concerned spy to his home station within 24 hours. Mr XX was demoted in rank and transferred to another non-sensitive location. His action of taking part in the "playback" operation came to his rescue. Mr XX was kept under surveillance for another three years, until he retired from a location in southern part of the country.

The concerned defence production department, in consequence of the operation, changed certain parameters of the ground-to-air indigenous missile. The enemy country was misled to believe that the Indian configuration was inferior to what they managed to get from another friendly country. On the contrary, the Indian configuration was much superior to the missiles obtained by the enemy country from its strategic friend.

In another successful EllInt operation in 1987 use of a micro pinhole video camera (no radio transmission but with audio recording facility) had helped an intelligence agency in documenting photos of top leadership of a Sikh guerrilla force and their hideout in a marshy location in Punjab. A Sikh operator having access to one of the guerrilla force was induced to cultivate his friend and earn his confidence by supplying certain material benefits. Gradually, he was given to understand that his friend could supply small weapons and ammunition to the guerrilla force, provided the friend could arrange a meeting with the chief of the force. A policy decision was taken to deliver two pistols as a token to earn confidence of the top leader of the dreaded guerrilla force leader. The government was kept in picture. After the intelligence operative earned confidence of the chief by presenting two pistols he was granted passage to visit the main hideout in the marshy tract.

The Operations officer developed a unique idea. He tried out implanting a micro-mini pinhole video camera (no transmission, but with audio facility) inside the turban of the trusted operator. The recording time was for about 6 hours. After the trial was successful in simulated conditions the camera was implanted inside the turban and the operator was directed to proceed to the target area.

Micro-mini Pinhole Camera 1.05 inches

The operator interacted with the guerrilla force chief and promised to deliver twelve pistols and 300 cartridges for an amount of rupees three lakhs. The deal cemented, a date was fixed for delivery of the weapon in a particular place of worship about three kilometers away from the hideout around 9 p.m. On the given day the operator approached the area and verified if the chief and his bodyguards were in position. After his signal was received the security forces surrounded the place of worship and after two hours gun battle the guerrilla chief surrendered with four bodyguards. For the first time a miniature pinhole camera was used camouflaging inside a turban. Later, a few more operations were carried out using the same modus operandi.

There are numerous uses of miniature cameras in intelligence production and counter-intelligence. Use of such cameras in "honey trap" operations is carried out only by the experts. Amateurish use can lead to "blow up" and the "honey" might come to physical harm. In recent times use of miniature cameras has become a handy tool with the scam-unfolding journalists and certain categories of politicians and private detectives. However, in intelligence operations use of such cameras is carried out after approval of the operations chief and the top decision maker of the agency. In certain cases even the top boss can be tasked by the political decision maker to use clandestine cameras on delicate occasions.

The top agency decision maker once directed that the hotel suite of a visiting foreign dignitary should be bugged and video camera should be used to monitor his activities. It was not known that a 'charming mole' was introduced in the game, who was also supposed to spend the night in the suite. Audio bugging was carried out in the guise of security checking of the room. Listening post was established in a nearby room. Since there was no opportunity to drill the walls to insert pinhole video cameras it was decided that two radio-capable video cameras would be installed — one camouflaged in the flower vase and the other inserted inside the frame of an artist's fine depiction of a mountain peak. The end results were not analysed by the operations team. These were passed on to the top decision maker for final consumption and likely future use by the political decision maker. It is not prudent to name the visiting foreign dignitary. Only comment that can be made is that soon after his visit to India certain aspects of bilateral relations between the two countries improved vastly.

On another occasion an opportunity was offered to use a micro camera hidden in a thick eyeglass frames. The camera transmitted signals to a miniature recorder secured in an inner pocket of the blazer. The tiny camera operating on mercury battery could record for three hours. In western markets more powerful eyeglass frame mounted cameras are available. Some clandestine listening devices are also implanted inside calculators, palmtops and iPods, etc.

Normal and miniature cameras have diverse utility in intelligence gathering and counter-intelligence operations. The only disadvantage with micro video cameras is that battery life is limited and under favorable circumstances certain cameras can function for about two hours. A specific operation requiring constant video recording and transmission for four days for 24 hours had presented a puzzle to the operating agency. After several research attempts it was found that the micro camera could be rigged and connected to an array of 6-nickel cadmium batteries suitably camouflaged inside a small honey beehive. Researchers collected a honey beehive by driving the bees away with smoke-torch. The hive was tooled to insert the battery pack and was concealed near the window ledge which provided a clear view of the main activity room of the subject under coverage; an intellectual suspected for his live connectivity with a group of terrorists. The fabricated battery served for the desired duration and the camera and the hive were removed after the operation was complete. The subject of coverage belonged to a northwestern state of India. The evidence gathered, it was reported, was able to neutralize the intellectual.

Besides use of photo technology, the intelligence agencies depend on radio bugs, both audio and video in ElInt operations. In recent times miniature radio-enabled bugs have revolutionized ElInt operations. Bugs are used to gain clandestine information from targeted subjects by implanting the electronic devices inside their homes, offices, cars and even on their person. Every intelligence generator is not trained in clandestine bugging operations. When an operation of this dimension is conceived by the operations chief and the controlling authority the Tech-ops operators are summoned and a compatible team is formed with personnel drawn from Int-ops and Tech-ops ranks. While the Tech-ops personnel should have the privilege to carry out the actual planting operation the Int-ops personnel maintain the right to decide where exactly the bug is to be planted, what camouflage would best suit the subject, decor of the room and accessibility. All such details are discussed by the operations chief and flexible decisions are taken with variable options.

Some bugs are supposed to be permanent or for long duration. In such cases, practically in all electronic bugging operations the disguise should be given top priority. In long term bugging operations the miniature bugs can be secreted inside a wall mounted electrical socket or plug. Connected with main electricity circuit such bug lasts for infinite period till retrieved or neutralized by bug detectors. In certain applications miniature bugs were connected to decorated lamps, ceiling mounted decorative lamps, inside television sets and telephones. In such cases also the planted bugs, connected to main electric supply system function for indefinite period.

Some of the micro bugs used in such operations are shown in the illustrations below:

Such bugs are not more than one inch dimension with inbuilt batteries, which can last for seven days, unless connected to main power supply with adaptable diodes and transistors. In an operation it was suggested that the main living room of the suspect required bugging for gathering sensitive information related to state security. Gaining access to the house and the room was rather difficult. Besides a housekeeper, presence of a vicious looking pet dog presented immense difficulties. An intelligence operator masqueraded as a domestic servant and over a period befriended the Garhwali housekeeper of the target. New to the area he was looking for a carpenter to repair some dining chair legs and a rocking chair that was dear to his master. Over a lunch the Garhwali was assured by the operator that he knew a good carpenter who he would bring along when his master was out of home.

A trained carpenter in the employment of the agency was taken along to survey the room and the furniture. He suggested that at least two days would be required to fabricate the dining chair legs and another day for replacing the rocking chair foam covers. A deal was struck. Three dining chair legs of the original design were fabricated in which two miniature radio-bugs were implanted. These bugs could be switched on from a distance of 800 meters and switched off when not required. A compatible receiver was placed within 800 meters and the room conversations could be recorded. A similar device was implanted inside the wooden frame of the rocking chair also. Such micro trans-receivers operate on Ultra High Frequency and depending on battery life can function from 5 days to 30 days.

Micro bug (right) and receiver (left)

Some bugs are planted inside the telephone and mobile phones of the targeted suspects. The normal problem of gaining access is insurmountable. However, for an ingenious intelligence operator it is not impossible to gain access even inside a defence installation. For line telephone two approaches are involved: gaining access to the target phone, replace with a similar phone treated with a bug or planting a bug in the line-pair of the junction box or the line connecting the targeted phone.

In a particular operation of political nature the controlling officer desired bugging of the residence phone of the target. Enquiry indicated that the target used a cordless Panasonic phone. Since access was not easily available a situation was created in collusion with the junction operator to render the phone line "dead". On receiving complaint two cover linemen of the telephone department visited the house and proclaimed that some transistors of the phone circuit had burnt out, if the owner desired they could repair it and return the phone in few hours. Certain amount would be charged. By using the ruse a similar Panasonic phone treated with a micro bug and connected to main power source was reinstalled by the linemen. The bug implanted is illustrated below:

However, luck does not favour always. In another case the line-pair connected to the phone was bugged and a receiver was placed within permissible range. There was no difficulty in recording all incoming and outgoing calls. This operation was done to monitor activities of an estranged daughter-in-law of a prominent political leader. It must be added here that intelligence operators cannot afford to have conscience-bites and weigh the morality of an operation. Most intelligence operations involve some ingredients of immorality. But the given job well done drowns the conscience pangs.

Bugging mobile phones poses serious problems. However, there are software in the market that can listen to Bluetooth enabled mobile phones, Black Berry mobiles and laptop computers. Besides conversation SMS also can be intercepted from the targeted numbers. Where the Bluetooth enabled phones are not used, depending on accessibility thumbnail sized (Israel made) bugs can be connected to the SIM card for monitoring all calls.

While on cellphone monitoring we propose to introduce some novel innovations that have reached the market. The cellphone interceptor is one of the latest inventions introduced. The primary aim of developing this unit is to intercept or capture mobile phone conversations taking place around. The person with this unit can call and listen to the sounds and voices in his or her surroundings, and this works even if the target is not using his or her own phone.

One of the most popular units ever introduced is the SecPro Cell Interceptor. It is one of the most effective GSM cellular interceptors that functions off-air. The SecPro is valued for several good features. In the first place, it possesses an intercept system that is very active. Notable about it is its characteristic of being non-detectable and highly performing. The unit can even be upgraded to carry a number of advanced capabilities. Other than that, this interceptor is powered with multi-channel and recording features.

Another model of a cellphone interceptor is the GSM Cellular Interceptor, designed with advanced monitoring features. This product is created to intercept cellular signals and traffic, and while SecPro is sophisticated in style, this too tops the list of the most advanced. Perhaps the best thing about this product is that it can be customized to fit certain specifications. Thus, users or buyers of this highly innovative technology can truly benefit from the capabilities that it has to offer, while enjoying the features they like.

There are many wonders in ElInt operations. The Wall Listening Device is a unique ElInt aid that can record room conversations from outside. This unique device is used to listen through walls. It is capable of listening through up to 20" of solid concrete, doors, windows, etc. The operator can also record by plugging in to recorder. This device is made for professional intelligence operators and is the top of the line for listening through the wall which allows the highest possible sound quality. However, if the wall is very thick and there is high pitch music in the room the interceptor may not work ideally.

Wall Listening Device

In some cases micro spy wireless Audio Bugs are planted in a target room. Most likely secreting spaces are green plant pots, picture frames and decoration piece. The wireless micro audio bug is a composition of oscillator transmitters and receiver. There is no need for GSM card and zero configurations. It works on fixed special FM frequency special signal transmission encryption so that other receivers are not able to listen to the audio signals. The actual size of the bug is half of the size of an AAA size battery. The radio broadcast can be picked up from a distance of 100 meters. Amazing miniaturized GSM Quadriband audio transmitter, for ambient locations such as vehicle or domestic room, remote unlimited audio surveillance are also used in advanced western countries. India is yet to introduce these sophisticated clandestine devices.

In Operation XYZ the controlling authority directed clandestine bugging of a politico-religious party in 1992. Physically, it was impossible to enter into the office complex because of several layers of security. After detailed survey, it was detected that the meeting room had a common wall with another residential building. The owner of the building was persuaded to allow use of the room for couple of hours on usual terms and considerations. Two parallel efforts were made to record the proceedings. In a night operation a micro hole was made in the wall and a wire-head camera was placed to capture the video of the proceedings. By way of ample precaution a wall listening device was also used to monitor the meeting. The results of the EIInt satisfied the decision making authority, though they had dithered in preventing the historic incident of demolition of a disputed structure.

There are innumerable uses of EIInt gadgets for collecting and denying intelligence. One of the handy devices is Pen Microphone. This is better used along with a micro cassette recorder that is hidden inside the coat and a wire cleverly connects the pen microphone and the recorder. Some cassettes can record for 120 minutes. This instrument simplifies the intelligence requirement of clandestine recording of interlocutions with a suspect.

In case it is not possible to gain access into a suspect location to plant a bug, the job can be accomplished by planting window bugs on the outside panel of the target room. The bugs are capable of picking up the sound waves and transmitting to a distance of 100 meters. The intelligence operators can physically handle a compatible recorder or a camouflaged recorder that switches on and off on receipt and tune-out of electronic impulses, can be secured inside a bush and can even be hidden in a green tree. Illustrated below are two typical window bugs which look like a beetle and a dragonfly. These bugs can perform for about 6 hours and given the security circumstances, can be retrieved and replaced.

Window Bugs

Besides such bugs there are sophisticated laser devices which can aim at a closed targeted window and pick up the vibrations and transmit to a receiver. Certain sensitive rooms are constructed with sound attenuation facilities. Some such rooms are designed to be rooms within a bigger room; thus providing buffer from snooping. In Delhi, it was noticed that a Persian Gulf country, while constructing its chancery building had provided complete lead-sheet wrapping of two rooms — the ambassador's room and the room of the cipher handling and communication-handling officers. Lead insulation of a room can minimize acoustic wave transmission.

The US government has prescribed certain standards for construction of highly sensitive rooms which are used for important project discussions. The federal government has several regulations for protecting sensitive conversations. They apply mostly to Secure Compartmented Information Facilities (SCIF) and are:

Defense Intelligence Agency Manual (DIAM) 50-3. Although this document is no longer the primary one related to physical security standards, the chapter on audio security notes the value of sound masking as a tool, but is not specific. This is the earliest publicly available document on the subject.

Air Force Pamphlet (AFP) 88-26, 1988. This document goes into great detail on the methods for creating sound attenuation around a secure room. However, it also states: "The employment of sound masking in wall voids, doors, windows, and overhead ducts may be a more economical technique to achieve acceptable transmission losses."

Director of Central Intelligence Directive (DCID) 6/9, 2002. This document is now the primary unclassified document on physical security in SCIF. Annex E pertains to "Sound Masking Techniques". It states: "...systems are designed to protect SCI against being inadvertently overheard by the casual passerby, not to protect against deliberate interception of audio." The author's experience with secure masking systems suggests that the military and its contractors as well as other government agencies are more concerned about the deliberate listener. It is likely that a publicly unavailable document exists that provides guidance for this higher level of protection. The DCID document does note that sound-masking devices may be used on doors, windows, walls, and vents or ducts, where applicable. Unfortunately, the document erroneously permits music as the sole source of masking. Music can be beneficial only when used in conjunction with sound masking.

Gramm Leach Blily Act. In compliance with this law, all financial institutions must protect the confidentiality of customer information and guard against any threats to the security of such information.

There are several sound-masking, sound equalizer and noise mixing equipment that can be used to minimize eavesdropping by intelligence agents and rival business competitors. The easiest means of denying eavesdropping facility is to play loudly a radio set to create ambience noise and continue the dialogue at as low decibel as possible. In India, there are standing instructions in the intelligence agencies and defence departments about acoustic security. However, in practice, these rules are more breached than observed. It is known that certain foreign embassies in Delhi have ElInt and SigInt facilities to intercept cellphone, satellite phone, computer communication and even eavesdropping facilities.

There is no end of the wonder world of ElInt. There are certain radio bugs which can be planted in a suspect car used by the target. His conversations with any accomplice can be picked up by another intelligence agency car following at a safe distance of 200 meters. In a sensitive case of a suspect from Kashmir it was noticed that he was taking lift from a car belonging to a political leader. Under orders from controlling authority the target car was bugged and conversations between the suspect and the political leader were recorded for four days. As the conversation verged on threat to national security, the matter was brought to the notice of the political decision maker. It was learnt that adequate measures were taken to sensitize the Union Law Maker.

Complete body mounted bugs is a listening device that is wired in the body of the intelligence operator. He can move around in the target location without any ostensible device in his hands, keep on recording conversations, and even live transmitting the same to nearby parked car. Dimension of the equipment is 1044 mm, operating time of the micro-headphone is 62 hours and service time of a micro headphone being 7000 hours. This convenient device has not been introduced in India. Instead, some enterprising officers hide a micro recording device on their body and tape the microphone to their hand, hidden under a coat. This is a cumbersome process.

Clandestine intelligence intrusion is basically a state activity, though many private players have started using ElInt equipment to serve private parties — matrimonial, divorce cases, corporate competition matters. However, bugging the apparel or shoe of a suspect is basically in the domain of government agencies. There are two distinct equipment which can be used to track constant movement of a person on foot or in a car. On occasions coat buttons are substituted by similar buttons with concealed ElInt radio device that emit radiation through GPS system hooked up to a satellite. Such radiations are picked up by a central control room and surveillance teams are directed to pick up the subject. Similarly, GPS enabled micro bugs are inserted inside belts and shoe heels.

In an operation in Punjab a situation arose when a person enjoying confidence of the agency and also of the terrorist organisation was required to be deputed to a hideout in Goindwal area in Amritsar. The area skirted marshlands of the Harike Lake and could be approached on foot. It was decided that a GPS enabled bug would be planted inside the scabbard of the *kripan* (small sword) worn by the Sikhs. The purpose was to keep track of the person and rescue him if the terrorists kidnapped and detained him. After three days constant tracking the person returned to his launching base safely. In a similar operation a youth was won over and persuaded to join a gang going to Pakistan for training and collecting weapons. Since the kirpan scabbard was a religious item of personal attire the same trick was applied and presence of the trusted youth was located in a forested area near Changa Manga near Lahore, where a camp was set up to train the Sikh youths. The gang was allowed to return to India without any encounter to secure safety and identity of the trusted youth. But the operation proved beyond doubt that Changa Manga was an important training facility of the Inter Services Intelligence set up for the Sikh militants.

The vast potential of ElInt operation was exploited by winning over confidence of a Naga militant, whose detachment of 150 well armed persons were entranced on a hilltop in Ukhrul area of Manipur. He was treated with a radio bug capable of transmitting to a distance of 150 meters by inserting the bug inside a Cross hung from his neck. The lithium battery provided 10 hours uninterrupted broadcast. A listening post was set up in a local school. The youth could come to the village frequently to collect ration items. That provided opportunity to replace the battery. The operation provided minutest details of the camp and safe approaches that could be taken to attack it by surprise. On an evening when the youth was out ostensively to collect some *madhu* (rice beer) from the village, army and Assam Rifles columns mounted a surprise attack and overran the fortifications. It may now be revealed that the camp was headed by Thugkalien Muivah (present CSCN-IM chief). This one ElInt operation has been recorded as one of the most successful counterinsurgency operation; courtesy a tiny radio bug.

For bugging a targeted car it is possible to insert a GPS enabled bug in the car of the suspect. Covert vehicle tracking can now be accomplished from the privacy of a computer using the new GPS satellite system. The system consists of a GPS Receiver and Cellular Modem, which is fastened to the target vehicle with two strong magnets. Power is supplied either by a field replaceable battery pack which powers the system for approximately five days. It is also possible to install a GPS bug connected to the main battery of the car. The GPS enabled bug sends signals to the control room enabling the intelligence operators to track the suspect car. However, in western countries even trucking companies use GPS systems to locate their truck plying long distance hauls.

The wonderful world of ElInt does not end here. In the famous Coomar Narain espionage case (1985) several contacts of Narain in the office of the President of India, Ministry of Defence Production, Industry were used to steal official documents and visit a shop in Khan Market for copying. These photocopies were passed to foreign intelligence officers by Coomar Narain. One of the documents was accidentally spotted by an agency officer in the Khan Market shop. This initiated an intelligence operation and arrest of a number of suspects selling government documents to foreign intelligence agencies. These days a secret foreign operator need not go through the hassles of using photocopying machines in a commercial establishment. All that he has to do is to use a miniature photocopier that can be hidden in pocket. Ten A4 size papers can be copied in less than five minutes. There are various brands in the market. But the most convenient one is the below illustrated pen photocopier.

This equipment is versatile and can be used for stealing, storing and physically carrying photocopies of bulky documents. Stored materials in laptop computers can also be copied by this equipment. It can be used as a USB.

The world of ElInt is full of surprises. Even as the spooks manage to eavesdrop, steal information with application of scientific tools there are tools that try to deny information and detect planted devices. The new Micro Audio/Video Bug Detector is a tiny but powerful RF vibrating detector small enough to be worn on body without being noticed. This tiny micro sized unit measures an amazing $2\,{}^1/_8$ inches long × $1\,{}^3/_4$ inches wide by ${}^1/_2$ inch deep. It's a full-featured dual bug detector that silently vibrates to alert about the presence of eavesdropping equipment. It can be used as a covert body worn detector with the included arm band or as a conventional bug detector to sweep a room or office. There are several brands of such micro-detectors in the western markets and in the markets of Korea, Japan and Taiwan.

Body Wire Bug Detector

There are many excellent devices to secure phone calls. But to secure room conversation one needs the Acoustical Privacy Jammer. This device will protect instantly from a "bug" even if you did not detect it previously. It works by generating unfiltrable random white noise — desensitizing any microphone — based eavesdropping. It protects from tape recorders, shotgun microphones, wired devices, and microwave and laser pickups, all the eavesdropper hears is a loud hiss. One homemade remedy is using a radio set at loud pitch to deny any room conversation access to an adversary. This simple method was tried on many occasions in theatres of operation and proved to be successful. A typical acoustic jammer may look like a small buzzing box, illustrated below. However, in large scale jamming operations, say, jamming Pakistani radio and TV beams directed towards a section of Indian people can be locally jammed by using jammers of bigger dimensions with multi-frequency jamming capability of short wave, medium wave and VHF frequencies. Certain embassies in Delhi use jammers to prevent suspected Indian efforts to use laser and radio beams for penetrating the firewalling of the audio facilities inside the diplomatic premises.

An Acoustic Jammer

A versatile bug detector that is compact and is capable of detecting minutest radiation is now available in the market. This bug detector not only tells if a listening device (bug) is present, LED bar-graph lets the operator zero-in on its exact location. It can cover radiation from 5 MHz to 2 GHz! This item is popular in VVIP security operations and other sensitive locations. Some of the corporate houses have also adopted this compact bug detector.

Super Sweep-Pro is a big equipment for bug detection. This countersurveillance Probe/Monitor provides five of the "most desired sweep functions" in one package.

a.   RF probe "sniffs" environment for hidden phone, room or body bugs, remote signals, computer, fax or telex transmitters, video transmitters, pulsed tracking transmitters, and even wide band frequency hopping or "burst" bugs.

b.   VLF probe tests AC outlets, phone lines or suspicious wires for very low frequency "carrier current" signs.

c.   Auxiliary audio input enables it to listen to telephones or lines for "hotmikes," hookswitch bypass and "infinity" bugs, also unknown wires and cables can be tested for wired microphones.

d.   After a sweep, the alarm monitor guards against new devices brought in, remote control activation, or someone tampering with installed equipment.

e.   The 24-hour "evidence" recording output will store suspicious sounds on a standard cassette recorder while you are away.

This equipment can quickly and silently detect all major categories of electronic surveillance, including:

- Room, phone, and body bugs that transmit conversations
- Video transmitters watching all moves
- Vehicle tracking beepers giving away location
- Infinity bugs, hook switch bypass or reversals "turned-on" to conversations
- Wired microphones listening inside a wall
- Computer, Fax or Telex transmitters "reading" information.

This equipment, it is learnt, has not been included in the inventory of Indian intelligence agencies. It is, however, not a very costly intelligence-denying equipment. There are several brands of such equipment.

Chapter 10

Signals Intelligence (SigInt)

Signals Intelligence is an important tradecraft in intelligence production and denial. In modern terminology, as used by the US army SigInt is a category of intelligence comprising either individually or in combination all communications intelligence, electronic intelligence, and foreign instrumentation signals intelligence, however transmitted. SigInt embraces vast parameters of intelligence collection tradecraft including ElInt, ImInt, FisInt (foreign instrumentation signals intelligence), and ComInt, etc.

In modern times the British were the first to use radio signals (HF) for field communication in the Boer War in 1900. If we recall history of development of communication system, I would not request you to see Hollywood movies where the aboriginals are shown to send signals through smoke, drumbeats and display of torch (non-electrical) and coloured flags from a high tree or tower. In reality these were the evolutionary processes through which human history has passed — communicating within the community, neighbouring community, in war and peace and festivity and mourning.

With the invention of radio broadcasting and practical application of the science in 1901 by Marconi (many others including JC Bose of India had experimented successfully), introduction of telephone in 1876 (AG Bell) and telegraphy in May 1844 (Samuel Morse) the world of electromagnetic transmission was opened up to human race enabling faster communication through the airwave as well as through telephone and telegraph lines. Gradual globalization of these inventions and later inventions of other modes of voice and data communication were subordinated to the needs of intelligence gathering about friendly and enemy nations. Modern SigInt operations took the first sure step into the books of intelligence tradecraft right from mid 19th century. This aspect of espionage and counter-espionage has become a vast subject that is scientifically too complicated to common minds. We propose to make it simpler by taking a common operator's approach and not a scientist's approach to the complicated matters of electromagnetic emissions, interceptions, etc.

In the earlier chapter we have spoken about ElInt (electronic intelligence). Those applications of electronic gadgets for obtaining and denying intelligence are mostly applicable in civilian intelligence management. These electronic gadgets are used to seek out clandestine intelligence from known and identified targets. However, ElInt has another side related to military applications, which is a subsector of SigInt.

Signals Intelligence operations encompass ElInt, TechInt, ComInt, MasInt, FisInt LasInt (Laser Intelligence), CryptoInt, and ImInt, etc. branches of intelligence tradecraft. Signals Intelligence (hereafter called SigInt) is a part of intelligence collection management of the country that may serve strategic, tactical and even internal security parameters. Signals intelligence involves intelligence gathering by intercepting signals used by friendly and enemy countries. It includes Communication Intelligence (ComInt) and Electronic Intelligence (ElInt) whether involving electronic signals not directly used in communication or combinations of the two. Most sensitive informations conveyed over the air are very sensitive in nature and often require encryption. To break these codes services of the cryptoanalysts are required. The most important part is played by the SigInt analysts. These analysts are well-trained professionals who decide, from piles of intercepted traffic, which are relevant to intelligence used by the strategic planners in the armed forces and the political decision makers.

A little elaboration of MasInt and FisInt, etc. is necessary. Measurement and Signature Intelligence (MasInt) is scientific and technical intelligence information obtained by quantitative and qualitative analysis of data (metric, angle, spatial, wavelength, time dependence, modulation, plasma, and hydromagnetic) derived from specific technical sensors for the purpose of identifying any distinctive features associated with the source, emitter, or sender and to facilitate subsequent identification and/or measurement of the same.

- Radar Intelligence (RadInt)
- Acoustic Intelligence (AcoustInt)
- Nuclear Intelligence (NucInt)

- Radio Frequency/Electromagnetic Pulse Intelligence (Rf/EpInt)

- Electro-optical Intelligence (Electro-optInt)

- Laser Intelligence (LasInt)

- Materials Intelligence

- Unintentional Radiation Intelligence (RInt)

- Chemical and Biological Intelligence (CbInt)

- Directed Energy Weapons Intelligence (DewInt)

- Effluent/Debris Collection

- Spectroscopic Intelligence

- Infrared Intelligence (IrInt).

FisInt, on the other hand is Foreign Instrumentation Signals intelligence from the intercept of foreign electromagnetic emissions associated with the testing and operational deployment of aerospace, surface, and subsurface systems. Since it deals with signals that are not exchanged by humans, it is a subset of ElInt which, in turn, is a subset of SigInt. Typical examples of such communication include: Telemetry data (TelInt), missiles, satellites, and other remotely monitored devices that often transmit streams of data concerning their location, speed, engine status and other metrics.

While in the USA, UK and other western countries the massive SigInt operations are mainly under operational control of the armed forces, NSA, the CIA, in India the picture was rather fuzzy since independence, and even now the fuzziness has not been cleared up satisfactorily. Before we discuss the scientific intricacies and other nitty-gritty of SigInt we would like to have a look into the mismanagement in intelligence management by the Indian agencies and the government.

In common perception, ComInt is monitoring of phone, etc. ComInt or communications intelligence is intelligence gained through the interception of foreign communications, excluding open radio and television broadcasts. It is a subset of signals intelligence, or SigInt, with the latter being understood as comprising ComInt and ElInt, electronic intelligence derived from non-communication electronic signals such as radar. During the early part of the modern intelligence era, the terms "signals intelligence" and "communications intelligence" were used virtually interchangeably, and therefore, much of what was described as Signals Intelligence in the Second World War is more properly understood as ComInt.

Image Intelligence (ImInt) is also generally misunderstood. ImInt is a product of imagery analysis. Imagery includes representations of objects reproduced electronically or by optical means on film, electronic display devices, or other media. Imagery can be derived from visual photography, radar sensors, infrared sensors, lasers, and electro-optics. ImInt includes the exploitation of data to detect, classify, and identify objects or organisations. It can be produced from either hard- or soft-copy (digital) imagery. Hard-copy imagery is synonymous with film, while soft-copy imagery is displayed on electronic terminals. Both types of imagery sources can be analyzed and interpreted for various purposes by different users.

The proliferation of space-based imagery systems permits a much greater use of imagery products by nations that previously did not have access to them. Currently, imagery can be purchased from a variety of sensors. These systems include the Landsat multispectral imagery (MSI) system operated by the United States, the French SPOT MSI and pan-chromatic imaging system, the European Space Agency's ERS-1 synthetic aperture radar imaging system, and the Japanese JERS-1 multisensor imager.

The Russians are selling 2-meter or better imagery from their space-based reconnaissance systems. The commercial imagery market is likely to continue to grow at an exponential rate, and additional collection systems are currently being developed. These will include imaging systems produced by US companies that will be capable of producing 1-meter resolution electro-optical digitized imagery. One-meter imagery is sufficient to conduct technical analysis of terrain, determine key facilities in an urban area, and conduct detailed analyses of industrial facilities. Other nations such as France, Germany, Japan, and Canada are producing advanced imagery platforms that could be used to target sensitive facilities. An additional factor that must be considered is the growing availability of sophisticated imagery work stations, and analytical tools. These capabilities will allow adversaries to conduct in-depth analysis for targeting and technical intelligence gathering.

The 1992 Open Skies Treaty also poses an imagery collection threat. The treaty establishes a regime of unarmed aerial observation flights over the entire territory of its signatories. The treaty was negotiated between the members of NATO and the former Warsaw Pact as a means to promote openness and transparency of military forces and activities. Observation flights can be performed from aircraft provided by the observing nation, the observed nation, or a third participating party. Aircraft can be equipped with panoramic and framing cameras capable of a ground resolution of no better than 30 centimeters, video cameras with a ground resolution of no better than 30 centimeters, infrared line scanning devices with ground resolution of no better than 50 centimeters, and synthetic aperture radar systems with impulse response rate resolutions no better than 3 meters. Ground resolutions of 50 centimeters or less provide significant detailed information for an imagery analyst. Using the imagery derived from Open Skies flights analysts will be able to identify particular types of equipment by type and capability, and perform detailed analyses of rail, port, industrial, and military facilities.

Imagery provides significant benefits to an adversary collecting intelligence against the United States. First, properly mensurated imagery can provide geolocation accuracies for weapon systems targeting, or other intelligence collection platforms. Second, imagery allows activity to be detected, target characteristics studied in detail, and equipment and facilities enumerated. Third, large areas can be covered by imagery sensors for mapping of areas of key importance.

Imagery also has limitations. Except for synthetic aperture radar, imagery quality is normally degraded by darkness and adverse weather. This allows the targeted organisation to use these periods of time to conduct activities that they wish to go unobserved. If an organisation is aware that it is being targeted by imagery systems, they can use camouflage, concealment, and deception (CC&D) techniques to obscure their activities or provide a misleading image to the observing party. Effective use of CC&D may result in the adversary drawing erroneous conclusions about the observed organisation's capabilities and activities. Finally, imagery intelligence collection usually requires a technologically oriented infrastructure. While this requirement may be lessened to some extent in the future, effective use of imagery will still require well-educated, technically competent analysts.

The Intelligence Bureau was the one and only intelligence agency of India, till after 1962 Chinese War and 1965 Pakistan War the Government of India decided to create a separate external intelligence wing styled Research and Analysis Wing (R&AW) of the Cabinet Secretariat; as a part of the office of the prime minister. The cynics in the intelligence fraternity had speculated that Madan Mohan Lal Hooja the senior man in the IB stood in the way of ambitions of Rameshwar Nath Kao, junior to Hooja, who was close to the Nehru-Gandhi family. They alleged that RN Kao was selected by Indira Gandhi because of personal liking.

Both IB and R&AW continued to work on the front of ComInt, ElInt and SigInt. The R&AW had its own Aviation Research Centre (ARC), the Radio Research Centre (RRC), Electronic & Technical Services (ETS) and National Technical Facilities (later transformed to National Technical Research Organisation—NTRO in 2004). The Intelligence Bureau responsible for internal security and security threats emanating from neighbouring countries could not afford to surrender its existing facilities of SigInt, ComInt, and ElInt, etc. Two organisations continued to function independently with very little exchange and sharing of information. Both agencies maintained their cryptology divisions in addition to Joint Cipher Bureau (JCB). The JCB is mainly responsible for cryptology development and key generation as well as providing guidance to better SigInt operations. This organisation basically uses Russian supplied equipment and PC compatible cipher generation and interpretation. In recent times some faster computers have been acquired. It is hoped that the JCB would acquire global standard in high grade cryptology.

Besides the IB and R&AW, the Military Intelligence (now Defence Intelligence Agency-DIA) is also responsible for SigInt operations for feeding the Electronic Battle Order as well as Military Battle Order on the basis of inputs received from own SigInt operations and feeds received from other agencies.

India's experiment with building an umbrella organisation for SigInt operations, as in the US, NSA has not been successful so far. In October 2004 the Cabinet Committee on Security (CCS) decided to have a centralized organisation modeled on the US's NSA for entire SigInt operations, including ComInt, EllInt, UAV operations and other aspects of Technical Intelligence. However, due to organisational rivalry the R&AW has not yet parted with the entire SigInt operations and the ARC. The Intelligence Bureau also continues to maintain its skeletal SigInt, TechInt, ComInt and EllInt operations for internal security purposes. The main objective outlined by the CCS has not been achieved and for the last five years multidirectional tug of war is going on between the intelligence agencies. This has seriously impaired the intelligence gathering capability of the country.

SigInt is a broad subject. It is simply not listening to clandestine radio broadcast by a targeted country. It involves data obtained by EllInt, ComInt and MasInt. An EllInt sensor may find a radar, and then guide a ComInt sensor for listening the talk between the radar and its remote users. Often a SigInt sensor can guide to a Frequency Domain MasInt sensor that can help identify the purpose of the signal. In case MasInt is not able to detect the source of emanation, the operations chief may request ImInt experts to carry out aerial photography of the area and even a specific satellite may be directed to zoom on and identify the likely source.

Experts involved in SigInt operations, analysis and interpretation cannot afford to scan the skies like astronomers. They require targets to tune in their own radars in HF, MW, VHS, and LF, etc. frequencies to detect the correct wave band used by the target source or country. Targeting is done by the SigInt operators on the basis of band scanning, frequency analysis, periodicity, regularity or irregularity of suspected broadcasts. Often certain EllInt, ComInt, MasInt and FisInt operations may give leads to the SigInt operators about the target source of emanation.

In Signal interception deployment of a single receiver is not sufficient. The adversaries mostly change frequency (wave band) of transmission and polarization. Polarization in SigInt means density of electromagnetism in the vector field that expresses the density of permanent or induced electric dipole moments in a dielectric material. Often solar disturbances disturb wireless transmissions. Often burst transmissions lasting for a few seconds are used. To avoid uncertainty the SigInt interceptors are required to use an array of receivers. The next important aspect of SigInt is determining the location of the suspect transmitter. This is normally done by the process of determining "time of arrival". This process involves reception of the transmission from more than three locations: say Simla, Hyderabad and Guwahati, and determining the time of arrival at each location. Wherever facilities are available, receiving stations may be located in Thailand, Maldives and Italy. A transmission takes its own time to swim through the airwaves for reception by the SigInt units. The USA has such facilities. India has no such facility. Perhaps the Andaman and the Lakshadweep islands can be used by the Indian agencies.

The other methodology is triangulation process. The triangulation process is determining the distance between points on the earth's surface, or the relative positions of points, by dividing up a large area into a series of connected triangles, measuring a baseline between two points, and then locating a third point by computing both the size of the angles made by lines from this point to each end of the baseline and the lengths of these lines. This involves intricate knowledge of trigonometry.

The other important aspect of SigInt is Direction Finding of the suspect transmitter. The common means of direction finding involves using directional antenna as goniometry, so that a line can be drawn from the receiver through the position of the signal of interest. A goniometer is an instrument that either measures angle or allows an object to be rotated to a precise angular position. The term goniometry has been derived from Greek words, *gonia*, meaning angle and *metron*, meaning measure. Unidirectional antenna may not be sufficient to identify the location of the transmitter. There are methods of setting up array of antennae to receive signals. The most well-known array system is known as Wullenweber array technique, named after its German inventor. In recent times western countries use aircrafts with electronic listening capability and even spy satellites to home in on a suspect transmitter and destroy it by cruise missile or other missiles, if situation demands.

Intelligence management hierarchy decides if certain transmitters are clandestine in nature and are required to be intercepted. Most high frequency clandestine transmitters serving the intelligence agency of other countries and even transmitters used by organised terrorist groups use cipher codes to transmit their messages. Who are the probable transmitters? The foreign embassies located in Delhi may transmit to their capital stations informing sensitive developments in the host countries. The capital station (including intelligence agencies) may transmit to the embassies in different countries about intelligence gathering, war, peace, arms race, nuclear programme, etc. subjects. Often Long Term Resident Agents (LTRA) also uses clandestine transmitters to communicate with the parent agency. Similarly, the parent agency may also use signals to communicate with the LTRA. Besides use of HF transmitters, they may use teleprinters, fax, email, SMS, voice communication over satellite phone and even transmission of data from satellite terminal to mother or sibling terminal. Portable satellite communication sets have made it possible to open a briefcase, rearrange the antenna and hook up to a designated satellite frequency and pass on ciphered data or use voice communication.

The US and other western countries use large intercept aircraft, such as the EP-3 or RC-135, which have the on-board capability to do some target analysis and planning. Other aircraft like GUARDRAIL are fairly small, and usually work in units of three to cover a tactical SigInt requirement. India also uses certain types of aircraft fitted with electronic equipment for monitoring clandestine signals and other communications emanating from suspect stations in neighbouring countries. India has gained the capability of using satellites for gathering, locating and identifying clandestine transmissions by suspected enemy countries.

The SigInt operators have stupendous responsibilities. Their high-calibrated receivers, multidirectional antennae, radar locators and interceptors, electronic equipment fitted aircraft and satellite resources scan broad spectrum of frequencies. Random interception and analysis by the cipher decoders lead to identification of target frequencies emitting doubtful signals and messages containing clandestine materials. Hundreds of frequencies are scanned and in consultation with the higher echelon certain frequencies are listed as "suspects".

For the purpose of national security it is not possible to disclose the Indian gateways from where foreign satellite signals are collected and their footprints are studied. Certain foreign satellites keep changing their transmission frequency and the footprint areas are also changed with a view to avoid detection. Satellite transmission is also susceptible to enemy attack. The USA and Russia have the capability of killing foreign satellites. China has also recently demonstrated such capability. India is also capable of killing foreign spy satellites, if the battle order demands such aggressive action.

A sub-category of SigInt is Telemetry Intelligence (TelInt). Telemetry is the set of signals by which a missile, missile stage, or missile warhead sends, back to earth, data about its performance during a test flight. The data relate to structural stress, rocket motor thrust, fuel consumption, guidance system performance, and the physical conditions of the ambient environment. Intercepted telemetry can provide data to estimate the number of warheads carried by a given missile, its payload and throw-weight, the probable size of its warheads, and the accuracy with which the warheads are guided at the point of release from the missile's post-boost vehicles. In case India launches an IRBM or ICBM from its usual launch site both the USA and China can monitor telemetry signals and can evaluate the military threat potential of the launched rockets. Such data are constantly studied by India whenever Pakistan launches new Ghouri type nuclear capable missiles. Such data are stored and regularly updated.

Another important aspect of SigInt is related to Radar Intelligence (RadInt). Any radar transmitting or receiving data and multimedia material emanates radiation and signals. The radar which emanates electronic signals — radio waves are susceptible to interception. Deflection of those signals allows the intelligence community to derive vital information that includes flight paths, velocity, manoeuvring, trajectory, and angle of descent. Locations of suspected radars are defined by signals interception, satellite search and search by airborne electronic gadgets. Once identified the suspected radar is kept under constant listening observation. In global context in 1950s the primary targets were the USSR and China's radars. Soviet radars remain a prime ElInt/SigInt target as it is a part of exercise for arms control verification aspect, since the 1972 ABM Treaty. Now for the West North Korea, Iran, and China continue to be the prime targets.

This discussion on SigInt cannot be concluded without some references to Laser Intelligence (LasInt). Non-imaging infrared sensors can detect the presence and absence and movement of an object by detecting and measuring temperature. This is thermal detection system now commonly used in warfare against the terrorists. Coherent light signal intelligence refers to lasers. Interception laser communications is an important part of SigInt. Laser signals can be intercepted by studying the method of transmission, the frequencies employed, and the cipher system used to conceal the signals originating from suspected targets, viz Russian and Chinese Laser transmissions under constant observation of the US intelligence community. Indian scientist community is experimenting with LasInt for application in defence uses. This aspect is yet to be integrated with usual intelligence gathering mechanism.

We have briefly mentioned about Satellite Intelligence (SatInt). SatInt is used for intercepting targeted countries as well as for communicating own data, multimedia contents to defined targets. A tremendous volume of communications is sent via satellite systems. Domestic and international telephone messages and military and business communications are regularly transmitted via satellite using ultra, very ultra, super ultra, and extremely high frequencies (UHF, VHF, SHF and EHF). The United States has major programmes for the interception of international commercial satellite messages. By locating satellite dishes at the proper locations, an enormous volume of traffic can be intercepted. The Ground stations send messages to satellites with antennae which are in very narrow wave band and transmit to the satellite with great accuracy. On the other hand satellite antennae are smaller and the signals they send has a larger footprint area—may be several kilometers.

Often, communications that are transmitted by satellite are sent via microwave towers through the rest of their path. Particularly telephone calls within a country may use microwave towers as the entire means of propagation and reception. Countries like Canada and the US use microwave to propagate majority of telephone calls.

In modern communications, telephone lines are not simply tapable line communication or signal communication. This may be a part of the entire message streams, which can contain nearly 1000 message circuits containing voice, telegram, telex and high speed data packaged together in enciphered or enclair format. Microwave signals can be intercepted by establishing ground stations near the invisible line connecting the two microwave towers, and by satellite collection systems.

Radio waves interception is an integral part of SigInt. Interception of radio signals often depends on the frequencies through which the signals are transmitted and geographic location of the transmitting station. Messages transmitted at lower frequencies, ELF, VLF, and LF, HF travel for long distances as they bounce off the atmosphere and come down in locations far from the transmitting and intended receiving locations. Data sent at higher frequencies pass through the atmosphere and out into space. To intercept such higher frequency signals, intercept stations should be located within the line of sight of the radio communications. The curvature of the earth can often make monitoring from ground-based sites impossible. This gap is now filled up by geosynchronous satellites. India has achieved this capability. This was a major "air warfare" between the USA and the former USSR. Even now the USA pays great attention to Chinese, North Korean and Russian radio channels.

It is easier to intercept VHF communication and walkie-talkie conversations that are used in surveillance operations or in war fields. However, in low and high frequency transmissions, if done in high grade cipher and through burst transmission, it becomes difficult for any intelligence agency to break the codes. Code breaking and making is another part of SigInt.

Space has been converted into a complicated battleground for intelligence collection and denial. In post-Second World War and during the Cold War period the USSR and the USA launched another kind of war in the space by placing low orbit satellites and geosynchronous satellites as a media to propagate open information, image location in target areas of any intelligence defined country, gathering Signals Intelligence from all kinds of emanations and relaying back to Ground Stations. The United States started the process of launching near-earth satellites termed as 'ferrets' for espionage and SigInt purposes. Since then the USA has launched several categories of 'ferret' satellites and geosynchronous satellites. The USSR/Russia has also launched unknown numbers of satellites. Countries like Germany, France, Britain, China and India also joined the race. In short, India has earned at least 50% capability to gather SigInt from its own satellites. It is anticipated that in another 10 years India would be self-sufficient in this aspect of SigInt operation.

Some US geosynchronous satellites named Rhyolite are beamed towards the Russian Federation, China and North Korea, etc. Rhyolite satellites were guided to varieties of ComInt activities. The satellites apparently were used to intercept Soviet and Chinese telephone and radio communications across the VHF, UHF, and microwave frequency bands. Walkie-talkie traffic generated by Soviet military exercises, which fall in the VHF-UHF range, was also regularly monitored by Rhyolite satellites. Beyond the Soviet Union, Rhyolite satellites intercepted communications from China, North Korea, Iran, Vietnam, Indonesia, Pakistan, and Lebanon. The US later launched Jumpseat and Vortex series of satellites to monitor Signals intelligence from Russia and China. Jumpseat has the capability of intercepting most Russian Laser Communications.

Satellite operations are supported by a worldwide network of ground control stations. A key element in the network of US SigInt system is the HQ Consolidated Space Test Center (HQ CSTC), formerly the Air Force Satellite Control Facility at Onizuka AFS, Sunnyvale. The HQ CSTC has ground stations across the globe— Hawaii, Greenland, the Seychelles, Guam, and England. The stations perform basic housekeeping functions—communicating commands to the satellites, altering orbits, checking the equipment on board. The stations also receive ELINT data from the Jumpseat and Ferret satellites. In addition to the HQ CSTC, several more specialised stations exist to control and receive signals from SigInt satellites.

Indian efforts in this direction are in adolescent stage. There are certain ground stations synchronized with the communication satellites and satellites used for harvesting and denying Signal intelligence. As commented earlier India has achieved about 50% capability in this sophisticated field of exploitation of the space for espionage activities and activities related to the armed forces. Indian satellite beams are yet to gain adequate proficiency in covering targeted aspects in Pakistan, China, and the Straits of Malacca and countries in the Persian Gulf and the Red Sea areas. These are important targets in India's geostrategic vicinity. India's capability of using satellites for ComInt was proved during Kargil invasion by Pakistan. Besides intercepting a satellite telephone talk between General Musharraf (in China) and his ISI chief Lieutenant General Ziauddin, Indian army and intelligence agencies also intercepted VHF and UHF communications between Pakistani rear bases in Gilgit-Skardu area and the high peaks surreptitiously occupied by Pakistan army personnel and jihadis. Such capabilities are being sharpened.

Eye in the Sky, or the concept of using airborne radars is generally understood as a military exercise. Airborne electronic, communication and other intelligence gathered by flying planes at high altitude has been added to the folklore of espionage by the downing of U-2 spy plane of the USA by the Soviet Union and capture of Gary Powers. Such airborne intelligence has a long history which we do not propose to discuss here. Moreover, the task done by U-2 spy planes is now being done by SatInt. It has already been stated that most countries, including India, use aircraft to collect intelligence about neighbouring countries. These electronically treated aircraft can cover up to some distance inside the target territory. These flights have trajectory problem and Indian flights are not equipped with advanced generation cameras. We may recall that such flight by the ARC unit of the RAW had failed to detect clandestine intrusion by Pakistani soldiers and jihadis in Kargil sector in early 1999. Their operations could also not detect military build-up at Skardu-Gilgit, Shigar and Badgam areas; though other sources of information indicated Pakistani build-up in the area, construction new roads, and helipads.

However, flying Airborne Early Warning System (AWACS) is a different concept. The USA has dozens of such flying AWACS platforms for gathering early warning about missile attacks, collection of missile telemetry and other ElInt aspects. Several versions of RC-135 AWACS planes are the main platforms for the US military and intelligence community. At present there are eighteen RC-135s in the US inventory. The USA has global operations using different kinds of planes flying from different locations, which cover Russia, China, Iran, Afghanistan and other target countries.

Some flights carry a crew of seventeen and flies at 35,000 feet for up to ten hours before it requires refueling. Its ComInt capability can be expanded from a minimum of six positions to thirteen depending on the requirements of the mission. The RIVET JOINT-ELINT (Code name) system comprises three collection positions— an Automatic ElInt Emitter Location System position supplemented by two manual operator positions. Some plane is equipped with a system known as COMPASS ERA, a system containing infrared thermal imaging, interferometer-spectrometer, and spectral radiometer sensors.

Some flights have additions to the forward portion of the aircraft including a large, drooped radome housing a seven-foot steerable antenna, high-frequency (HF) probe antennae on each wingtip, and a trailing wire, HF antenna on the bottom of the fuselage. Antennas for post-mission data transmission and satellite transmission also have been added. Data collected by these sensors are mainly used in space programme of USA and rival countries. These equipment also keep watch on rocket experiments conducted by countries like North Korea, China, Russia, India, Pakistan and Iran.

As compared to this India has started an ambitious beginning in 2009. The first AWACS system was mounted on a Russian Iluysin-76 plane by Israel as a force multiplier. Two more similar AWAC systems fitted with modern Phalcon type radars are likely to join the inventory soon. The Israeli Phalcon AWACS will enable the IAF to carry out tactical surveillance over a radius of 400 kilometers and collect surface target information deep inside Pakistan even as the aircraft operates within Indian airspace. An electronically steered beam emitting from a solid-state phased array Elta EL/M-2075 radar, mounted on a radome above the fuselage, provides 360 degree coverage around the aircraft. It is also suggested that the AWACS will eventually be networked with other air force assets through a dedicated satellite. India has an indigenous AWACS programme being developed by the Defence Research and Development Organisation (DRDO), which signed a deal last year with Brazilian aircraft manufacturer Embraer for the purchase of three EMB-145 aircraft for use as an AWACS platform.

In June 2006, Pakistan finalized the purchase of six Saab 2000 turboprop aircraft to be equipped with the Saab-Ericsson ERIEYE Airborne Early Warning System. On April 3, 2008, the first Saab 2000 Erieye AEW&C was rolled out and presented to Pakistan during a ceremony in Sweden. Now China and Pakistan are collaborating in developing modern AEW & C system.

The US, UK and other advanced western countries employ three main SIGINT collection systems designed for the U-2/TR-I: type flying platforms: SENIOR RUBY, SENIOR STRETC.H, and SENIOR SPEAR. SENIOR RUBY is a near real-time ELINT collection, processing, and reporting system that provides information on radar emitters within line of sight of the U2-R. The SENIOR RUBY system can handle a large number of emitters simultaneously and send its data to a

Ground Control Processor that is suitably located with the Transportable Ground Intercept Facility (TGIF), used in conjunction with real-time U-2 missions.

SENIOR STRETC.H is another near real-time ComInt collection, processing, and reporting system. The airborne receiver subsystem consists of a multichannel microwave receiver, remotely controlled via satellite link from the Remote Operations Facility (ROFA). The data collected is transmitted via DSCS satellite back to the ROFA.

SENIOR SPEAR is also a near real-time collection, processing, and reporting system that provides a line-of--sight collection capability — out to 300 nautical miles — from the aircraft. U-2/TR-I missions are flown from several bases mainly against Cuba and certain Latin American countries. Two additional airborne SigInt systems are army systems: GUARDRAIL V and Improved GUARDRAIL V. GUARDRAIL is a remotely controlled airborne and ground-based intercept and radio-direction finding system, designed to exploit HF-VHF-UHF voice communications, mounted on RU-21H/GUARDRAIL V and RC-12D aircraft.

Eye in the Sky is not the final frontier of Signals Intelligence. Signals Intelligence is also collected from Ground Stations. A country like the USA has several ground stations on its own soil as well as on soils of friendly countries. The network of Ground Stations is run by the NSA. There are about sixty stations in twenty countries. In addition, several radar stations, operated by the Air Force Space Command, are involved in detecting and tracking Russian, Chinese and North Korean missile tests and space launches. The stations collectively conduct intercept operations across the VHF-UHF-HF bands. Approximately thirty stations collect HF, strategic COMINT while others focus on VHF-UHF tactical communications. Other stations target various forms of electronic emanations. Outside USA Ground Stations have been located in Germany, Italy and Turkey mainly to cover France, East European countries, part of the Middle East and Russia. Stations located in South Korea, Thailand and Japan monitor SIGINT emanating from China, North Korea and partly from eastern Russia.

China has Ground Station based SigInt collection facilities near the borders with Koreas, Vietnam, Tibet and Russia. Some of the reported Ground Stations are at Xinjiang, Xizang (Tibet), and Tianjin, Wenzhou, Kinmen, and Yangzhou, etc. locations. Technical details are not available.

Known Pakistani Ground Stations are reportedly located at Makli, Sanghar, Samsi Airfield (Baluchistan), Skardu and Rawalpindi. These stations are directed at India for detecting emanations from Indian stations.

India has the capability of monitoring emanations from China, Pakistan and Bangladesh. For obvious reasons Indian Ground Stations have not been identified. However, efficacy of these Ground Stations had been questioned after the Kargil attack. Besides the failure of the airborne ElInt facilities our Ground Stations also failed to detect any emanation from Pakistan's capital region and from the Northern Area. During seaborne attack on Mumbai on 26/11/2008 also Indian listening devices, ElInt mechanism had some initial input about Lashkar-e-Taiba's location in Pakistan's territorial waters. Thereafter the ElInt assets miserably failed. Taking these instances in consideration some experts have expressed that the NTRO should be given complete authority to carry out total SIGINT operations. The government also tinkered with the idea of installing ship/boat detecting radars along the vulnerable coastal areas. The principle of radar operations has been widely researched and tremendous advances have been made in this field. In simple language radar works on the basis of transmits electronic impulses, which return to a receiver installed nearby the transmitter after the impulses hit any object. Ship to Ship and base to ship and vice versa radars are in common use. A simple illustration may clarify the conception behind Ground Station operations. In scientific terms India's ElInt operations failed during the seaborne attack on Mumbai.

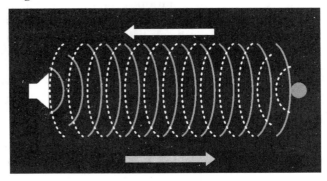

Besides the above SigInt methodologies western countries, Russia and China maintain Covert Listening Posts (CLP) in the embassies in some selected countries. This is in addition to other HF, VHF, UHF interception methodologies and other COMINT operations carried out by embassy based intelligence operators. The United States is known for running such operation in its Moscow embassy. They successfully intercepted open and encrypted car telephone talks of important leaders like Brezhnev, Kosygin and Podgorny. Though not officially admitted it is learnt that the US, Russian, Pakistani and Chinese embassies in Delhi carry out CLP operations and also carry out software based mobile phone interception of talks of the important political leaders, military bosses and intelligence operators. In the light of CLP and other monitoring capabilities of certain foreign embassies India may re-examine its shielding efforts through physical and electronic measures.

In addition to other measures as mentioned western powers, Russia, China, etc. countries gather SigInt from surface ships and submarines. The naval fleets of these countries have special electronic intelligence gathering facilities. India has not, so far, deployed spy ships for SigInt. But normal naval ships do sometime gather useful intelligence signals. Taking into consideration the geostrategic location of India in Indian Ocean Zone, presence of US and allied fleet in the Indian Ocean and emerging strength of Chinese navy, India may have to decide about use of spy ships for gathering strategic SigInt. Some of the Indian battleships have EllInt and SigInt capabilities in certain designated areas. The Indian Navy has undertaken onerous tasks of intercepting and tackling the Sea pirates in Red Sea areas, near Seychelles and Mauritius. It has strategic involvement in guarding the Straits of Malacca and the Indian Ocean Zone in the Bay of Bengal, Laccadive Sea, Maldives areas, Andaman Seas and even in adjacent areas of the Gulf of Thailand.

With the acquisition of the Phalcon AWACS system India has advanced to the realm of unifying the SigInt system embracing the low orbit and geosynchronous satellites and the Ground Stations. The Indian Navy has moved forward to acquire a sea-based Phalcon like system to beef up its own LINK II system operational in ships and aircraft. The LINK II system was manufactured by Bharat Electronics Ltd.

The Indian Navy will also have to experiment with the Phalcon for maritime operations and air battle management at sea. The Phalcon radar has the capability to transmit a very short pulse to reduce the sea clutter and detect moving and stationary ships. The Phalcons would also be able to guide MiG-29K aircraft from the aircraft carrier INS Vikramditya, or from shore to carry out anti-ship strikes and interceptions. The Navy is in the process of acquiring Boeing P8-I Multi Mission Aircraft from the US to improve its EllInt and SigInt capabilities. The IAF Phalcons can also make available data for Over-The-Horizon (OTH) targeting of ships and in the ultimate, may even form part of India's ballistic missile shield from the seas.

Recently China launched a new electronic surveillance ship from one shipyard of the Hudong-Zhonghua Shipbuilding Company. The ship is designed by No.708 Institute of CSSC (China State Shipbuilding Corporation). This ship is designed for collecting electronic intelligence (EllInt) off the coast of other countries. This ship is believed to be the successor of previous Type 851 electronic surveillance and missile tracking ship.

Advanced western countries have the capability of gathering SigInt from submerged submarines. The US had adopted the technology code named HOLYSTONE, way back in 1959 mainly directed against the USSR, China, Vietnam, etc. According to US strategic studies the special equipment placed on submarines for HOLYSTONE missions included the WLR-6 Waterboy Signals Intelligence System. The WLR-6 is in the process of being replaced by a more advanced system known as SEA NYMPH, described as advanced, automatic, modular signals exploitation system designed for continuous acquisition, identification, recording, analysis and exploitation of electromagnetic signals. India has not yet equipped itself with such undersea SIGINT capability. Another undersea intelligence capability relates to attaching signals emitting waterproof bugs to the undersea communication cables.

The wonder world of SigInt is expanding horizons and achieving higher space calibrations. However, the human element that is involved in analyzing the SigInt and ElInt data are as important as the data collecting machines are.

ElInt collection, processing, screening, analysis, reporting, and information management require fine human minds synchronized with real-time displays support, simultaneous live display of multi-channel spectral, DW, and DIF data. The Graphical Analysis Report (GAR) format, editor, and associated storage and search tools have revolutionized the ElInt report dissemination through Data Assessment and Screening facilities. New generation of SigInt tools support remote analysis.

While SigInt is responsible for interception of foreign transmission, the SigInt operators are also responsible for assuring absolute secrecy of India's own transmission. There may be several points of origination of wireless transmissions—the armed forces, external affairs ministry, internal, external intelligence agencies, etc. The cardinal principles are: avoid voice transmission, use high-grade cipher pads, one time cipher pads, burst transmission, use of auto-cipher mechanism attached to trans-receivers, etc. As indicated earlier, most cipher pads are originated by the JCB. Use of cipher pads are strictly controlled and supervised by senior officers.

In many respects, HumInt depends on supportive roles from ElInt and SigInt. In the realm of scientific studies SigInt is a vast and intricate subject. However, in this chapter we have dealt with the subject as succinctly as possible.

Chapter 11

Open Source Intelligence (OSINT)

There is a saying in the intelligence community that 60% of intelligence comes from open sources. Open source intelligence (OsInt) means information not gathered through covert and clandestine manner and that are available freely in the open; in print, electronic media, printed literature of various social, religious, sectarian and camouflaged associations or bodies. A matter of national security concern can circulate as a piece of gossip in a well knit society, which may not come to the knowledge of the intelligence operators.

Allen Dulles had commented on OsInt in his book: *The Craft of Intelligence* that "the collection of foreign intelligence is accomplished in a variety of ways, not all of them either mysterious or secret. This is particularly true of overt intelligence, information which is derived from newspapers, books, learned and technical publications, official reports of government proceedings, radio and television. Even a novel or play may contain useful information about the state of a nation."

OsInt has been defined by the US Department of Defence and Director of National Intelligence as intelligence "produced from publicly available information that is collected, exploited, and disseminated in a timely manner to an appropriate audience for the purpose of addressing a specific intelligence requirement." *As defined in Sec. 931 of Public Law 109-163, entitled, "National Defense Authorization Act for Fiscal Year 2006."*

In India there is no Act of the Parliament governing the intelligence agencies. No notification also exists defining and authorizing collection of OsInt. Collection of unpublished OsInt related to defence departments, intelligence community are treated as espionage and treason, even when collected through open enquiry by a journalist. He or they can access published government documents.

Open Source Intelligence sounds to be contradictory to the concept of intelligence being a secret/top secret clandestine activity of the trained sleuths. The overt parts of the ingredients that go in for intelligence production are as important as covert information gathered at great cost. OsInt requires few basic understandings: the intelligence hunter and the analyst should be able to comprehend the totality of an information that is required to be catered to the consumer. OsInt is like an elusive maiden; it may knock the user's door, fleet around and a non-conscious user may not recognize the piece of information knocking at his door. The ground hunter and analyst have to apply their trained intelligence gathering tradecraft to know where to look for the pieces of information relevant to their culling, assessing and producing the finished product. They may also take into consideration that printed materials are as profuse as the materials circulating in the www domains. Most of these materials are not in Hindi, other vernacular language and even English. These could be in Arabic, Persian, Hebrew, Urdu, Russian, Chinese, etc. In the context of India it is necessary to have dedicated trained staff to scrounge the printed arenas and www domains for internal and external security related OsInt.

Discovery of Open Source Intelligence is like stumbling against King Solomon's Mine. Deliberate searching is necessary. Once the materials have been detected the hunter-gatherer and the analyst have to use discrimination to determine if the OsInt is relevant to the subject under development, whether it is outdated, mere propaganda or real piece of views and facts about any given organisation and its action programme.

After application of discretion the hunter and analyst may find tons of information on a given subject. For example certain English and vernacular newspapers and magazines may cater pieces of information about Maoist guerrillas in certain areas of the country. Besides incident reporting certain interpretations are also published on the basis of interviews given to chosen journalists and academia by the guerrilla leaders. In addition the electronic media may also flood the air with their own versions of an incident and offer different interpretations. At the same time the www sites may offer additional information. From the confusing battle royal of OsInt the analyst has to distil the entire information coming from different OsInt sources. The analyst himself may carry out the distillation work or he may hire an outsider expert to work under oath of secrecy and piece together the information that can be used for final production process.

Once the product has been finalized the analyst should try to compare the product with any covert information available on the subject.

Where to look for OsInt? The obvious spaces are newspapers, magazines, radio, television and Internet search. Web based communities; social networking (Tweeter, etc.), Video sharing (Orkut, etc.), blogs and user generated contents are some of the open sources from which targeted information can easily be obtained. Several published documents can be obtained with ease. These are government reports, state budgets, census operations and demographics, court hearings, legislative debates, press conferences, and public speeches.

Amateur radio operators, amateur aircraft observers, radio monitoring buffs and satellite observers often come across valuable observations and they publish or relate their experiences. Besides these keen observers of open sources like Google Earth, Geographical Information System, which include information on coastlines, maps of certain areas, ports, transport system can gather valuable information sitting in the confines of their room.

Open Source Centre, Lexis Nexis sites (LexisNexis is a division of Reed Elsevier. It offers a widely used, searchable, and identically named archive of contents from newspapers, magazines, legal documents and other printed sources.) are considered very important resources for OsInt gathering. The Open Source Centre is specific to the USA. The Director of National Intelligence Open Source Center (OSC) was established in November 2005 under the overall command of the Director of National Intelligence. This organisation absorbed the Foreign Broadcast Information Service (FBIS) functioning under the CIA. In the former KGB and present FSB and SVR, the Russian intelligence systems have units embedded in their intelligence post in different embassies which exclusively collected OsInt and shared with Moscow for intelligence analysis purposes. Certain segments of Indian political community in India were funded by the KGB for procuring OsInt for them. They were also paid heavily for publishing materials, periodicals and dailies espousing Moscow's line of world views. Even after dissolution of the USSR, Moscow is engaged in gathering OsInt from targeted countries. Subjects of coverage are wide, including trade, environment control, NGO operations, etc. This unit of the FSB is also responsible for interacting with journalists, politicians, opinion makers, and members of the Parliament. They often manage to get closer to several community organisations.

China has an ambitious policy towards India in matters related to collection of OsInt. Units of the Guojia Anquan Bu (Ministry of State Security–MSS), the Second Department of the People's Liberation Army and the New China News Agency (Xinhua) are actively engaged in collection of covert and overt intelligence. For OsInt purposes they gather all published materials, scan the www sites, infiltrate the community organisations, universities, etc. and all the gathered and analyzed information are passed on to Beijing for ultimate utilization by the MSS and the PLA.

India does not have any specific OsInt collection agency like the one created by the USA in 2005. The Central Monitoring Service of All India Radio monitors all radio broadcasts in India as well as all foreign radio broadcasts which can be received in India. The operations are secret in nature and there is no streamlined system for sharing gathered information on line with the real users. However, if a specific demand is made by intelligence agencies the CMS tries to cover that area and cater to the output with the concerned agency. The Intelligence Bureau has a system of monitoring TV news channels. The NTRO has, however, gone for an ambitious arrangement for both Radio and TV monitoring which cover both Indian and foreign wave bands. The RAW representatives posted abroad are supposed to gather OsInt and share with the HQ analysts.

The Press Information Bureau (PIB) under the Ministry of Information and Broadcasting is supposed to gather open source intelligence and share with the concerned ministries. They are supposed to maintain archival records as well. In reality, the PIB has not digitalized its information gathering and storing system. The PIB's OsInt resources do not receive priority and PIOs attached to different ministries are not considered gatherers and suppliers of OsInt. These information officers prefer to act as PRO of the concerned ministries.

Since India is in the process of establishing core organisations for fighting terrorism, like the National Security Council, Joint Intelligence Committee and Joint Operational Command, many intelligence researchers feel that there is need for establishing exclusive OsInt collection units in the internal and external intelligence agencies. The ministry of defence is also required to have an agency under the DIA to gather OsInt from target countries, in addition to what is now gathered by the military, air and naval attaches.

Besides collecting OsInt through open means, the Inter Services Intelligence and Pakistan Intelligence Bureau located in their Mission in Delhi certain unorthodox practices are also resorted to by these agencies. While Joint Signals Intelligence of the ISI, located at Malir Cantonment area of Karachi, is engaged in collection of Signal Intelligence, the field operators task the border smugglers to collect specific Indian newspapers and news magazines. Several such cases were detected during sample operations on Indo-Pak borders. Even in the age of Internet such demands are made by the Pakistani agencies from their contacts amongst the petty border smugglers. Besides collecting OsInt, Pakistan often hacks the www sites which carry strident criticism of affairs in Pakistan. The author has experienced two instances of hacking of his www site by suspected Pakistani hackers; most probably encouraged by the ISI.

OsInt has played crucial roles during the First and the Second World Wars and the Cold War era. We will traverse that field later in this chapter. However, the hardboiled Intelligence communities all over the world give importance to clandestine secret intelligence based on different intelligence tradecraft. According to Stephen Mercado (A Venerable Source in a new era: Sailing the sea of OsInt in the information age, part of the book *Secret Intelligence, A Reader*, p. 82), "With open sources so accessible, ubiquitous and valuable, one would expect to see OsInt occupying a commensurately large space within the Intelligence community. This is not the case. Too many people still reject OsInt as intelligence. Worse, too few are able to gather and exploit open sources. Worst of all, the Intelligence community assigns only a handful of those capable people with the task."

From personal experience, I can support Mercado. In India there is an obsession for HumInt or SigInt based intelligence. Officers considered to be useless for other important intelligence production operations are deputed to OsInt, which mean to them cutting paper clippings and submitting to the boss. Most of them are not even literate in foreign languages and even various Indian vernacular languages. They are also not trained to surf the suspected www sites for gleaning out OsInt. Some of the iHindu, iMuslim and iKhalistani sites spew venom. Systematic study of these sites can give fair estimate of the ferocity of electronic warfare in www domains. This open domain of intelligence is not properly and adequately studied in India. The situation is worse in Postal Research operations, where suspected letters are intercepted and analysed. Once a letter written in Dari, (spoken by Iranian Zoroastrians), created tremor in the Postal Research section. Experts opined it was in Baloch, Hindco, Seraiki (all in Pakistan). The sensation was solved after a Persian knowing friend was consulted. He immediately translated it, which turned out to be a family related exchange from a Zoroastrian living in Eastern Iran with his cousin living somewhere in Bombay.

OsInt has certain built in advantages and disadvantages. The advantages are: it is openly available, can be located with little effort and expenditure, can be adduced as evidence in a court (clandestine information is not generally produced in a court). While highly classified intelligence is compared to a narrow beam of focus, OsInt has a vast footprint area, which is often shared by the media in a planned manner with the targeted audience. For instance countries like India and Pakistan present collaged information and visuals and broadcast for the targeted audience in Kashmir. Similar is the case with a number of TV channels which focus on greatness of Islam and propagate fundamentalism. "You Tube" is another visual media which is exploited by individuals and government sponsored groups to propagate their points of view. Such OsInt propaganda warfare is an integral part of intelligence operation and psy-warfare.

OsInt has become increasingly accessible, ubiquitous and can even compete with clandestine HumInt products. OsInt provides early warning. Two case studies can justify this approach. As far as India is concerned gathering clandestine HumInt and SigInt intelligence in respect of Pakistan is preciously difficult. Pakistani intelligence personnel calculatedly tailgate Indian diplomats, often hitting their bumpers, pinching the diplomat's wives in shopping malls and even gesticulating threatening postures. There were several cases when Indian diplomats were physically tortured. Indian diplomats are not allowed to visit certain areas of Pakistan. Under such circumstances language knowing officers, diplomat and non-diplomat, can access open source intelligence with greater ease. Besides newspapers, magazines and television channels they can access several printed materials circulated by different religious organisations, *tanzeems* and even government agencies. All over Pakistan, senior pro-jihad religious leaders deliver *taqrirs* (lectures) on *Jumma Namaz* (Friday prayer) days and on other special occasions. Someone on behalf of the OsInt gatherer may attend these public speeches and deliver the recorded material to his friend in the Mission. In fact, OsInt has emerged as the main intelligence input for the Mission based diplomats and intelligence operators.

In the case of Koreas, especially the Communist DPRK the USA faces more difficult situation than India faces in respect of Pakistan. The DPRK is virtually a closed country, much more closed than Cuba. The country has only two newspapers, both managed by the government and the ruling party – Nodong Sinmun and Minju Choson. Even though the DPRK media are strictly controlled, Pyongyang's strategy is to use the media for indoctrination of the masses. But the intelligence experts can cull out prioritization of state policy from the print media, radio and controlled TV broadcasts. In fact, for the international intelligence community the DPRK is a black hole. State controlled print and electronic media are the only sources of reliable information. The USA has to depend on third countries like Poland, Malaysia, Indonesia, Algeria, Bulgaria, FRG, and Egypt, etc. to gather information from DPRK. Indian embassy in Pyongyang maintains a low profile and from all accounts it has not been successful in tracking North Korean-Pakistani connection in strategic supply of IRBM and nuclear technology. North Korea is an example as to how a country can impose information blackout by restricting OsInt materials to outside observers.

During the Cold War the USSR was also treated as a closed country–Iron Curtain. Some top level clandestine agents, some infiltration and some OsInt used to the general sources of intelligence in addition to elaborate SigInt, ComInt, ImInt, EllInt, etc. Sometimes defecting KGB officers provided excellent intelligence. There have been several such cases. The case of Stanislav Levechenko a KGB officer posted in Japan is unique. He defected to the USA in 1983. His interview with a Japanese journalist later published as a book threw more light on the USSR and KGB operations than the CIA could collect over a decade.

In India too certain ISI operators functioning from within the walls of the embassy had provided valuable information about ISI's broader schemes against India. Major General Zahirul Islam Abbasi (expired in July 2009) was posted in Pakistan embassy in Delhi in the rank of a brigadier in 1988–89. He was running a flourishing spy ring on behalf of the ISI. He was caught red handed while handling a retired officer of the Indian army. His interrogation provided plenty of data about ISI operations in India. There were few more cases of exposé of long term resident agents of Pakistan in India, whose interrogation had thrown immense data on ISI tradecraft applied in respect of India. Interrogation reports, interviews, etc., though often treated as secret/ top secret are basically OsInt materials. In USA and other countries such materials are declassified after a few years. Unfortunately, in India declassification of such restricted data is prohibited.

Open source data has started encroaching into the territory of hitherto classified HumInt, ImInt and SigInt domains. One can task individuals to gather information about any organisation, person and groups of people. Certain MNCs and big business houses commission people to carry out area study, risk factors, law and order situation in an area where they are interested in setting up industrial complexes. Recent Special Economic Zone (SEZ) fiascos in West Bengal and other states were due to failure of the authorities to gather open information about the mood of the people and their own perception of priorities. Sample open surveys can bring out startling factors. It is not even necessary to task the intelligence agencies to gather such open information. An MNC executive can order collection of such data, satellite imagery and software to conduct analysis of different parameters and even traffic analysis.

Open source intelligence has encroached into the hallowed territory of ImInt. A Japanese magazine frequently focuses on satellite imagery of North Korean nuclear sites, palace of the leader, Kim. France, Russia and other countries offer commercial ImInt products to state or non-state buyers. The NSA and CIA often procure open source ImInt. However, the National Geospatial-Intelligence Agency of USA performs more delicate ImInt tasks. The NGA serves the NSA, but it performs top secret military commissioned missions. It performed amazingly during Cuban missile crisis. On the other side of the ImInt force in USA special mention can be made of National Imagery and Mapping Agency (NIMA).

During the last couple of years India has made a good beginning in ImInt operations. However, failures of the intelligence agencies and remote sensing satellites to detect Pakistani build-up in Skardu-Gilgit areas and infiltration in Indian held areas was inexplicable. In 1999 ImInt of specific areas were available in open market, especially from France, Germany and Russia. There was no doubt that the intelligence agencies and the armed forces failed to anticipate the stealth applied by Pakistan in unfolding a sudden war on India in a very sensitive sector. The Kargil saga should be taken as a landmark of ImInt and ElInt failure of India. To be candid, the Indian intelligence agencies display lackadaisical attitude towards OsInt.

One of the important sources of OsInt is strategic books written in foreign languages. In India books in this category are abundant in English, French, German, Russian, Chinese, Urdu and Japanese languages. Before the final collapse of the USSR took place many authors in France and the USA produced research based books indicating and even forecasting that under the emerging circumstances it would be impossible for the Soviet Russia to maintain its unity. Now that Pakistan is showing tendencies of a collapsing nation, very few Indian thinkers are producing research materials that can be studied to follow the furrows which this sick nation would take. Very few studies have been made to forecast what would happen to Afghanistan and Pakistan, when total Talibanization takes place and what would be the impact on India and South Asia. Funnily enough, the Government of India has virtually banned writing and publishing books on intelligence matters. The western countries are flooded with such books and revealing ones. Such are the hazards to knowledge in a stunted democracy. In the name of secrecy most of the dirt and failures are shoved under the carpet.

Very few senior intelligence managers read strategic books in English and hardly other such books in French or Chinese are translated into English and vernacular languages. The cutting edge intelligence producers are not encouraged to read strategic books, books on intelligence tradecraft and spatial and global strategic matters. Around the time our generation joined the intelligence fraternity (1960-68) senior intelligence managers used to task newcomers to read certain prescribed books and present a summarized appreciation. Some of them even discussed the book with the rookie officers. This practice has been discontinued. A discerning visitor's foray to the libraries of these agencies would betray the assumption that intelligence agencies are storehouses of knowledge. Without most uptodate knowledge, application of hackneyed tradecraft becomes infructuous and unproductive.

Some critics opine that clandestine intelligence gatherers/ operators suffer from tunnel vision. They prefer to look at a given problem through the eyes of agents reporting to them. Secret intelligence is rated very high and reliable. But a given piece of information that the Maoists in Nepal were in the process of resuming armed depredation and China was ready with supplies of weapons would seem to be an excellent piece of secret intelligence rated either A or B category of reliability classification. Even if the intelligence was gathered from horse's mouth the analyst would be required to evaluate the information in the light of various OsInt available to the agency and reverification of geostrategic approach of China to Nepal Maoists.

A piquant situation had arisen in 1972–73 when a desk analyst conveyed to the government, on the basis of unverified ground intelligence that 700 Naga underground volunteers had left for China for collecting weapons. The Army intelligence contested the information as they had no ground information from their detachments. The field unit of the agency did not agree with the analyst. To maintain inter-agency relationship a deceptive method was resorted to: showing return of the Naga group in installments and making satisfactory accounting for 700 ultras claimed to have left for China. In fact, in 1972 only 200 Naga ultras had left for China and they returned in small groups after collecting weapons. This was an educative instance of tunnel vision developed by the analyst, who insisted on accuracy of his intelligence product based on unconfirmed ground reports.

OsInt, if properly gathered and assessed, can help better calibration of secret intelligence. OsInt also offers an overview while secret intelligence is target specific. At the height of armed insurgency in Punjab, secret intelligence operations played important roles. However, open informations about the *Ragi* and *Kirtani jathas* (groups of religious singers), *Pathis* (readers of the Holy Book), *Dhaddi jathas* (folktale singers) moving in the interior villages, urging the people to fight for independent Sikh homeland produced most valuable informations about the mood of the people. Even, recitation of the *Ardas* (last prayer) of the Sikh congregation in a Gurdwara used to mention the ongoing upheaval, eulogize Bhindranwale (the progenitor of the separatist movement) and urging the Sikhs to fight for Khalistan and avenge the death of their leader in army action. Such valuable OsInt were as sensitive as any secret information that could evaluate the mood of the people and the strength of motivation they nursed.

Intelligence managers often spurn OsInt on gerunds of suspected reliability. This is a valid attitude. In intelligence fraternity no input should be accepted without evaluating the information and analysing these against the overall perspective. Intelligence operators like to remain hooked up to their tradecraft rote and stick to grading of the given piece of intelligence– A = reliable and from a trusted agent, B = somewhat reliable, require verification; C = doubtful authenticity; D = not reliable. Grading intelligence is in vogue in all intelligence agencies. However, the staunch protagonists are of the view that OsInt can be graded A if it is supported by other circumstantial open source information.

Often strident comments are pronounced by critics on the issue of classification of information. Thomas Quiggin commented in his book *Seeing the Invisible: National Security in an Uncertain Age* "One result of overestimation is the building of bureaucratic bunkers or caves. In order to protect their classified information, bureaucrats build compartmentalized systems that in effect, cut them from the rest of the world."

Robert David Steele in his book on Intelligence, also commented harshly on the intelligence community for over-cautiousness and for sticking to their orthodox ideology of intelligence: "We have created a security bureaucracy which has lost sight of the purpose and has no idea to deal with the changed circumstances of a world in which the US intelligence community no longer controls the bulk of the information. Worse, we have an entire community of intelligence professionals — good people trapped in a bad system — who have been trained by rote to stay inside their little box, and literally have no understanding of the vast wealth of information available to them outside of the bunker, often for no more than the price of a telephone call." Though harsh, the comment is not totally irrelevant in the context of US failure before 9/11, Indian failures before attack on the Parliament and the ghastly incident of seaborne attack on Mumbai. If we examine carefully Pakistan's centre of gravity as a nation has started shifting poles mostly because its chief intelligence agency was allowed to function as a core part of the state management. The ISI is the prime planner and executor of terrorist attacks against India.

Nonetheless, with asymmetric growth of security threats the world intelligence community, especially the Indian intelligence community may have to give more attention to OsInt. Long before a ghastly incident of terrorist attack takes place the open source materials throw up tidbits of information about the building up of forces that are capable of unleashing catastrophic terror attack. The most recent case of attempted terror attack on a US North West airliner as it was approaching Detroit is a case of cave dwelling intelligence operators failing to activate their radars. There were advance intelligence inputs from Nigeria and Yemen that Umar Farouk Abdulmutallab was allied to al Qaeda and was assigned to attack US targets.

Similarly, no major attack has taken place on India from Pakistan and Bangladesh based jihadi terrorists after 26/11. A queer combination of luck, Pakistan's preoccupation with its internal affairs, US pressure, etc. has slowed down Pakistani thrust against India. But if one studies the English and Urdu newspapers of Pakistan and peruses several leaflets circulated and the *taqrirs* (addresses) delivered from the ramparts of mosques leave no doubt that Pakistani jihadi *tanzeems* are waiting restlessly to mount concerted attack on Indian targets. Recent revelation by a follower of Hakimullah Mehsud, the Pakistani Taliban chief, that they had plan to attack the Indian border post at Wagha was lost to the Indian intelligence community. Only now it has come to notice that David Headley's collaborator Tahawwur Rana had visited several places and even published advertisements in local newspapers for recruiting young Muslims in the ruse of offering jobs in Canada and US. These ads were inserted well before the 26/11 attack on Mumbai. The intelligence community had obviously ignored the OsInt material that could have been pursued to the attackers on Mumbai.

Ignoring open source intelligence can often lead to a blank canvas situation, total intelligence blackout. Regarding US President's daily brief (PDB) former Secretary of State Colin Powel had tersely commented in his memoir, *My American Journey* "I preferred the *Early Bird (US Defense Department's early morning newspaper)* with its compendium of newspaper stories to the President's Daily Brief, the CIA's capstone daily product."

The same comment can be made on the Daily Summary of Information that is submitted by the Indian agency to the prime minister at the beginning and end of the day. These are mostly summaries of incidents and known plans of action of certain disruptive groups. To be true to the profession, a simple compilation of information published in *Mainstream* and regional papers can also be as good as the daily Summary. During the scandal ridden years of Rajiv Gandhi's regime newspapers like *Indian Express* adopted a vanguard attitude in attacking the prime minister and several alleged acts of corruption. A system was devised to collect the printed papers by 2 am and prepare a summary of information targeting the government and send the same to the prime minister's office before eight in the morning, presenting the report as early morning summary of information. These comments are not meant to belittle the immensely important clandestine sources of information. Reminding the intelligence managers about the utility of OsInt as sources of believable and reliable information is also a part of the exercise carried out by the scholars, critics and flash-nuggets presented by former intelligence operators.

From practical ground experience I may add that when posted in the Indian Mission in Canada during the peak period of Sikh turbulence in 1983, I realized that a few English speaking Sikhs were not good enough to gather information on the impact of the Bhindranwale separatist phenomenon on the Sikh Diaspora. A good number of Punjabi daily and weekly papers were published from London, Birmingham, the UK and Toronto, Vancouver and other places in Canada. They were managed by pro-Bhindranwale groups. A staffer in the Mission often translated a few items and presented to the Dy. High Commissioner, a Malayalam speaking person. The realization that I was missing the enormous OsInt sources prompted me to learn the Gurmukhi script and the language within three months with the help of a staffer. Thereafter, I did not have to go thirsty; OsInt regarding the Sikh affairs in Canada and USA flooded me. The Mission had to get an additional hand to help me to examine the OsInt data and prepare the distilled reports. The High Commissioner and the bosses in Delhi were overjoyed with the flood of information reaching them. Later, in 1987, my skill in the language helped me to discover the inner cores of the terrorist groups and help the government in taming the wild fire of separatism. This personal example is cited here, as an illustration. The same method was applied by me in Manipur, where Meiteilon is the reigning language, in Nagaland, where Nagamese is the lingua franca and Nepali, in Sikkim, which is the state language of Sikkim. My knowledge of these languages had helped me both in covert and overt intelligence productions.

While working on Pakistan related matters I noticed that my agency was dependent on a fortnightly compendium called POT, collection of news items in Pakistani newspapers and magazines. The product used to reach my desk after good 15-20 days of the incidents happening in the neighbouring country. This was an infructuous exercise. As there was no internet connectivity we developed the idea of getting three-four day's old Pakistani newspapers (English and Urdu) through border smugglers. These became a good source of OsInt. However, in the absence of Urdu knowing staff we had to depend on another unit of the agency. That unit, managed by inefficient officers always worked behind the arrows of the clock. The problem was sorted out by singling out an officer who used to present regular translation of the Urdu newspapers. I also gathered some working knowledge. Now the Internet has demolished that Berlin Wall of OsInt gathering capability. Moreover, use of internet has given access to different World Wide Web sites which provide tons of information on insurgent fundamentalist jihadis patronized by Pakistan.

Since there is abundance of OsInt in languages other than English, it is imperative that the intelligence agencies should have a division of languages, especially languages like Chinese, Urdu, Arabic, Persian, Spanish, French, and German. In the context of India, Bengali, Urdu, Tibetan and Myanmarese languages are required to be studied. Agencies in the USA, UK, France, Spain, Germany, etc. have adequate language experts. The major Indian agencies are yet to create adequate facilities to scan tons of OsInt generated daily in the print as well as electronic media. Systematic studies of the www domains are still to match up to standards practised in countries like the USA.

Some commentators on OsInt are of the view that intelligence agencies over-classify their clandestine inputs with a view to protect their turfs. This appears to be a sweeping observation. Most clandestine inputs are required to be graded confidential, secret and top secret depending on the source of origination, quality of the information, and impact of the information on national security matters. Often such informations are graded high to protect identity of the agent. Protection of the information is as important as the protection of the agent who catered it. Adversaries are capable of identifying an agent in case they can lay hand on the information through leakage, theft and other means. Certain information in a target area can be accessed by handful persons in a target organisation. Through the process elimination the suspect agent can be identified. After proper surveillance his activities can be scanned and if necessary he can be neutralized.

OsInt has no such in-built security mechanism, some scholars feel that 'one result of overestimation is the building of bureaucratic bunkers or caves. In order to protect their classified information, bureaucrats build compartmentalized systems that in effect, cut them off from the rest of the world,' *Seeing the Invisible*, Thomas Quiggin. Robert David Steele (*On Intelligence*) is of similar view. These and similar other opinions appear to be peripheral comments by persons not having inside knowledge of treatment of classified information by the intelligence agencies.

It is possible that information obtained from clandestine sources are not properly analysed and the strings of pearls are not put together to arrive at a clear picture enabling the policy makers in taking decisive action. The US agencies had plenty of intelligence on the probable al Qaeda attack on US soil, though not specifically on the Trade Towers. They failed to communicate with each other and string the pearls thus allowing al Qaeda to stage 9/11. Even the recent failed attack on a US plane over Detroit could have been prevented had the CIA and the FBI analysed, assessed and stringed the pearls to complete the valuable intelligence. India too had some information inputs about attack on Mumbai on 26/11 and recent Lal Chowk (Srinagar) hold up on 11.01.2010. Perusal of Urdu and Kashmiri language papers of the period depicted correct mood of the people. Even during recent troubles (June-July 2010) ample indications were available in the local language papers. Obviously, the wing of the MHA handling OsInt in J&K has not earned their bread honestly. Indian agencies had also failed to analyse and assess the pieces of information allowing the fatal incidents to hit the country badly. But, to comment that estimation of information is bureaucratic is perhaps not the correct approach. Classified information has certain limitations when the agencies fail to communicate with each other claiming sovereignty on the information and not analyzing and assessing the same to complete the whole picture. This is system failure and not failure of the intelligence. In recent times various countries have started institutionalising focal points as parts of unifying the intelligence processing command. Human failures are likely to be repeated in the intelligence agencies, but the degree of precision can be improved through repeated drill and learning lessons from failures.

OsInt can be misused by some unscrupulous intelligence operatives. To produce the bulk they often utilize OsInt as secret information. There are two motives behind this, proving productivity and claiming secret service amount on regular basis as long as the product results are accepted by the analyzing officer or desk officer. Taking advantage of proficiency in local vernacular languages some operatives gather kernel of the information and write down a graded secret report, which may be of topical or national interest. I have had the experience of such intellectual deceit in certain stations inside India and abroad.

In one instance a senior level officer, recipient of daily summary of information (DSI), forged the signature of a top Naga underground leader and pedaled as supposed original letters from the exiled leader to his lieutenants in Nagaland. It was considered to be a prized source of information. However, comparative study of the DSI informations and the contents of the letters betrayed the craftiness of the intelligence operative. He was exposed. A similar instance took place in station where Bengali is the local vernacular. A senior officer used to sit down with a couple of newspapers and produced a couple of secret reports every day. He hardly ventured out or guided his grassroots operators to gather real secret intelligence. Such intellectual and professional dishonesty is not uncommon. It should be mentioned that bulk of the daily intelligence production are channeled to different desk officers. There is no central unit to oversee all OsInt or secret information. Such compartmentalization often makes it feasible for the fabricators to go scot free.

Open media information has another disadvantage. In the money spinning age certain print and electronic media are controlled by certain interest groups and lobbies. Political entities, both in the Open Countries and Close Countries try to influence the media. Chinese media, whatever pretence of openness might be claimed, is basically controlled by the state. Arab countries finance several print and electronic media to project their views. There are allegations that Jewish lobbies also control a large numbers of print and electronic media. Intelligence agencies using OsInt from such controlled media generally weigh the balance and accept only the kernel. Propaganda literature is usually shunned, but are examined to analyze how certain political views and ideologies (both internal and external) are trying to influence the masses. In the seventies and eighties USSR dumped its literature in several Indian languages to promote the ideologies of communism. Religious groups also circulate literature to propagate their faiths and even to spread hatred. Communal literature is another area which tries to provoke racial, ethnic and communal violence; these require close study by the concerned desk officers. Some communal attacks on Christian institutions in Karnataka were allegedly provoked by hate literature circulated by a neo-convert to Christianity against Hindu gods and goddesses. Such OsInt are easily available and it is obligatory on the part of the intelligence operators to collect these, alert the local administrative authorities and inform their controlling authorities. As commented earlier, OsInt plays vital roles in intelligence production and nearly 60% of intelligence is available in the open. Discerning eyes and minds are needed to gather such information as corollary to classified information.

Chapter 12

Analysis

Intelligence gatherers are miners. They dig in and collect intelligence nuggets. This is called collection. The same or similar information may come from different sources and stations as well as from OsInt. It is the duty of the desk officer to collate all the intelligence and prepare the collage for the analyst. Often the desk officer is designated as the analyst. In certain cases specialist analysts are consulted to polish and fine cutting of the edges of the final production. This process of collection, collation, analysis and dissemination is the crux of the tradecraft of intelligence. Analysis is a part of the Intelligence Cycle — collection, collation, sifting, digesting, analyzing by professional analysts before the final product can be presented to the top boss and in turn to the political consumer.

There are professional and trained analysts in various walks of life — system analysts, business analysts, project analysts, market analysts etc. All these professionals are intimately wired to the grassroots and the higher management structures. We are concerned with the Intelligence Analysts. Intelligence analyst works for the government controlled intelligence agencies — say in the USA for the Central Intelligence Agency, National Security Agency etc and in the UK for the Government Communications Headquarters (GCHQ) and the Security Service (MI5) and Secret Intelligence Service (MI6). While the GCHQ use the tag of analysts, the MI5 calls this as Intelligence Officers, the MI6 styles them as Operational Officers. India follows the British pattern and very often the Station Chiefs (presiding over a large contingent of collectors) themselves assess the melange of information and submits to the higher management formations. The Intelligence Bureau and the Research and Analysis Wing do not specifically recruit and train the analysis officers. In USA and other countries there are courses for Analysts in certain universities and institutions managed by the armed forces. In India a senior desk officer scrounges through all available information on a given input, uses his intellect, knowledge about the subject, area and the people and the historic background related to the inputs. Unfortunately, some of the desk officers/analysts are taken for granted as experts simply because they belong to a particular service. There is no provision of in-house training for the analysts. Such desk officers are just data collectors and collators.

Before we proceed further we may examine the job requirement of an analyst. The Intelligence Analyst is primarily responsible for supervising, coordinating and participating in the analysis, processing and distribution of strategic and tactical intelligence. Some of his duties as an Intelligence Analyst may include prepare all-source intelligence products to support higher formation; providing support to the Intelligence procurement, surveillance pattern, and reconnaissance (physical, electronic and satellite) synchronization process; receive and process incoming reports and messages; assist in determining the significance and reliability of incoming information; establish and maintain systematic, cross-reference intelligence records and files and integrate incoming information with current intelligence trends and prepare and maintain graphics wherever necessary. He should be able to prepare prognosis for the future. Suppose he is in charge of analyzing intelligence input on Nagaland–on the prolonged talk process and likely impact of breakdown of the truce and repercussions in the neighbouring states. This analyst should be capable of generating a few prognosis offering alternative lines of action by the governments, armed forces and the political bodies. Such futuristic studies are rarely taken up.

An ideal analyst is required to undergo special training to make him mentally capable of interpreting vast collage of field intelligence collected from different sources. Some of the fundamental training aspects may include: critical thinking capability; preparing maps and charts, understanding military symbols used in combat as well as internal security duties, preparing intelligence reports by picking up the essence of the subject and interconnectivity of the reports with past events and correlating the product with future prognosis. The analyst must be proficient in using computer systems. The trainers should also take into account certain other qualities in an analyst. He should be interested in understanding the process of intelligence gathering. Unless he is exposed to the intelligence gathering process through various tradecrafts he would not be able to appreciate the generated raw intelligence and grade its reliability. He should have the cranial capability of a diamond evaluator to understand which one is genuine, and which padded. As commented earlier padding a piece of intelligence by the originator with his idiosyncratic perceptions is a common feature. Often the agent also pads information with a view to earn a little more. The analyst should be able to organize all the intelligence on a given subject and weave a pattern out of the chaos and present himself in crystal clear language and display his capability to think, speak and write clearly. He should be trained to prepare himself to be capable of supervising intelligence surveillance, collection process, analysis, processing, and distribution activities as speedily as possible. In most cases the time factor is important. The ultimate consumer demands quickest possible dissemination of assessed intelligence. Properly assessed and analysed intelligence often enable the top policy maker to take certain decisions.

The Sherman Kent School for Intelligence Analysis is the prime analyst training institute of the CIA. The institute trains selected CIA and defence intelligence staff in Career Analyst Programme. It is the basic training programme that encompasses basic thinking, writing, and briefing skills. Some aspects include analytic tools, counter-intelligence issues, denial and deception analysis, and warning skills. It also offers a wide range of intermediate, and advanced level training for analysts and managers on analytic methodologies, substantive issues, and leadership skills. Some aspects of leadership training are also included. Some selected analysts are also trained in chosen foreign languages to enable them to proficiently handle country specific and region specific desks. In the UK the MI6 has a similar training programme. Similar practices are carried out by the French Direction Generale de la Securite Exterieuer (DGSE-external intelligence) and Direction Centrale du Renseignment Interieur (internal security). An examination of the Bundesnachrichtendienst (BND) of Germany and the Federal Security Service and Sluzhba Vereshney Razvedki (foreign intelligence service) indicate that these countries also train their analysts with meticulous care. Often fresh recruits are trained as analysts over a period of time.

Some proponents are of the view that analysis and intelligence production (final product) can better be performed by staff trained in intelligence cycle. They can have the privilege of supervising intelligence collection from diverse sources and even directing them what to look for. Some scholars are of the opinion that the analyst should not emotionally or procedurally get too closer to the collection process. Ground level intelligence collectors are focused workers and they are assigned targets according to norms and requirements of intelligence tradecraft. The analyst may request the Station Chief for certain specific inputs to complete the analysis process. His involvement in collection process may blind him of the intrinsic as well as wider picture. The other school is of the view that analysis and production can be performed by a separate analysis centre. But it must be understood that intelligence is a distinctive trade and outsider, even if he is an eminent scholar, will not have any idea about secret and top secret services of the organisation. A trained intelligence personality guards his turf more jealously than a young lover protects his love.

William E Odom, former director NSA has justifiably commented in his book *Fixing Intelligence–For a More Secure America:* "The two approaches can be mixed by augmenting the intelligence staff sections with separate supporting analysis and production units. For some types of analysis and production, large national may make sense, but the principle of analysis and production by intelligence staff sections is obviously preferable because it is better to be attuned and responsive to users' need."

This sounds to be a balanced approach. For instance, an Indian intelligence agency coming across intelligence about affairs of the nuclear sensitivities of the country may well be advised to associate one or more senior nuclear scientists and analysts to weigh the intelligence in the light of technical parameters of the input. An intelligence operative cannot understand certain technical matters in the domain of nuclear science. Such specialized consultation is more required in the cases of threatened biological warfare, air attack by the terrorists and certain other specialized areas.

Allen W Dulles has aptly commented in his book *The Craft of Intelligence* that: "Analytical process within an intelligence Organisation, ranging from the initial sifting and evaluation of information received to the preparation of high-level studies, calls primarily for a well-trained mind free of prejudice and immune to snap judgment. A man who is more interested in intellectual pursuits than in people, in observation and thought than action, will make a better "analyst" than an "operator." For this reason, it is no surprise that people from the academic professions fill many of the analytical jobs." Dulles distinguishes the analyst from grassroots gatherer-hunters. "The "operator" or, as he is frequently called, the case officer, is the field man, the collector of secret intelligence from agents. It is he who locates recruits and handles the primary sources of information. The operators are drawn from everywhere. There is really no norm and no pattern. The main thing is that they be lively, curious, tireless and endowed with a keen sense of people."

There are some misplaced perceptions and confusion between assessment of intelligence and analysis. Like analysis, assessment passes through different stages. The HumInt operator who collects the raw intelligence from his agent or the SatInt and ElInt operators who gather certain information have to assess the intrinsic value of the information in relation to internal and external security of the country. The assessment process is repeated at the level of zonal in charge or station in charge and graded after interactions with operating officer. Assessment depends on operating officer's performance on record, quality and performance of the agent and an understanding that the given information fits in the pattern and known propensities. Grading of information depends on the assessment of reliability of the information.

In some cases a single source information in the direct knowledge of an agent is taken seriously and passed on to higher echelons for immediate action. This is tactical in nature. For example, in 1988 an agent, a border smuggler, rushed with an information that 30 Sikh youths belonging to a rebel *jatha* (group) were hiding in a forest near Mustafa Abad area adjacent to Lahore-Kasur road. A contingent of Pakistani Rangers was escorting them. Mustafa Abad is just two hours march from Indian border in Amritsar district. As no air reconnaissance facility was available the information was assessed on the spot after grilling the agent and the handling officer. The agent's past inputs were also examined. After spot assessment the agency was advised to activate the border security. The desk analyst opposed the idea of activating the international border on the basis of a single "un-assessed and unanalysed" single source information. The officer and his peers had never served in the field and had no expose to the turbulence in Punjab. The top boss was persuaded to use his intuition on the basis of the chief operations officer's personal impeccable record and the agent's past performance. He decided to act. Both the BSF and Army were alerted with some additional inputs of known routes adopted by the rebels and their Pakistani facilitators. On a new moon night a Pakistani post opened up indiscriminate firing on the Indian posts to facilitate infiltration. Pre-planned battle order of the Indian forces had succeeded in intercepting part of the gang infiltrating from Pakistan and adequately replying to Pakistani firing. This incident has been accepted a copy book case of instant assessment of single source information of tactical nature. However, in strategic nature of informations a single input may not always be taken unless an ImInt or SigInt changes the texture of operational obligations and force the decision maker to order the forces to act immediately.

Analysis, as has been said in earlier paragraphs requires scientific approach. Analysis is the process of collating known information about situations and entities of strategic or tactical importance, evaluating the known intelligence, weigh with other inputs from HumInt, SatInt and ElInt etc, and formulate a cohesive probability thesis about actions to be taken by the policy maker. The analyst has to pass through certain stages, both physical and intellectual, to prepare the final product.

The analyst has the enormous responsibility of blending the known and identified information with different, ambiguous and unconfirmed reports. It must be taken into account that a piece of intelligence passes through several mind frames – the agent – ground operator – immediate supervisor – station chief. Each one of them has separate mind shape, neuronal spectra and mirror image disadvantages. Scientific studies support that in a common given situation five persons may react in five different ways, often adding their own interpretation and even imposing own thought process on the original information. The analyst may not have any chance to interact with the agent but the other personalities are his peers. He can, if any doubt arises, communicate with them and clarify doubts.

The main psychological faculty of the analyst should take into account that the agent who caters the intelligence may be a victim of deliberate deception by the adversary of the agency and the country. It is common in intelligence parlance to face the inevitable fallacy of facing planted, doctored and deceptive intelligence. It is imperative for the assessing officer as well as the analyst to weigh carefully if a piece of intelligence is planted, doctored and a part of deception played by the adversary.

Sometimes the analyst gets trapped by what is known as "cognitive traps". Cognitive traps have various manifestations. The most dangerous aspect is that the analyst gets trapped by mirror imaging problems. His own mental process, thinking capability, range of knowledge and idiosyncrasies and ego influence his recognition problem and he starts analyzing an issue in the light of his own mental image. Analysts often fixate on a hypothesis and refuges to open mind's windows and doors and accept fresh ideas. They often fail to draw a total picture from minor tidbit intelligence from various sources and fail to link them into a texture. It is now said that 9/11 attack on the USA was caused by such "recognition failure" and "cognitive traps" as the several intelligence agencies failed to communicate with each other and take cognizance of an emerging pattern.

Analogy is an important tool in the hands of analysts to explain a situation and prepare a comprehensive analysis. However, analogy is not always logical. Two humans do not behave similarly. Organised human groups, with malintentions, also do not behave in the predictive manner. It happened in the recent past when a veteran counter-intelligence officer came up with a startling information of a group of Maoist guerrillas assembling somewhere near Brinda, near the mining town of Gumla (Jharkhand) with the object to attack a police station. More information started trickling in gradually. The station chief in the area analysed the information and concluded that the Maoist were likely to take the Gumla- Silam (NH 78) road to mount the attack. He placed trust on a similar attack about a month back somewhere near Chaibasha (Jharkhand). His controlling officer agreed with this analysis. The forces ambushed around the main road leading to Gumla. The Maoists, through their information network discovered heavy troop movement near the highway. They abandoned the NH 78 approach and followed the contours of NH 23 that also leads to certain areas of Gumla. The Maoists abandoned the plan to attack the police station and raided a mining facility and looted away 3000 pieces of gelatin sticks and detonators. The big faux pas happened simply because the analyzing officer was anchored to analogy of a similar attack in the area. Moreover, he was influenced by his own mirror image defect; declining to take into account that the Maoists had several alternatives to approach the target.

Organisational culture is an important aspect that influences analyzing process. That India can be attacked by sea-borne terrorists was not new to Indian intelligence agencies. This was proved beyond doubt when Pakistan based mafia and terrorist groups brought in huge quantities of explosives for conducting extraordinary acts of terrorism in 1993. In spite of some advance warning the central intelligence agencies and the state intelligence department failed to appreciate that coastal areas could also be exploited for acts of terrorism. This failure had resulted in March 12, 1993 serial bombings in Mumbai

In spite of these events Indian intelligence agencies had not taken up systematic survey of the vulnerable coastal areas, counting all the minor ports, landing sites, creeks travelling deep inland and sparsely populated broken creeks where smaller boats can berth. The concept of coastal policing was not adopted as a national policy. The shallow water policing was left to the Coast Guard, which suffers from resource crunch to dominate the entire shallow water and land part of coastal security. The intelligence agencies and the political policy makers had not taken seriously the warnings that organized terrorists could attack India through coastal areas as well. Failure of Organisational culture had blinded the local agency stations and the state intelligence to appreciate the possibility of such attack. This had resulted in the daring sea-borne attack on Mumbai on 26.11.2008. This was a mini Kargil type attack on India. The Indian defence forces and the intelligence agencies had also not developed Organisational mindset to apprehend massive attack by Pakistan from the Kargil-Drass sector. Surprises are often welcome in personal life; but Kargil and Mumbai type surprises indicate that Organisational culture of Indian security and intelligence edifices require vast reorientation.

There is another factor that often perplexes the inference drawing process of an analyst. Most societal cultures have different value systems. An apparently small incident may be construed as a major issue by certain communities. I recall a sensitive incident that happened in 1971 in a village near Bishenpur, in Manipur. An Assam Rifles patrol pursuing an alleged gang of terrorists entered the house of a priest and kicked a structure that was the seat for Meitei God, Sanamahi (equivalent to Vishnu). When the report reached me through a field officer I consulted a local officer. His view was that the issue should be immediately brought to the notice of the Lt. Governor as

Sanamahi was a household deity and Meiteis considered the deity more important than imported Vaishnavism. After I shared the concern with the Lt. Governor he summoned a meeting in which the Brigadier in charge of the Assam Rifles pungently remarked that intelligence had made mountain out of a mole. It was not a mole at all. After three days about 5000 Meiteis assembled before the Raj Niwas and demanded prosecution against the accused Assam Rifles personnel. The event rolled down to a general strike that ended with a few broken limbs and heads because of police action. In this case the Assam Rifles chief and police chief failed to take into account the proportionate reaction of the Meiteis as they were not exposed to the nuances of the cultures of the people.

In strategic field also the analyst must not be swayed away by his own cultural bias and pattern of reaction of a given group of people susceptible to strategic preparations of the defence forces of the country to which the intelligence analyst belongs. It would be improper to equate the response manifestations of Pakistan, Bangladesh, Nepal, Myanmar and China on issues like strategic road, port, and airport construction near about disputed border areas. Similarly India's response, particularly at political level may be different from the reaction levels of the intelligence agencies and the armed forces. Indian intelligence agencies and army often report factual violation of borders by Pakistan and China. They seldom prepare a long-term prognosis and make forecast covering strategic period of over ten years. China and Pakistan are known to make long term strategic intelligence estimates and calculate progressive prognosis. India's political culture has been slow-reactive since independence relying more on philosophical perceptions. Intelligence agencies also have been trapped by the political culture. As a result the analysts have also been oriented by the trap of political psychology of the ruling parties and prominent individual leaders. Intelligence chiefs and analysts often try to tailor their approach to the political and strategic thrust of the leader. This was amply proved during the reign of Indira Gandhi, who pursued an aggressive policy in most of her strategic dealings.

Imposing self-perceptions on a given issue is technically described as mirror imaging. An analyst should take care that he does not impose on a given strategic scenario his own perception and known reaction pattern of his country. Scholars have Analysed the reaction pattern of Ho Chi Minh, Vietcong leader and those of Lyndon B Johnson and McNamara. The US intelligence and strategic analysts assessed that Ho would react in the manner US troops and command were reacting. Imposition of mirror image on the Vietnam issue, as it progressed, had finally ended in humiliating withdrawal by the US troops. In such cases of intelligence assessment cultural values, national traits and unorthodox war strategies of a group of people are required to be evaluated before a definitive conclusion is drawn and a forecast is made.

The target organisation and individual as well as countries often adopt deception as tool to mislead the adversaries. In Russia they call it Maskirovka. There are several real life stories of deception actions adopted by the Allies to mislead Hitler. Deception material may come through HumInt, SigInt and even through published materials. Around 1990 High Frequency radio interception monitored a female voice announcing numerical ciphers. It was a period-segmented broadcast – morning or evening or late in the night. Through deciphering process it was ascertained that the broadcaster was located somewhere in Tajikistan and the messages were meant for misleading the US, Pakistan and Mujahideen forces about deployment and instructions to the USSR forces. The OsInt researchers and SigInt analysts are generally trained to differentiate between a genuine intelligence input and a piece of disinformation. During the Second World War various deception technologies were applied by the Allied forces against Germany. However, during the closing months of the war Hitler's intelligence forces were heavily infiltrated by the British and the Americans. They wanted quick defeat of the Fuehrer. Those who were committed to Hitler were so bloated with confidence that they failed to distinguish between reality and deception tactics. A trained analyst is required to sift all available information and isolate the disinformation. This requires higher mental capability and deep knowledge about the subject dealt by him. It also calls for training in the tradecraft of identification of decoys, deceptions and traps.

Sensationalism is an arch-enemy of intelligence analysis. Field intelligence is often padded up either by the agent handler or his supervisor with a view to lure the analyst to pay instant attention and credit the source of origination. Many unscrupulous field operators have such tendencies of dressing up an ugly bride as most attractive. It is for the desk analyst to apply elimination process while collating various inputs on the subject. Padded intelligence is as dangerous as disinformation coming from hostile sources. It requires an illustration. It happened in Sikkim in 1976. An agency officer posted at the remote outpost at Dongkong near China border sent wireless messages about concentration of Company strength of Chinese troops near Indian border. Indian army had no presence in that area. After three messages were received, it was felt necessary to share the information with the HQ desk. However, simultaneously, a small contingent of expert Sherpas were deputed to survey the exact border peaks to confirm the binocular observation of the post officer. The Sherpa leader (agency employee) wired back after four days that there were no Chinese troops at the location observed by our officer. They were gothwallas, grazers, tending the yaks and camping at a distance of about six kilometers from Indian border. Though the Indian army column had proceeded toward Dongkong and arrangements were made for aerial survey when the weather cleared up, the reports of the Sherpa group removed doubts about the panicky reports of the post officer. On debriefing it was found that the binocular supplied to him could recognize human features up to a distance of two kilometers only. He was chided for sensationalism, but his binocular was changed to a more powerful one along with a directional microphone to pick up distance chattering of the Chinese.

An analyst has to be bold and sincere to his conviction. He should under no circumstances cave down to his superior's assessment of a situation. But he should not be adamant and inflexible. Inflexibility is an anathema to practical and objective analysis. He must start from the point of the emerging pattern out of diverse inputs. Gradually, he should build up a mental process to determine if he agrees with the emerging picture. In case he is happy with the adequacy and conformity of the contents he should start building up a composite picture. If necessary he should consult his colleagues dealing with the subject and brainstorm with them without any bias. Out of such brainstorming new ideas may emerge and add new dimension to the thesis under construction.

Agreement on the contents of the inputs should be arrived after all possible sources have been exploited. An agent report may be required to be vetted by a SatInt input and even SigInt input. For example, HumInt input about construction of bunkers by Pakistani troops near Indian border in Punjab sector may require precise SatInt inputs and even analysis of signal intelligence gathered by the agency may throw newer lights. After comparing all available inputs the analyst may draw a conclusion about number, type and location of the bunkers under construction. Only such a refined product can be shared with the consumer.

The analyst should be able to grade the information from his own point of view in addition to grading done by the originator. In case the input is graded A, the analyst must vet it in the perspective of other inputs received from different sources. His mental process should not get coagulated. The inference process should flow freely establishing connectivity within his cranium in such a manner that his mind does not fog up and he is not subjected to self-pity, confusion, bias and fear psychosis. He should be objective and his reasoning process must contain the elements of induction, deduction, abduction and the scientific method.

Induction is the act or process of reasoning from a part to a whole, from particulars to generals, or from the individual to the universal; also, the result or inference so reached. A process of demonstration in which a general truth is gathered from an examination of particular cases, one of which is known to be true, the examination being so conducted that each case is made to depend on the preceding one; – called also successive induction. (Borrowed from Brainyquote). In intelligence analysis process induction is an important step, which includes identification of the relevant particulars and from those pieces to arrive at a general conclusion.

On the other hand the Deduction process of reasoning is rather opposite to Induction, in which a conclusion follows necessarily from the stated premises; inference by reasoning from the general to the specific. Some intelligence analysts may like to depend mainly on induction process as it is based on raw data. Some specialists deride deduction as an oracle process. Deduction is a scientific process. It is not analogical process. It is not even the intuitive capability of the analyst. An analyst making a deduction must be versatile in his trade with long experience. However, a healthy blend of induction and deduction process may help the analyst in arriving at a more scientific conclusion.

In this regard an illustration may be necessary to repel the confusion between induction and deduction process. Two human assets had reported in September 1994 about berthing of a Chinese ship in Karachi and unloading of about twelve 8 to 9 meter long tube like objects under heavy military guard. Pakistan had developed Hatf I missiles in a factory established near Rawalpindi. The desk officer first declined to process the input on the plea that Pakistan is in the domain of another agency. He could at best share the information with that agency as chance finding by a friend. The operations handling officer was of the view that the tubes could be missiles gifted by China. His view was ruled out on the ground that China would not flout CTBT and indulge in weapons proliferation in South Asia. The argument given by a specialist sounded like a deduction based on his past experiences. Fortunately, during this assessment impasse the same human source managed to supply a photograph of the tubes taken at great risk. On examination it was established that the tubes in reality were M 11 missiles supplied by China that began the missile race by Pakistan with Chinese and North Korean collaboration. The final analysis prepared with the help of Military Intelligence and another intelligence agency opined that Pakistan had received M 11 missiles capable of carrying 700 kg nuclear warhead. The consequential steps taken by India are not a subject of this illustration. However, it must be stated that the transaction between China-Pakistan-North Korea took place under the nose of US surveillance.

Experienced analysts often apply the tool of intuition to map up the present and probable near future developments in a particular area or a specific subject of national interest. Such intuition comes from deep personal knowledge of an area, its people, problems and the likely repercussion of the given people to certain developments. From given sets of ground intelligence input the analyst can often predict that a particular historic event may lead to certain other complications. The year 1974 witnessed several historic events — Pokhran nuclear test, upheaval in Sikkim leading to merger (1975) and Naga peace agreement at Shillong (1975).

Events those preceded the Shillong Accord between the Government of India and the Naga Federal Government and NNC in November 1975 were characterized by negotiations between the insurgent groups and the government of Nagaland. However, a point was made to the Governor and the Government of India that though Phizo group was ready for negotiations a small breakaway group was still in China and they were not willing to support Phizo, who probably wanted to return to his homeland and govern over its affairs. The breakaway group was headed by Muivah and Isaac Swu, respectively a Tangkhul and a Sema leader. They were sent to Vietnam for witnessing the people's war and were ready to accept Maoist ideology. It was also pointed out that though the home minister of the underground government and Phizo's brother had signed the agreement, a good number of second rank leaders were opposed to the accord. Z Ramyo, the charismatic Tangkhul leader and a rival of Muivah was in bad health and would not be able to thwart the revolt by Muivah group. The government in Delhi was in a hurry to add another laurel. Analytical reports that the breather would not last longer as the Naga movement had splintered and the anti-agreement leadership and ideologues were likely to rally behind Muivah-Issac axis were not entertained. These warning reports to the government were originated by an intelligence operator who had spent about 10 years in the area and had intimate knowledge of the tribal people. His intelligence coupled with intuition forecasted the near future scenario of chaos. This was not acceptable to Delhi, though it witnessed the rise of NSCN (I-M) in late seventies, around 1978 with Chinese and Pakistani patronage. This exemplifies the positive effect of good combination of ground intelligence and studied intuition used by intelligence operators in forecasting certain developments from the womb of ongoing developments.

In American intelligence parlance the terminology of Linchpin Analyst is used to illustrate analysis on the basis of confirmed intelligence. It is based on the scientific theory that given the precise input to a problem condition there exists a unique solution, which depends on the consistency and quality of the input. The system was introduced by deputy director for intelligence in the CIA (1993-1996) Doug MacEachin. Linchpin analysis basically depends on confirmed information and includes the process of elimination of improbable alternatives and parallel hypothesis.

Heuer Richards J Jr (1999) in his book *Psychology of Intelligence Analysis*. Chapter 8: Analysis of Competing Hypotheses", History Staff, Center for the Study of Intelligence, Central Intelligence Agency, (http://www.au.af.mil/au/awc/awcgate/psych-intel/art10.html, retrieved 28.10.2007) mentioned about Analysis of Competing Hypothesis that is involved in making analysis near perfect. There cannot be any perfect analysis and assessment in intelligence parlance. According to him an analyst should follow the following steps:

1. "Identify the possible hypotheses to be considered. Use a group of analysts with different perspectives to brainstorm the possibilities.

2. Make a list of significant evidence and arguments for and against each hypothesis.

3. Prepare a matrix with hypotheses across the top and evidence down the side. Analyse the "diagnosticity" of the evidence and arguments — that is, identify which items are most helpful in judging the relative likelihood of the hypotheses.

4. Refine the matrix. Reconsider the hypotheses and delete evidence and arguments that have no diagnostic value.

5. Draw tentative conclusions about the relative likelihood of each hypothesis. Proceed by trying to disprove the hypotheses rather than prove them.

6. Analyse how sensitive your conclusion is to a few critical items of evidence. Consider the consequences for your analysis if that evidence be wrong, misleading, or subject to a different interpretation.

7. Report conclusions. Discuss the relative likelihood of all the hypotheses, not just the most likely one.

8. Identify milestones for future observation that may indicate events are taking a different course than expected."

These guidelines are treated as path-leading lights by professional intelligence analysts. However, the analyst is required to know the minds of his consumers. The policy makers in the government have certain ideologies, outlook and constraints of complex decision making in a multiparty democracy. The intelligence agencies are generally aware of political complexions of the ruling party and general trend of political alignment in the country. They are required to cater to intelligence and submit Analysed reports and assessments to tailor with the political views and style of functioning of a leader. But, the agencies cannot completely ignore the general policy framework of the top policy makers of the country. Analysed assessments should be based on certain circumstances plaguing the country and also should have certain periodicity. Normally strategic assessment and analysis are submitted to the government on quarterly basis, followed by yearly assessment and guarded forecast for the coming months. However, the top policy maker has a right to receive daily briefing by the intelligence agencies on matters confronting the nation on continuous basis.

Intelligence agencies often fall prey to the whims and whacks of the top government authority. Though intelligence officials in the USA and the UK are insulated from the political vagaries of governance and administrative controls they surprisingly succumbed to the pressures from the office of the President of the United States and the Prime Minister of the UK and tailored reports, analysis and assessments to suit the illegal war declared on Iraq on the unsubstantiated issue of WMD. The fraudulent Iraq war was the basest geostrategic decision by the USA, the UK and their allies. The doctrine of regime change was supported by the CIA and the MI6 with concocted intelligence. Fortunately, there are built-in accountability factors controlling the intelligence agencies of the USA and the UK. Some enquiries have been conducted on the propriety of declaring war on Iraq on the basis of concocted intelligence.

However, in India there is no such accountability factor. Political parties have failed to introduce Parliamentary legislation for the internal and external intelligence agencies. It is well known that preceding and during the emergency regime of Indira Gandhi intelligence agencies bent down on knees where a mere bow was sufficient to express loyalty to the ruling leader and her cronies and office managers. The same intelligence and investigative communities prostrated where bending was enough to placate the Janata Dal leaders in harassing and prosecuting Indira Gandhi. Basically Indira Gandhi introduced the system of staffing the higher echelon of the intelligence community and the key administrative posts with her band of faithful. The avalanche of corruption started overwhelming the country as soon as Indira Gandhi evolved the doctrine of loyalty and blind endorsement of her policies by the iron-frame administration and the intelligence community.

The analyst may often feel frustrated when the top decision maker fails to take cognizance or act upon the Analysed advice on a matter of grave national importance. Two instances will clarify such failures of the ruling policy makers. The intelligence agency sent daily, weekly, fortnightly and special reports to the prime minister's and the home minister's offices since 1988 about intention, preparation and training by the RSS and other Hindu entities to build up a movement on the issue of Ram temple at Ayodhya after demolishing the standing structure, Babri mosque. Special reports numbering over 75 were submitted to the prime minister during 1992 about secret preparation for demolition of the mosque. For whatsoever reason the top policy and decision maker of the country did not act on the reports. The prime minister stood as a mute witness as he was outmanoeuvred by the Hindutwa forces governing Uttar Pradesh and the allied affiliates of the RSS. The scar caused by the event cannot be wiped out even if hundreds of concessions are offered to the aggrieved community. The event had widened the cleavage between the Hindu and Muslim communities. The intelligence community was demoralized by this and subsequent events. But they did not have the right to explain the situation to the country and even to themselves.

The Indian system is, in a way, obscure and unscientific. In the IB the Indian Police Service Officers are inducted and given basic and advanced intelligence training, including training in desk management and analysis of information. The same practice is followed in the RAW, where there is a melange of officers coming from different services and they have to work with RAW Service officers of diverse ranks. The kind of training given to the prospective officers is inadequate. The first incompatibility rests with the system of baking the officers in the kiln of different kinds of experience. During sixties and early seventies most IB officers were from the IPS at an early stage of their career under the earmarking scheme based on their performance during training and evaluation of their suitability. They were later trained in the IB and they did not carry with them the baggage of police experience. Policing is altogether a different domain than Intelligence operations and mastering intelligence tradecraft. This system was abolished and exclusivity of the IB was eroded by treating it as one of the Central Police Organisation like the CRPF or the BSF. More or less since 1967–70 the earmarking scheme was abandoned and officers were categorized as hardcore and soft-core. The IPS officers started coming on deputation even at the rank of a DIG and IGP. Very few of such officers migrated to the IB with the intention of making intelligence as their career. Officers from some of the uncomfortable states in the northeast and other states where they were not in the good books of the authorities preferred to make IB a transit station before they migrated to other CPOs or other central government jobs. Very limited number of such officers made IB a permanent home and even the seeming hardcore opted to return to the home cadre to become Director General of Police. Destruction of IB's exclusivity and treating it at par with other CPOs has devalued the cutting edge efficiency of the top level officers for whom IB was the only second home after their family nest. No unbiased assessment has so far been carried out what damages were done to the IB by robbing its exclusivity. Twisting the system often blunted the edges of assessment and analysis of tactical and strategic intelligence, which are essential for immediate and long term security parameters of the country.

In the higher management formation IPS or RAS service officers are given basic training in tradecraft and other related issues and are made to work on a desk job for a limited duration. In the IB they are posted out to stations inside the country and after some ground experience they are rotated to other stations and the HQ Desks. Resourceful officers manage to cling to the HQ or go through the ritual of doing one or two soft stations.

These categories of officers cannot be described as professional analysts. For example, an officer of Malayali origin may get his first field assignment in Punjab or Manipur. He does not know the languages, has no knowledge of the historical and cultural traits of the people, and has very little idea about their problems and tribulations. For him it is easier to handle a tactical intelligence — say advance information about activities of a militant group. He can simply brief the local authorities and share the same with his desk officer in the HQ. It is rather impossible for him to put together an essay on the aspects of restlessness in the segments of the people in Manipur and advise the government on lines of action. It never occurred to the intelligence bosses that before an officer is posted to a station he should undergo minimum six months intensive training about the region and pick all basic knowledge and some proficiency in the regional language. Most station in charges posted in inconvenient stations and dangerous areas often mark time and get out at the earliest opportunity to a greener pasture.

His counterpart in the desk, the supposed primary analyst may not have any idea about the trials and tribulations of the people of a state, say Manipur. He has no basic idea which tribe is related to neighbouring tribes and the nature of their social and cultural connectivity. The tribals are broadly divided into Naga and non-Naga stems. The Naga stem has over ten different sub-stems. Among the non-Nagas the stems may be described as Kuki, Hmar, Paite, Simte, Gangte etc twelve odd sub-stems. Each sub-stem has vastly different languages, cultures and traditions. Unless a station in charge can enter into the maze of the labyrinth and identify himself with the major stems and sub-stems he cannot either be an efficient field officer or a desk analyst.

It has been experienced that an Indian intelligence analyst (desk officer) does the collation, cleaning and tailoring jobs and push up a collage to his superior, who polishes it and pushes up to the next higher manager. He may be the final figure to accomplish the final analysis, often dotting the Is and cutting the Ts and changing words and style of presentation. By the time he presents the product to the Chief and takes his clearance, the destination consumer may become informed through OsInt, political colleagues, media persons and other sources. Such delay is involved in strategic analysis of a given problem, say, Lashkar-e-Taiba and ISI plans to create fresh disturbances in the country or likely impact of certain government policies of different segments of the people.

However, in tactical information (actionable) delay may jeopardize national security. For example, a piece of information that some Indian Islamic militant group has been planning to send a group to Pakistan for training and they have started recruiting members and collecting funds may come from a single source. There may not be a second source to verify the information and technical operations may take longer time to gain useful input. In such cases the analyst must decide very quickly, by churning the received piece of intelligence with historical data, personalities of the leading figures and other related matters available with other agencies and station chiefs. In such cases analysis must be instant and sharing with the political and executive consumers as fast as possible.

The desk analyst generally accomplishes the analytical task on the basis of received inputs and collated data. There exist communication gaps between him and the SigInt, ElInt, ComInt and ImInt managers. A system is required to be evolved to feed automatically all relevant SigInt, ElInt, ComInt and ImInt data and assessment made by the generators/managers with the subject oriented desk officer. Such on line exchanges can enable the analyst to map up the largest possible canvas and build up a nearly perfect hypothesis. Such mutual exchanges happen, when it happens, at the manager level and passed onto the desk analyst much later. Keeping in view the security ambience in the country and in the neighbourhood a new matrix for instant exchange of information and assessment is required to be developed.

There are arguments in support and against specialist analysts. It is argued that senior level officers, say the IPS or RAS are recruited from the cream of the educated youths and they are exposed to diverse circumstances and they are able to digest the inputs in the light of their vast experience, command over the grassroots operators and capability to liaise with other wings of intelligence generating facilities. On the other hand, it is argued that there should be a separate group of well trained analyst officers who are well exposed to tradecraft technology. They should be treated as specialist analysts in various streams of intelligence — HumInt, ComInt, ElInt, SigInt etc. Processing of HumInt borrowing from the matrixes of other wings of intelligence inputs may make the final analytical product more comprehensive. This debate has not yet come out from the confines of rooms and not yet debated by the intelligence community and the policy makers. However, an efficient analyst conversant with HumInt, SigInt, ComInt, ElInt etc and having sufficient grassroots experience is the strongest column of intelligence edifice. He is not bao. He is a thinking machine with open-minded approach to any intelligence input and is capable discerning the kernels and presenting a cogent picture fearlessly.

Chapter 13

Counter-intelligence: Principles and Practices

Spying on the spies is the essence of counter-intelligence. This branch of intelligence tradecraft has built-in infrastructures and techniques to target, locate, identify and neutralize enemy or foreign country's agents trying to steal intelligence secrets of the country. It is a branch of the intelligence hierarchy which is concerned with keeping information out of the hands of foreign and domestic enemies. Allen W. Dulles describes Counter-intelligence or Counter-espionage as he calls the trade as: "The classical aims of counter-espionage are 'to locate, identify and neutralize' the opposition. 'Neutralization' can take many forms. Within the United States an apprehended spy can be prosecuted under the law; so can be a foreign intelligence officer who is caught red-handed if he does not have diplomatic immunity. If he has immunity, he is generally expelled. But there are other ways of neutralizing the hostile agent, and one of the best is exposure or threat of exposure. A spy is not of much further use once his name, face and story are in the paper." *The Craft of Intelligence.* p. 119.

Dulles perceived counter-intelligence as a defensive trade of intelligence though the methodology of defence may be aggressive. Frederick L. Wettering in his essay on counter-intelligence (*Secret Intelligence- A Reader*), avers that: "The obvious first responsibility of counter-intelligence is to protect information, usually classified and hereafter referred to as secrets considered important to national security. Two aspects of this function are: physical security, which involves keeping secrets away from all except those who need to be aware of them, and personnel security, which involve making sure that the people who are made aware of secrets protect those secrets responsively."

Both the definitions lay emphasis on defensive character of the concept of counter-intelligence. However, the history of intelligence in modern era, especially during the Second World War and the Cold War has unveiled the various facets of counter-intelligence. Besides physical security, which is defensive in nature, aggressive counter-intelligence is an integral part of locating and neutralizing enemy agents operating inside the host/target country. Frustrating activities of foreign intelligence agencies from stealing national secrets involve application of almost all the traditional tradecrafts of intelligence generation, application and innovation.

Most nations have designated intelligence agencies or wings in the existing agencies to carry out defensive and offensive counter-intelligence. FBI is the nodal agency for counter-intelligence in the USA, though the CIA has its own counter-intelligence wing, National Clandestine Service (NCS) of which James Jesus Angleton was a legendary figure. In the UK the Security Service (MI5) discharges the duty of counter-intelligence in collaboration with the Special Branch. In Russia the FSB is responsible for counter-intelligence activities.

In India the Intelligence Bureau and the Research & Analysis Wing of the Cabinet Secretariat are primarily responsible for counter-intelligence. In the states the respective intelligence branches and special branches have the mandate of carrying out counter-intelligence activities.

At the national level the Intelligence Bureau (IB) is the nodal agency. The agency has basically followed the British pattern and later added on newer tradecraft from lessons learnt during the Cold War period. While during the British rules Russia, China and Middle East affairs drew general attention of the Central Intelligence Bureau, the agency was also responsible for locating and neutralizing COMINTERN thrusts in India and linkages of Indian independence struggle with German, Italian, Japanese and Russian intelligence agencies. The classical example is of Subhas Chandra Bose's linkages with German, Japanese and Italian intelligence agencies and his efforts to cultivate the agencies of the Soviet Union. Bose is also a classical example of collaboration between the NKVD of the USSR, a section of the German secret service Abwehr, and the Indian communists in frustrating Subhas Bose's activities in Germany. Churchill made full efforts to keep Bose confined in some place in Europe as another Indian renegade Subhas Pasha. Even Mussolini tried to neutralize Subhas Bose.

Churchill's secret agents in India and the Viceroy also fed the Congress leaders with doctored intelligence about German and Japanese designs on India and their linkages with Subhas Bose. These inputs had vitiated minds of several top Congress leaders including Nehru, Patel, Prasad, etc. On the other hand, the XX Division of the

MI5 were supplying inside information of the British cabinet to Jinnah. They needed Jinnah more as the British Indian army was 75% Muslim. The only person who could stop or thwart Jinnah was Subhas, who had acceptability amongst all the communities, including the Dalits. Keeping Bose confined in Europe or allowing him to link up with Japan was in the full knowledge of British intelligence. Churchill had simply ignored the importance of an Indian renegade linking up with Japan. He was more than happy that the firebrand popular leader was away from India and it was not possible for him to manipulate Gandhi, Jinnah and Nehru. This aspect of British counter-intelligence has not been researched well so far; the scholars were simply immersed in the developments around important political personalities. That aggressive counter-intelligence can also shape the course of history had not been taken into consideration by most of them.

In post-independent India the IB was basically preoccupied with Communism and Russian penetration in Indian political, societal and cultural entities. Pakistan, having been born out of hate-campaign and communal dissension, remained glued to its so-called unfinished agenda of the partition. Pakistan's wars on Kashmir and other hostile activities had oriented the Indian intelligence to focus on Pakistan counter-intelligence. Besides the USSR, Pakistan and the USA, China was also brought under the counter-intelligence cover, though a little late in history. India's one-sided bonhomie with China was perhaps based on utopian expectations.

In short, the Intelligence Bureau and the RAW have country-specific counter-intelligence units, which play both defensive and offensive roles. Security apparatuses form an important part of the counter-intelligence wings for ensuring access control, security of personnel, documents, security of communications and all perceivable aspects of physical security of the agency, its operations and operatives. There are existing policies and practices to allow access to information on 'need to know basis,' periodical internal verification of the staff, selective surveillance on them, occasional estimation of wealth and properties accumulated by them and their immediate family members. 'Leakage' of information is systematically investigated and open or discreet contact of operatives with suspected foreign intelligence officers are also investigated by the agencies. The prime intelligence agencies practise access control and physical security. However, they have not yet opted for biometric access control. Online communication security is also in primitive stages. Protecting own SigInt edifices, ElInt operations and denying the intruding intelligence agencies the pleasure of stealing these sources of operations are being tightened up. But, aggressive thrusts by foreign intelligence agencies in stealing information from computers, signal units and other means of communication are on the increase and Indian agencies are yet to build up strong firewall against such poaching.

There is an embedded understanding that counter-intelligence is only aimed at invasionary thrusts from foreign intelligence agencies and their agents. In this age of uncertainty ethnic, religious and ideological insurgency and terrorism should also be covered by counter-intelligence units. Both in the USA and the UK there are clear drawn lines between intelligence and law enforcement. In India too this practice is in vogue. However, the 26/11 attack on Mumbai and other jihadi terrorist attacks on India by forces commanded by foreign intelligence agencies have proved beyond doubt that Indian intelligence agencies are required to extend the parameters of counter-intelligence beyond the borders; which I prefer to call forward-counter-intelligence and counterterrorism. It is necessary for India to build up strong forward-counter-intelligence and counterterrorism edifices which should be empowered to look beyond the border, not for collecting classical intelligence, but advance intelligence about the activities of foreign intelligence agencies and forces controlled by them to enable the nation to anticipate and prepare for defences against acts of wanton violence. This is an important aspect of counter-intelligence, which many scholars term forward intelligence operations inside target countries and agencies.

Counter-intelligence has certain built-in practices woven around defensive mechanism. Defensive mechanism is necessary to protect the agency from intrusion, invasion and penetration by foreign intelligence services and their Indian collaborators. This branch of the agency edifice is normally described as security wing of the counter-intelligence mechanism. These are broadly classified as: physical security, personnel security, security of installations, communication security, information system security and operations security.

Physical security includes peripheral and boundary security as well as access security. Securing the building locations include perimeter security by means of raising walls, fences and if necessary laser fencing in very high sensitive locations. This job should not be left to watch and ward section only for physical patrolling. Installation of close circuit TVs and monitoring from a central station is an important ingredient of physical security. Once the outer periphery is secured the agency has to consider access control by issuing digitalized personal identification cards, which may be checked at the main entrances or some system of electronic reading of the card should be in position to allow access to the identity card holder. In certain cases biometric identification methods are also used to allow access to very sensitive areas of the agency. Besides walking through specially wired security doors the staff should also be checked if they carry any file or document when leaving office. Certain category of officers are allowed to carry certain files to their homes after certifying which files they are carrying for processing at camp office.

Besides access control the physical security department has to ensure that doors and windows opening outside are fitted with proper security system. Every building should have the assigned number of people to carry out physical security check of the doors and windows. They have to deposit the keys with a central custodian in the building. Only vetted janitors should be employed for housekeeping jobs under supervision of staff assigned for such duties.

Certain sensitive rooms may be required to be encased in lead sheet below the outer cement coating for denying electronic eavesdropping and other electronic invasion to pick up voice vibrations and transmitting the same to a nearby receiving post. All important meeting rooms should have thick curtains for similar reasons. The officer occupying a office room is responsible for maintaining security of his cupboards and closets which contain classified files. It is his duty to ensure that the closets and cupboards are locked by him personally and all waste papers are finely shredded in his presence. The physical security department is required to gather all the shredded papers and burn in an incinerator the same day.

Personnel security concept has different layers. Antecedents of a person recruited in the agency are thoroughly vetted by the agency itself and police departments are also consulted for background verification. After recruitment and training the officers are subjected to periodical in-house verification and scrutiny to ascertain if he has been contaminated by enemy agencies. There was a time when youths having political connectivity with the Communist parties and the Rashtriya Swayamsevak Sangh were not recruited to the intelligence agencies. This regimen is still in vogue. So also was the case with Muslims. However, under changed circumstances Muslims are now recruited to the agencies unless they are otherwise found unsuitable.

Personnel security is often compromised by greed, lure of easy money and promises of better placement in life. During the peak of lottery mania in Delhi around nineties it was noticed that some employees of an agency were addicted to buying lottery tickets. One of them, having heavy financial commitment at home, gambled heavily and lost regularly. He was contacted by the intelligence officer of a FIS and lured with money. The employee working in the record section of the agency was tasked to steal certain files and pass over to the FIS operator. His sudden affluence drew attention of the surveillance team and after closer watch it was found that the employee used to meet the FIS operator once a week. He was intercepted and after due procedure was penalized. The FIS operator was also intercepted and prosecuted according to proper legal provisions. The agency however suffered certain grave damages and the record keeping system was overhauled.

Personnel security is also compromised when Indian frontmen try to win over lower employees on behalf of FIS operators. In the famous Coomar Narain case of 1985 as many as 12 former staff of the Prime Minister's Office (PMO) and the Rashtrapati Bhavan Secretariat were sentenced to 10 years' rigorous imprisonment. Those who were awarded 10 years' rigorous imprisonment are : S Sankaran, then Senior PA in the President's Secretariat; Jagdish Chandra Arora, then PA to the then Secretary, defence production; Jagdish Mittar Tiwari, then Senior PA to the then Additional Secretary, ministry of defence (MoD); Amrik Lal, then Senior PA to erstwhile Joint Secretary (Supply) MoD; VK Palaniswamy of the ministry of shipping and Transport, HN Chaturvedi, then Assistant EP (LSC), Ministry of commerce; TN Kher, PS to the then Principal Secretary to the former Prime Minister, Rajiv Gandhi, Mr PC Alexander; P Gopalan, then Senior PA and KK Malhotra, then PA to the Principal Secretary to the PM; Swaminath Ram, UDC in the office of the Principal Secretary to the PM; KC Sharma, then PA in the Planning Commission and SL Chandra. Coomar Narain, a businessman with links with FIS bribed these officers to smuggle out valuable documents and share with him. Narain used to get these photocopied and supplied to his FIS benefactors.

The court verdict observed that the accused persons had entered in conspiracy with Lt. Col. Mexi Morvan and Lt Col A Bain Bioley of the French Embassy and some officials of the Polish Embassy and the Embassy of the then German Democratic Republic (GDR) in Delhi and collected, obtained and communicated secret official codes, secret and classified documents and information pertaining to defence, shipping, transport, finance, planning, Research and Analysis Wing (RAW) and Intelligence Bureau (IB) reports, official codes and other classified top secret and confidential information and passed the same to foreign agents.

The famous case of KV Unnikrishnan, RAW operative in Chennai was penetrated by the CIA. The recent case of Ravinder Singh, Joint Secretary of RAW is a pointer that high rank is no barrier for an officer to succumb to FIS overtures. With some help from the CIA, Singh escaped from India to the safety of USA. The recent case involving Brigadier Dasgupta, SS Paul and Mukesh Saini of the cyber department of the National Security Council is a pointer that FIS operatives are always on the prowl and any susceptible senior or junior officer may succumb to allurement. There was, another media reported case (1997) in which a very senior officer of the counter-intelligence department of the Intelligence Bureau Ratan Saigal was suspected for working with the station chief of the CIA. It is learnt that Ratan Saigal was honourably retired with all benefits as there was no clinching evidence. There were allegations that he was let off because of his connections with former Director IB and other influential persons. However, on India's request two US diplomats were withdrawn from India.

Personnel security has other dimensions. A particular near-top level officer had acquired within ten years properties worth forty million rupees. He was overseeing operations in an eastern neighbour of India. Indepth enquiries revealed that he had misappropriated nearly 30 million rupees out of seventy million granted by the government to a political party in the neighbouring country for contesting a national election. The officer was not prosecuted, as the money was drawn from secret service fund. He was eased out of the agency only to buy out another post in a uniformed organisation. The aspect of misappropriating secret service funds is a contagious disease, if it is imbued by senior echelons the lower strata make merry with smaller loots. Secret service fund is a sacred trust of the nation just like ammunition issued to a battlefield soldier. If one fritters away the bullets he gets exposed to enemy bullets.

In one case it was noticed that the daughter of a middle level employee had secured a job in a foreign embassy. He had not disclosed the fact to the agency. The matter came to notice when a diplomatic car visited the residence of the employee to drop his daughter, a lady with good looks and excellent personal qualifications. The observation was confirmed by surveillance reports. On discreet questioning the employee admitted that he had no control on his grown-up daughter and he was unable to force her to resign. Procrastinations over the issue were finally resolved when the daughter married a foreign national of the embassy and later migrated to a western country. In another case an officer of IPS rank working with the RAW declined to return home while working in a North American country. He left the job and after some years took up appointment in a provincial government.

Similarly, it is often noticed that wives and daughters of agency officers posted abroad undercover take up employment in the host country. Often wives and wards of diplomatic and non-diplomatic staff also avail of employment without keeping the government informed. In an embarrassing case wife of an undercover officer posted in North America had taken up job with a company known as the front of an intelligence agency of the host country. When accosted the officer agreed to be repatriated to home base; his wife and children stayed back in the host country. Such tendencies are endemic amongst certain categories of RAW and non-diplomatic staff of the ministry of external affairs. In fact, no correct assessment of such cases has been made by any independent agency. The correct statistics may expose the unholy craze for settling down in western countries. No objective studies have been made so far about the security implications to the intelligence agencies and the country as a whole.

The physical and personnel security of the CIA is supervised by units tagged to the Directorate of Operations. The Office of Security, while it assigned the security of operations to multiple groups within the Directorate of Operations: the counter-intelligence staff and the area of general security are also overseen by this agency. In Britain the MI5 and the MI6 have their own security wings. In the British service, the cases of the Cambridge Five, and the later suspicions about MI5 chief Sir Roger Hollis caused great internal dissension. Clearly, the British were penetrated by Kim Philby, but it was never admitted in any public forum. In the US service, there was also significant disruption over the contradictory accusations about moles from defectors Anatoliy Golitsyn and Yuri Nosenko, and their respective supporters in CIA and the British Security Service (MI5). Golitsyn had exposed Philby, and was generally believed by Jesus Angleton, the CIA counter-intelligence baron. There are several such international cases which still form the bones and marrows of juicy spy stories.

Security of installations like clandestine radio stations, radar formations, and aircraft for electronic espionage, satellite installations and cryptology offices are most vital segments of SigInt. The adversary intelligence agencies are always on the prowl to locate these installations, penetrate the employees and operators. For China it is very important to gain access to the satellite and radar formations somewhere in Assam. They would be ready to spend fortunes to gain access and steal the algorithms, digital encryption codes and other trans-receiving details. An algorithm is an effective method for solving a problem using a finite sequence of instructions. Algorithms are used for calculation, data processing, and many other fields of data sequencing and transmitting. Algorithm was first invented in India. Al-Khwârizmî, Persian astronomer and mathematician, wrote a treatise in 825 AD, *On Calculation with Hindu Numerals*. While translating in Latin the name of the Persian author was mutilated as Algoritmi, and later the system of calculation with Indian numerical came to be termed as algorithm.

Similarly, Pakistan has been found sniffing around Indian installations in Punjab, Himachal Pradesh, Leh, Gujarat and even Karnataka. In a curious case detected in 1992 it was noticed that a supposed barber from Bihar had set up a saloon very near to a satellite installation in Rajasthan. Located in a market area no one doubted the bona fides of the nearly perfect Maithili speaking person. His good and cheap cut drew good number of clientele, some of them from within the satellite station. Over period he befriended some of the employees and on special request he obliged the seniors by visiting their homes for haircutting. A chance interception of his telephone call to a number in Pakistan gave the game away. After prolonged surveillance he was picked up. He turned out to be a barber from

Bulandshahar in Uttar Pradesh. He was trained to converse in Maithili, a language in Bihar and set up a shop for penetrating the satellite station. Though the case was solved satisfactorily, it remains the paramount duty of the intelligence agencies to revamp physical security of all such installations. The Military Intelligence, however, are responsible for their sensitive installations. But, the present security situation in and around many cantonment areas, located in thickly populated civilian areas cannot be said to be satisfactory.

For securing sensitive installations both physical and electronic surveillance is necessary. Physical surveillance is limited to guarding, carrying out enquiries, and constantly verifying antecedents of people working in sensitive areas; say the enrichment plant area of an atomic reactor. However, electronic surveillance has the advantage of being unobtrusive, subtle with enlarged focus on given areas and personnel. Beyond the concept of close circuit TV, there are electronic eyes and sensor which can detect movements, identify people and raise alarm if there is unauthorized intrusion. For example, invisible laser beam barriers cannot be violated with impunity. Once this Laxman Rekha is violated, automatic alarm is raised attracting attention of the physical security contingents.

Document security is always under attack of FIS agents. The cited Coomar Narain case gives an eye-opener to the lack of security system in the government offices. The other case is of the senior most military officers ever to be convicted of espionage, the Larkins brothers, Air Vice Marshal (retd) KH Larkins and his brother Major General (retired) FD Larkins, and two others, Lt Colonel (retd) Jasbir Singh and arms dealer Jaspal Singh Gill. They were charged with passing on classified military documents to US intelligence officials. The spy ring was detected in April 1983, but the government ordered further surveillance for another seven months in view of ramifications involved in arresting such senior officials. FD Larkins was caught red-handed on November 18, 1983, while passing documents to an American. KH Larkins was also arrested the next day. A 2003 report had mentioned that both the brothers were not traceable to their addresses in India. It was reported that one was living in Australia and the other in Sri Lanka.

In both the cases departmental document security was flagrantly violated. Coomar Narain had bribed the officer and office staff to take out files, photocopy the papers and pass on to him. Of all places they selected a shop in Khan Market to copy the papers. Chance detection of one such page led to series of counter-intelligence initiatives leading to detection of the case. In case of the Larkins government insistence on watch and observe had delayed the process of detection of the case.

Document security and information security should not be bunched together. There are paperless information sources, which may be in the minds of the intelligence generating officers, his cut-outs and even with the source of information. The FIS operators often target these sources also. There is an instance of an intelligence generator in early nineties who was assigned the task of penetrating a fake passport manufacturer's gang located at Khatauli, near Saharanpur in Uttar Pradesh. He did the job appreciably, but lured by easy money he started disclosing to a FIS intelligence officer about the scheme of operation of the Indian agency. He, simply speaking, turned a double agent. Suspicion arose when the foreign embassy concerned changed its policy and format of allowing the travel agents and visa agents approaching the consular section. The game was busted when a lady agent was detected carrying classified information hiding a page inside her holy book. This tradecraft was taught to the agency's operations officer assigned to Khatauli area. This link initiated a process of counter-intelligence procedure leading to dismissal of the officer from service under Article 311 of the Constitution.

Physical documents are to be stored in secured places. The trick of stealing one or two pages includes removal of the unnumbered papers and replacement of two similar papers in the file. In most government departments files are not properly docketed, page numbered and a summary of the file and each page are not recorded on the master page. Often file registers are not updated. Agents take advantage of this situation and steal key papers. After the series of correspondence are complete, say a file related to agent XX, the Guard file is consigned to Record Room and certain matters from the file are also copied in microfiche and stored in designated archives. Files are tampered with when the ideal procedure to prepare, handle to store a file is not followed. Dual key security system is also not usually observed. In this scheme the master key remains with the Desk in charge and a duplicate is kept with the section officer in charge. Often 'safety vault' locking system is also introduced: insertion of one key followed by the other can only open the lock. Such ideal situation does not exist even in the offices of the intelligence agencies. Modern photocopying gadgets look like normal pens. The physical security officers should check pens, cellphones with cameras and any other micro camera being carried into the office by unauthorized employee. In fact, certain categories of officers dealing with secret papers should not be allowed to bring in their camera enabled cellphones inside the office.

Communications security (COMSEC) is a vast subject. We have discussed some aspects in the chapters dealing with SigInt and ComInt. In this branch of security some measures and tradecrafts are applied to deny unauthorized persons access to classified information derived from SigInt and ComInt procedures to ensure that unauthorized interceptors and intruders cannot break in and steal classified information. Communication security encompasses security of crypto materials, real time trans-receiving security, emission security, traffic-flow security and physical security of communication equipment. We have discussed these items earlier.

Security of Crypto materials and their secure handling involve the scientific community who generate the ciphers, the custodians and end users. The Joint Cipher Bureau is under the ministry of defence that generates crypto materials for use by the defense forces and intelligence agencies. The intelligence agencies often generate their own cipher key system for exclusive use. Cipher documents are transported under strict security and the user officers are to certify that all the pages and keys have been used and the remnants have been destroyed by burning and by smothering the ashes.

The aspect of Emission Security has been discussed earlier. In short, the FIS operators try ceaselessly to gain physical access into the SigInt and ComInt installations. They try to identify the equipment, their analog and digital variants, and aerial installations, trans-receiving manuals, networking system and crypto documents.

Traffic security is ensured by masking the communication in cipher text (alpha-numeric, alpha or numeric). Monitoring of radio transmission is a common game, but the manner of masking, keeping the circuit busy and various observing other traffic-flow security and transmission security like frequency hopping, spread spectrum diversion and burst transmission. Each foreign spy agency has more than one Alibaba to steal the open sesame secret. Indian military and civil intelligence agencies have in place certain security devices which are not subject of discussion of this book.

Information security is defined as security of information that are stored, communicated through electronic/computer network. It requires protecting information and information systems from unauthorized access, use, disclosure, disruption, modification or destruction.

Computers, single ones or networks become vulnerable once the users communicate through Internet and World Wide Web systems. Right from the organisation that uses network to the hardware and software of the computer is under threat from electronic viruses, break in, hacking, stealing through on-line technology as well as through installation insecurity, personnel insecurity, unauthorized access, carelessness of operators, programmers and data processors and many other means. Normally a network works through secured wireless WiFi system or Local Area Network. For instance, in the same building networking is normally established through Infranet. In case there are several workplaces of the same organization in the same city networking is achieved through point to point linking process. Organizations in various cities at geographical distances are networked through Internet Protocol devices—static or dynamic. The diagram below illustrates the likely quantum of attacks.

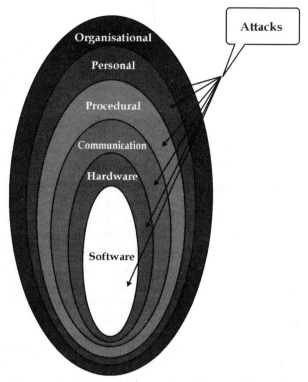

Information security is concerned with confidentiality, integrity and availability of data regardless of the form the data may take: electronic, print, or other forms. Information can be pilfered from outside a computer. On the other hand computer security can focus on ensuring the availability and correct operation of a computer system without concern for the information stored or processed by the computer. Confidentiality, integrity and availability are the main concerns of the counter-intelligence experts. Confidentiality relates both to the information and the persons handling the information. A piece of information, especially in intelligence agency, can be confidential, secret and top secret. According to the grading of the information it is tagged and stored as per procedure laid down by the organisation. Confidentiality can be breached if a person working in the organisation leaks out the secrets, smuggles out a printed-paper, gives away the IP address of the computer network system and the configuration of the TCP/IP of a local network. An officer losing his laptop computer through neglect or motivated theft can breach confidentiality of the information stored.

Certain procedure is required to be strictly followed while organising the security parameters of the organisational information security. These are basically counted as: security policy, organization of information security, personnel management, asset management, physical and environmental security, security management of communications and operations, access control and regulations regarding who can access which information.

The concept of threat from "insider saboteurs" is an important factor. Insider activity might involve such incidents as compromising, manipulating, exceeding authorized access to, tampering with and disabling departmental information resources, workstation, or network. Trusted insiders often abuse non-technical vulnerabilities, such as general rules and organizational policies, rather than vulnerabilities in information systems and network. It is essential for organisation management to secure confidential information resources from unauthorized access by employees at all levels. However, innovative technology providing for data content analysis and intelligent monitoring may also be of great help.

Unauthorized data access and transfer is another great threat. Data is transferred outside or stored in an unauthorized location. The data that can be copied into a word processing application, email or instant message or transferred to another format is usually the most vulnerable part of sensitive information security. Information can be easily transferred outside the network to a portable device, compact disk, pen drive, micro storing devices in cellphones or some other repository. User access policy should provide rigid adherence to access controls procedures. Every piece of confidential data should be secured and the amount of data access privileges should be extremely limited. Files containing sensitive information should be stored in a specific location. It should be immediately detected if any data was transferred across the system network or to an external device. To reduce insider theft risks, it is essential to monitor and audit user activity across the entire network on a regular basis. Sometimes entire laptops and hard disks can be stolen too.

The use of cyber forensic tools can often deter stealing of information. Many types of software are available. For example, GFI LAN guard Network Security Scanner (NSS) allows scanning, detecting, assessing and remedying any security vulnerabilities on network. The administrator has to deal separately with problems related to vulnerability issues, patch management and network auditing, at times using multiple products. With GFI LAN guard NSS, the main concerns of vulnerability management can be addressed in one package. Using a single console with extensive reporting functionality, GFI LAN guard NSS's integrated solution helps to address these issues faster.

GFI LAN guard NSS use state of the art vulnerability check databases based on OVAL and SANS Top 20, providing over 15,000 vulnerability assessments when network is scanned. GFI LAN guard

NSS gives the information and tools to perform multi-platform scans across all environments, to analyse network's security health and effectively install and manage patches on all machines across different operating systems and in different languages. This results in a consistently configured environment that secures against all vulnerabilities. However, if sensitive information is mailed to an inimical receiver in the format of an attachment it may not be possible to retrieve the data from the registry of the computer, in case the sender deletes the mail along with the attachment. Such betrayers also delete the mail address of the receiver from the computer mailbox address and contact lists.

It is necessary to manage hard disk security by the organisation. Systems management is a complicated procedure. This may include Hard disk encryption device. This procedure can delete the data if detached from the unique computer identification; data file encryption should not work if opened from another computer ID; device lock: hide or restrict access to removable media devices such as CD, DVD, floppy, flash and USB drives, and deny access to partitions of your hard disk drives with the programme. The management should prevent copying data between removable media and hard disk drives, deny access to removable media, protect PC against unauthorized software installations and prevent data leaks through removable media.

Data grouping is a method in which data stored on workstations and servers according to information security level and define users that may access that information by users' access level. It will prevent both accidental data leakage and intentional data theft.

As far as computer information security is concerned the organization should train and educate all users to lock their PC when leaving it — even for two minutes. Administrators should connect PCs to a network to lock after a certain number of minute's idling situation, followed by auto-locking. Otherwise if a PC is left even for ten minutes another person can access files and folders on the network. Employees should not be allowed to carry any storage device like pen drive, etc. They should be thoroughly frisked and their cellphones, especially Blackberry systems should be kept in a safe location to be taken back by them while going back home. It is necessary to ban carrying of Bluetooth, Infrared, email, video-still photo capable cellphones to work stations. Security teams should search Operations Room operators for suspected pen-copier, pen/button cameras and cellphones and wrist watches with voice recording facilities. It is absolutely necessary to draw up strict access control manual and implement the same religiously. Constant supervision by physical and hidden cameras is suggested to detect unethical activities by personnel handling sensitive information. The management should keep checking for the behavioural changes in employees who have access to critical data. Additionally a log of file access pattern of the employees should be maintained by the management. It is also necessary to expose the employees to inimical intelligence thrusts and management's counter-intelligence measures.

Often an important aspect of separation of duties is neglected by the management. Separation of duties ensures that an individual cannot complete a critical task by himself. For example, an employee who submits a request for reimbursement should not also be able to authorize payment or print the check. An applications programmer should not also be the server administrator or the database administrator— these roles and responsibilities must be separated from one another.

There are various layers of data security. The following example may illustrate the layers more succinctly:

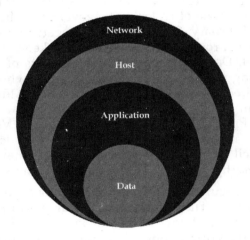

The data core must be protected by all means. Information security must protect information throughout the life span of the information, from the initial creation of the information upto to the final disposal of the information. The information must be protected while in motion and while at rest. During its life time, information may pass through many different information processing systems and through many different parts of information processing systems. To fully protect the information during its lifetime, each component of the information processing system must have its own protection mechanisms. The building-up, layering on and overlapping of security measures is called defence in-depth. A few other precautions are: to restrict physical access of employees; Biometrics like iris scan, thumb impression scan can help; to keep users out of systems that don't concern them; restrict rights that directly impact computer access; deny access to some computers from the network. These stand-alone computers can build up excellent firewall; hardening of log on and deny log on rights to unauthorized personnel and restriction of number of systems to minimize administration and the probability of configuration errors.

The classic case of breach of information security in India was detected in 2005 when the Naval authorities got whiff of huge leakage of classified information from the Naval War Room computer and other related storages by responsible naval officers in collaboration with arms dealers.

It was alleged that nine people were involved in leaking classified information relating to Navy's planned purchase of a wide array of sophisticated equipment from the war room or Directorate of Naval Operations. Three officers – Captain Kashyap Kumar along with Commanders Virender Rana and Vinod Kumar Jha – were dismissed from naval service in October 2005 after it was established that they had sold classified information for commercial benefits. Kumar, described as its mastermind, headed the Directorate of Naval Operations, at the time of its leak. The government handed over the case to CBI in February, 2006 following allegations that middlemen involved in the war room leak case were also linked with the Scorpene submarine deal. Developments led to the arrests of five people in April, including Commanders Rana and Jha (who were earlier dismissed), retired Lt. Cdr. Kulbhushan Parashar, Mukesh Bajaj and Rajrani Jaiswal. Lt Cdr Ravi Shankaran, a nephew of navy chief Admiral Arun Prakash was also arrested. Abhishek Verma, son of a former MP was also arrested in this connection. Besides the National Security Council (NSC) data leakage, this was one of the biggest information security breaches in India in recent times.

Operations security is another important aspect of counter-intelligence warfare. The Second World War poster said 'enemy is listening, he wants to know what you know, keep it to yourself.' This aspect is the cornerstone of operations security. Operations security helps to avoid disclosure of sensitive information. Such data concerns an agency's secret missions, capabilities, research and development. It also includes training which could prevent the compromise of military operations.

Intelligence and military operations are worked out with maximum possible secrecy. Intelligence briefing rooms and war rooms are restricted areas, where access is allowed on need to know basis. However, in many other matters of governmental activities certain degree of confidentiality is required to be observed. It would not be an ideal situation if the Maoist leadership pilfers classified information about types and quantities of weapons the government was planning to acquire and deploy against them. Even the foreknowledge of joint operations by several Maoist affected states to regain the lost ground can contribute to the failure of the operations. The very same thing happened when the state and central governments announced about joint operations in Chattisgarh and Jharkhand. The guerrilla forces are trained to vacate an area under attack by superior forces and regain back the lost territory whenever the government presence is relaxed.

In war operations and intelligence operations the chief planners comprise a compact team. With inputs from the analysts, data processors, and political policy makers, the compact team conceives of intelligence operation to attain certain objectives assigned and defined by the state. Similarly, the armed forces are given a task by the policy planners either for defensive or offensive actions. To formulate a scheme of operations that would facilitate to attain the objective, the Military Operations Directorate may form a compact team to examine the offensive and defensive priorities of the mission.

In the same vein it is necessary to assess, identify and classify which areas of activities of the intelligence agency or the military establishments are likely to be targeted by the inimical foreign intelligence agencies. To draw up a defensive charter of areas to be protected the expert team formulates certain parameters and evaluates the weakest links through which the enemy agency may attack. These weak links are fortified to prevent leakage and operations compromise.

Most intelligence agencies observe a set of guiding rules with local variations. These are identification of critical information, which involves analysis of the value of the intelligence to national security. Certain categories of information obtained through open sources may already be in the possession of the inimical agencies. But what covert operations were taken up in the wake of the OsInt input is classified and can even be graded top secret.

This is followed by analysis of threat from adversaries. It has been noticed that Pakistan is constantly focused on India's army, air force and naval movements, deployment of radars, missile batteries, construction of border defenses, etc. On the other hand they are highly sensitive to Indian approach towards the minority Muslim community and their religious and public domain institutions. Countries like China target intelligence regarding Indian defence forces, economic progress and ideological contamination amongst certain segments of the Indian society.

After the likely targets and areas are identified the agencies carry out analysis of vulnerabilities. Each forward and counter-intelligence moves are evaluated by the operation groups and possible weak areas are identified and precautions are taken accordingly. On the basis of these evaluations the Operations Directorate adopts certain insulating and certain diversionary measures to protect the core areas of the operation and to misdirect the inimical agency. Finally, an operations chief employs measures to reduce risks to an acceptable level, either by eliminating indicators or vulnerabilities, disrupting the effective collection of information, or by preventing the adversary from accurately interpreting the data. The most effective measure tends to be simple, straightforward, and inexpensive procedural adjustments that fit the solution to the need. Countermeasures are drilled in on the personnel to protect the vulnerabilities having the most impact. It may often be necessary to adopt multiple countermeasures to guile, mislead and misguide the adversarial agencies.

Counter-intelligence Practices

In the Indian context counter-intelligence thrusts are expected from countries like Pakistan, China, the USA. UK, France, Russia and major countries as far as strategic defence, commercial, entrepreneurial and other official secrets are concerned. Countries like Japan, Korea, Taiwan, Germany and certain other countries are more interested in commercial intelligence and information pertaining to global tendering for strategic purchases or infrastructural investments.

India is, basically, a Pakistan and China centric country, though it is a fertile ground for US, UK and Russian classical and operational intelligence concerns. To address all such counter-intelligence concerns the Indian Intelligence Bureau and the Research and Analysis Wing have certain built-in infrastructures, which are country specific and sometimes subject specific.

Soon after independence, India paid maximum attention to counter-intelligence operations conducted by the KGB and NKVD of the USSR. India had inherited the British bias against the USSR and activities of the Indian communist parties, their front organizations were studied meticulously and counter-intelligence operations were also directed against Moscow based or Delhi embassy based intelligence operators. Some giants of the Indian intelligence graduated out of the Das Capital and other works of the international communist movements. It took India over fifteen years since 1947 to shift the focus on China and nearly eighteen years to determine that China and Pakistan were the strategic enemies and Indian counter-intelligence responses are required to be directed against the intelligence apparatuses of these two countries. Though Pakistan's Inter Services Intelligence (ISI) was operating in India from 1952 onwards, both from home bases in Dhaka and Islamabad and embassy based intelligence hubs in Delhi, Mumbai and Shillong, Indian responses were focused on Pakistan's counter-intelligence thrusts generally from 1960 onwards. The USSR centric stalwarts grudgingly started giving some concessions to the counter-intelligence desks covering the USA, UK, China and Pakistan.

The prime intelligence agencies of India generally follow the British and US system of structuring counter-intelligence units after evaluation of intelligence thrusts from different countries. India's nonaligned status and perceived leanings towards Moscow had prompted both the Iron curtain countries and the Free World nations to aggressively pursue intelligence missions in India. The fierce competition between the USSR bloc countries and the US, UK and allied countries were palpably perceivable. On the one hand the USSR made sustained efforts to infiltrate several political parties and their leaders. Besides the Communist Party and its fronts there are allegations of several Congress leaders being on the pay roll of Moscow. The Soviet satellite countries like Poland, Hungary, and East Germany, Bulgaria, Romania and Czechoslovakia acted in unison as proxy intelligence collectors for the Committee for State Security (KGB), People's Commissariat for International Affairs (NKVD), and the Second (II) Main Directorate of the General Staff of the Armed Forces of the Russian Federation (GRU). The Russian embassy in Delhi had (has even now) an elaborate espionage network which penetrated almost all walks of life encompassing parliamentarians, legislators, ministers, several layers of bureaucrats, media leaders, intellectuals and other opinion makers. Certain gaps, which the Russian agencies could not cover, were looked after by the agencies of the satellite countries heavily infiltrated by the Soviet apparatchiks.

Similarly, the USA and the allies (the French preferred to walk alone) also had established wide network in India to steal intelligence as well as to influence the opinion makers among the politicians, bureaucrats, industrialists, media persons and social organizations.

Pakistan and China had their respective strategic interests in India. Pakistan was involved in inflicting thousand cuts on India by supporting and assisting the ethnic insurgent groups in the northeast. Pakistan Intelligence Bureau and the Inter Services Intelligence trained, armed and motivated the insurgent groups to keep India busy in the troubled northeast. China also supported India's ethnic insurgent groups like the Nagas and the Mizos by training and arming their cadres. Between 1960 and 1971 Pak-China collaboration on this front had generated serious security situation in the remote northeastern areas of the country.

Pakistan has other priorities: penetration of the armed forces, gathering intelligence about defence installations, subverting the Indian Muslims, spreading terror network in India and influencing the media leaders, intellectuals, political leaders and other opinion makers. Several sections of opinion in Pakistan still propagate the ideology of reunification of the subcontinental Muslims under a single umbrella of Islam. Systematic subversion of the Indian Muslims constitutes an important part of Pakistan's state policy.

The Chinese, on the other hand, put emphasis on stealing intelligence about the armed forces, force and weaponry deployment, nuclear and rocket sciences and increasing naval presence of India in the Indian Ocean rim countries. Though the Indian Maoist guerrilla groups flaunt the ideological tenets and war strategy of Mao Zedong, the Chinese Communist Party and the People's Army have rendered only indirect help to the Indian insurgents. Obviously this is a fertile ground and in case India falters in handling the growing menace China would not hesitate to exploit the boiling cauldron.

Keeping these broad contours of threat perceptions Indian intelligence agencies have defined certain priorities to organize the counter-intelligence edifices. Some of the focal points of emphasis are:

- To effectively and efficiently manage and oversee the national counter-intelligence enterprises targeting the countries logged as known pirates of national secrets.

- To synchronize intra-departmental counter-intelligence activities across the country, in coordination with the provincial intelligence community.

- To manage priority counter-intelligence plans and projects in fulfillment of national, departmental and defence force's requirements.

- To select and develop unique counter-intelligence operational support capabilities and make them available to the wider intelligence community.

- To effectively prevent, thwart and aggressively pursue the intelligence operatives of foreign countries from stealing national secrets, identify and to neutralize them through lawful means.

- To identify, develop and deploy advanced technologies for counter-intelligence.

- To create a joint, interoperable and synchronized approach to counter-intelligence as a distinct intelligence discipline.

- To assess the feasibility of a joint operational element in collaboration with the defence counter-intelligence units and other sister-organizations.

- To train and put in position counter-intelligence analysts and technical and scientific experts to build up sinews of combat preparedness for preventing the FIS agencies from penetrating the secrets of the nation.

- To share feedback with general intelligence and counter-terrorism branches with inputs obtained during counter-intelligence operations.

- Charter of duties, besides the broad principles, varies depending on the country and the agency under coverage.

In India the focal counter-intelligence units are located in Delhi with skeletal units located in certain state capitals. The state police intelligence units, in some states, operate holistic 'foreigner's desk' to cover activities of the suspected foreign nationals. The states have not synchronized their counter-intelligence activities with the agencies of the Union Government. This has caused a big void in organizing counter-intelligence coverage in certain sensitive parts of several states. Because of ultra-thin deployment of counter-intelligence staff in subsidiary units of the Intelligence Bureau and the RAW, in most of the states counter-intelligence works are neglected and often vital intelligence leads are lost. It is not impossible for foreign agents moving the length and breadth of the country under some guise, guile, and steal vital intelligence. In this area India is vulnerable.

To understand this it is necessary to comprehend the methodology and modus operandi of the foreign intelligence agencies engaged in intelligence stealing operations. Most foreign intelligence services (FIS) locate their intelligence operatives in their respective diplomatic premises with undercover diplomatic status. These undercover diplomats are senior employees of the FIS with varying ranks from minister to second secretary. Several non-diplomatic staff is also posted in the consular, commercial, education, publicity, etc. divisions as well as with the offices of the military, naval as air attaches.

The Consular division dealing with visa, education division dealing with student visa, scholarships, studies abroad, the information, cultural and publicity divisions dealing with media, cultural affairs make sustained efforts to spot talents for recruitment as agents for supplying the embassy based benefactors with secret information in their respective fields. There are innumerable instances where prominent media persons, literati, artists and intellectuals were won over 'by offering the correct price' to work for the FIS. While the undercover diplomats handle the classy individuals the job of tracking, locating and cultivating lower talents are left to the non-diplomatic FIS staff.

In the States, wherever consulates are in existence the same pattern of intelligence operations are followed. States not having consulates or trade representative offices are covered by the undercover diplomats during visits to places of pilgrimage, historic sites, normal tourist spots and conferences, congregations which draw the literati, intelligentsia, media persons and sympathizers. Some talents are cultivated on the basis of recommendations from veteran contacts of the FIS. A prominent media person, in regular contact with US diplomats was known to have acted as a recruiter and talent spotter. Running a ragtag news agency he made millions and went unpunished. The government did not have the guts to advise and prevent the celebrated journalist. Another editor level person working in a prominent daily was kept under surveillance and his connectivity with the CIA was established beyond doubt. It was also found that certain electronic media received funding from Middle East sources. They are known for tilted reporting in favour of a particular religious community.

In addition to diplomatic mission based operations certain FIS make sustained endeavors to gather HumInt by deploying and positioning 'short term resident agents, 'itinerant agents, and 'long term resident agents.' These operations are mostly guided from the 'home bases' of the Foreign Intelligence Services. For example, a university scholar, a scientific researcher, and an aid volunteer (Peace Corps), etc. may be deputed with a fixed mission to study a given problem area, say development of Cryogenic rocket engine, and obtain inside intelligence during the process of study, collaboration and also by befriending Indian scientists working in the concerned area. The foreigner's desk often has to collaborate with counter-intelligence wings and the government and convey its reservation about allowing a 'tainted' scholar taking up research work in a given area. Obviously, such restrictions are opposed by the intellectual community.

A short-term resident agent is recruited, trained and briefed to locate himself in an area of interest, work for a limited period, say for three years, and return to home base after accomplishing the intelligence tasks. They come with long-term visa and repeat visit visa like David Coleman Headley (Lashkar-e-Taiba/ISI operator) did for his repeat visit to India. He had even started a travel agency business as plausible cover. His accomplice Tahawwur Hussain Rana had visited India on the plea of recruiting youths for foreign jobs. Similarly a US geophysicist or a glaciologist may be deputed to study certain areas of rock formations, glacial behavior in the Himalayas for short durations. Their hidden agenda may include study of uranium exploration and mining by India and funding groups to oppose such mining in a given area and to study what military preparations India might have undertaken in the Himalayan region on Pakistan and China borders. The uranium mining uproar in Meghalaya, some sources suspect, is inspired by a Beijing based FIS having diplomatic presence in Delhi.

Long Term Resident Agents are deputed after detailed training and briefing to settle down in a compatible location, acclimatize with area and the people, adopt a natural cover and merge with the background. He may even be allowed to 'take a station wife' and start living as a normal resident pursuing some vocation. A searching mind can locate numbers of Jewish, German, French, US and other nationals settled in Kulu, Manali and other Himalayan tracts in Himachal Pradesh, Uttarakhand, etc. states. They are treated as drug addicts who make charas out of Ganja plants (*Sativa Indica*), consume the same and also indulge in some trading on the sides. Not much intelligence watch is kept on this thriving community by the central and state intelligence units. A large number of them do not even register themselves with local foreigner registration officer. Several Pakistani nationals visiting India stay back as 'illegals' and disappear amongst the Muslim masses. They work as long term agents handled by home based operators. The number of missing Pakistani nationals is over 5000. There were occasions when some Pakistani LTRA were located and identified in Western Uttar Pradesh. Such unmasking requires prolonged surveillance, secret enquiry through agents, and by infiltrating own agents in the spy ring.

This requires an illustration. The name and fame of Faqir Ikramuddin Chisti was not heard in Saharanpur area till 1989. Suddenly he appeared at an abandoned Dargah near village Khatauli and claimed he was a descendant of Khwaja Muinuddin Chisti and he was directed by Allah to serve the humanity from the Dargah of one of the Chisti saints. He started healing operations and regularly addressed the people when they congregated on Fridays. The Faqir had both Hindu and Muslim followers. He issued *taviz* (protective amulets), holy water and ash from a fire that burnt in his abode for twenty-four hours. Soon his name and fame started spreading like wildfire. He was invited to cities like Meerut, Ambala, Delhi, Jhansi and Jodhpur.

A chance detection of the Faqir's meeting with a Pakistani undercover diplomat at Ajmer Sharif aroused suspicion. The Faqir was kept under surveillance and all his movements were covered. Soon it was discerned that a lady visa agent visited the Dargah twice in a month. She was known as a talent spotter of the embassy based intelligence operator. She was quietly lifted and interrogated. Her revelation led to the arrest of the Faqir for spying activity. In real life, Muniruddin Qureshi, was a resident of Karachi. He was trained by the ISI, given the cover of a Faqir and directed to communicate through Pakistan embassy by using the intercepted lady as cut-out. He was allowed to meet embassy official only at Ajmer or Nizamuddin Dargah in Delhi. It took nearly a year to bust the LTRA operation launched by Pakistan.

Experience has proved that certain foreign missionaries, research scholars, anthropologists, etc. are planted by the western FISs for collecting political, demographic, economic, industrial data and even aid and abet ethnic insurgents under the guise of preaching and teaching. Several such incidents were unearthed in Meghalaya, Tripura, Orissa and other parts of tribal India. Such incidents are not related alone to the contentious issue of proselytisation, but the more complicated issue of funding and encouraging the ethnic restive groups seeking separate political identity.

However, to understand how intelligence stealing operations are conducted from within the mission based operatives it is necessary to understand that security and intelligence services of major countries depute their operatives either under open post or undercover post. For instance deputation of FBI personnel in the US embassy is an open post action. They are designated and presented to the host country as security personnel with varying ranks. The Indian external affairs ministry also deputes security officers from varying ranks to certain foreign missions. These officers are not undercover spies. They look after security of the mission, its personnel and liaise with the security division of the foreign office of the host country. Such exchanges are covered under Vienna Convention on Diplomatic Relations adopted in April 1961.

However, such type of deputation of security personnel depends on mutual agreement between the deputing and the host country. Similar is the case of deputation of military, naval and air attaches to different missions. Like the open security personnel the military attaches are also not supposed to indulge in clandestine intelligence collection. However, in most cases, these officials and the support staff normally scoop out military intelligence. Several such cases were detected by the Indian intelligence agencies. The most prominent case was that of Brigadier Zahirul Islam Abbasi (later Major General), who had served in the ISI also, was caught red-handed in Delhi by an Indian intelligence agency while exchanging documents with a retired India army officer. He was the senior most officer to be exploded while engaging in clandestine intelligence operations in 1989.

The undercover operators are hardcore intelligence officers who are given diplomatic cover of varying ranks with supporting staff to work in a foreign mission under command of the station chief, also an undercover intelligence operator. Most major countries maintain elaborate intelligence set-up in important countries. The CIA, MI5 and MI6, FSB, SVR, GRU, Inter Services Intelligence and the Chinese intelligence services maintain considerably large intelligence contingents in India.

For counter-intelligence response India has structured its responses by maintaining country specific units to unearth clandestine intelligence operations of the FIS embedded in the diplomatic premises. Indian efforts on own soil is defensive in nature. Indian agencies normally do not try to infiltrate the intelligence edifices in the foreign missions and win them over for long-term intelligence relationship.

Even for defensive actions the agencies have to observe certain routine protocols like obtaining background information about each and every diplomatic (open or covert) personnel in the mission. History sheets of the previous postings are also obtained in most cases through own agency enquiries or through friendly agencies and miscellaneous sources. This is the process of establishing the real identity of an undercover intelligence operator. Their suspected movements are also kept under surveillance. The process of surveillance, secret enquiry and certain agent operations lead to identification of a suspected undercover spy. Once his identity is confirmed, he is classified as an Intelligence Operator (IO) and he is brought under surveillance and other tradecraft technologies to unearth his modus operandi, agents and his clandestine actions.

There are certain undercover operators whose credentials cannot be easily traced and identity established. They are treated as Suspected IOs (SIO). These categories are also brought under tradecraft operations. The main tradecraft tools used are: Surveillance, EIInt, HumInt, SigInt, etc. operations. Use of double agent, honey traps, infiltration of own intelligence assets are also prescribed. Though Indian counter-intelligence on its own soil is defensive in nature, often certain aggressive measures are resorted to unearth deep penetration by undercover FIS operatives. There are instances of successful application of the 'honey trap' tradecraft.

It would not be out of place to make a passing reference to "honey trap" operation. The term means planting an attractive woman of a FIS target after it is determined that he has tremendous weakness for the fair sex. In one case a career diplomat was noticed hopping from one Delhi socialite to another. Some of the names belonged to impressive families. In this particular operation, besides surveillance, EIInt operations were used to record the diplomat's activities on celluloid and printed photos. As his operations reached peak and he succeeded in penetrating some defence perimeters, permission of the government was obtained to declare him as a persona non grata. In this important case a beauty was used to entice him.

In another case a notorious non-diplomat intelligence operator of a country came to notice for causing severe damage to defence related securities. His fondness for women was testified from his visit to certain pleasure holes in the walled city. A beauty was planted on him and she performed her duties admirably. Finally, the FIS employee was accosted with the evidence and intercepted when he was found meeting a defence department employee in one of the parks in Delhi. The "honey" was rewarded amply.

Since it is not possible to record in details the operational modus operandi of the major FIS active in India we propose to discuss certain case studies of the Inter Services Intelligence of Pakistan, which pursues very aggressive tradecraft technologies to steal Indian secrets and subvert sections of the people. The ISI and complimentary military intelligence units apply arrays of tradecraft technologies to identify, win over and exploit Indian contacts and agents. The most important window is the consular section, which is mostly manned by the personnel of the ISI. The peculiar situation of religious compatibility, keenness to visit Pakistan to meet parted relatives, necessity of matrimonial relationship prompt many Indians to visit Pakistan from all corners of the country. The professional visa agents, touts and existing contacts and agents indicate the likely targets and probable softies. Such visa seekers are cultivated, given sample tasks and are gradually drawn into the network of espionage. Some of such talents are trained in various tradecrafts, once they reach Pakistan and tasked with certain well defined clandestine operations. Some of them graduate to "sleeper agents", who operate silently for years together. Some are also trained as talent spotters.

In addition, the non-diplomatic operators move around various defence installations and office complexes and try out hit and pick tactics to hook up lower level defence employees. They prowl near bus stands, eateries and locations where the staffs normally spend time during lunch break. The ISI operatives remain on the lookout for employees who work till late hours, try to offer them lift and build up relationship. Existing contacts and agents also feed information about the needy, distressed and emotionally disturbed defence and other key government officials and their family members. Some of the undercover operatives take advantage of their diplomatic immunity, move around different parties, invitees in the embassy premises on national day, etc. functions, and fraternize with media persons, intellectuals and even the lawmakers. Talent spotting is done in the process of powwowing, chatting and conversing with identified talents when they visit the embassies to attend occasional parties. Their dossiers are prepared carefully through local enquiry by enlisted sub-agents and social circuits. 'Everything has a price' is the slogan of all intelligence agencies. Such prices may include hefty cash payment in India or abroad in escrow fund. This is supplemented by free gifts of alcoholic drinks and other incentives.

A hard nut to crack by monetary incentives, a bureaucrat was hooked by Pakistan embassy by dropping a honey trap. The bureaucrat employed in Indian defence ministry had weakness for the fair sex and had entangled himself in a couple of extramarital relationships. A socialite from Pakistan was flown in as a junior diplomat and released on the trail of the bureaucrat. It did not take more than a fortnight to allure the officer to an electronically treated bedroom. The result was devastating. When confronted with the still and video clips the bureaucrat caved in and agreed to work for the ISI. His handler was the tantalizingly beautiful junior diplomat. However, counter-intelligence efforts tracked the footsteps of the bureaucrat visiting a posh guesthouse in Delhi's Sundar Nagar locality rather frequently. A counter sting operation amassed evidence to nail down the bureaucrat. The government adopted disciplinary action by transferring him to an innocuous location temporarily before he was dismissed. The junior diplomat-beauty suddenly disappeared from Delhi. Employment of a socialite in a diplomatic post for a specific operation was an exceptional tradecraft experiment by the ISI. Such local and imported socialites are generally employed for honey trap operations, but conferring diplomatic status was a new experience. For reasons of national security the name of the bureaucrat is being withheld.

The embassy embedded diplomats, particularly of the South Asian countries, pick up clandestine agents during their purported visit to religious shrines and historically important monuments. All diplomats are supposed to notify the ministry of external affairs before they visit any place outside Delhi. However, this norm is more breached than observed. In 1992 it was observed that a particular diplomat visited a religious shrine in Rajasthan almost every quarter on the plea of soliciting mercy of the Sufi saint to have a child. Counter-intelligence efforts unearthed the sinister intelligence operation of the undercover diplomat when it was found that two *khadims* (service persons) of the shrine worked as his conduit to a few intelligence contacts from areas where important defence installations were located. Surveillance, electronic operations and bugging finally unmasked the well-planned operation by the ISI in Rajasthan areas bordering Pakistan. While five Indian nationals were picked up for prosecution the undercover diplomat was declared persona non grata and was given 24 hour's time to leave Delhi. Such instances are too many and cannot be incorporated except for illustrating the operational tradecraft employed by the FIS personnel and efforts of India's counter-intelligence preparedness.

In addition to Mission based operations Pakistan generally employ shallow penetration itinerary agents to gather strategic and tactical intelligence pertaining to India's defence preparations, identification of troop formations, locating bunkers, foxholes and other forward war tactics. This category of agents can either be Pakistani or Indian nationals who crisscross the border for smuggling purposes.

Often deep penetration itinerant agents or short-term residents are deployed, who enter India legally or illegally, move around selected locations for locating defence installations in the hinterland areas and defence production facilities. This category of agents normally moves under cover of mendicants, petty traders, faith healers and festivals in the families of their relatives in India. They are not required to communicate with their handlers in Pakistan. They collect all the evidence and escape to Pakistan after the mission is accomplished.

The long term resident agents are selected carefully and trained elaborately in intelligence tradecraft. They are infiltrated into India illegally and allowed time to locate themselves initially with their extended family members and gradually their cover is woven up for locating them in prime areas for periods longer than five to ten years. They are assisted to take cover of petty professional, trader, and impersonate as a caste Hindu. Often they marry local girls. Set up family and build up relationship in the neighbourhood. Gradually they build up intelligence network and start production. They are required to communicate with their handlers in Pakistan through electronic channels — wireless, fax, email, SMS and MMS. We have discussed the aspects of SigInt, forward and counter-intelligence operations in an earlier chapter. While it is possible to monitor fax and emails the aspects of monitoring SMS and MMS are yet in infantile stage. India's counter-intelligence efforts are yet to be equipped with the sinuses of counter-intelligence combat situation by deploying advanced electronic equipment. However, such long term agents are frequently compromised when they commit mistakes in their locational areas and in employing tradecrafts. Surveillance, telephone and mobile phone monitoring and exercising control on the public communication hubs (PCOs) which are variably used by the long term agents for sending emails and fax messages. In the age of laptop computers, blackberry systems, wireless internet facilities and wifi zones in certain public places it is difficult to zero in on all such communication devices. Indian counter-intelligence efforts would require enhanced capabilities to cope with advanced communication devices flooding the market.

With thin and sparse counter-intelligence deployment it is rather difficult to locate and neutralize a long term resident agent. Real hard nuts merge with the background perfectly and hardly betray their actual mother tongue, religious practices, food habits and behavioural pattern. In addition, Indian intelligence management does not have regional and provincial hubs (some states are bigger than some European countries and thickly populated) to monitor Signals Intelligence, collect electronic communication data and monitor other EIInt equipment. A city like Bangalore and Hyderabad is without any facility for monitoring EIInt, SigInt and other aspects of ComInt. With such handicap counter-intelligence efforts are mainly confined to the capital city and in skeletal manner in a few provincial capitals.

Often it is reported that certain terrorist modules and cells are active in different parts of the country and foreign jihadi organizations like the Harkat-ul-Jihad al Islami (HUJI), Lashkar-e-Taiba (LeT) and Indian Mujahideen activists are active in certain parts of the country. That jihadi modules are intricately connected with the intelligence modules is not clearly understood by Indian agencies. Not even the terrorists and suicide bombers can be effective in intelligence void situation. They require advance intelligence and tactical current intelligence. Some of the resident agents help Pakistani agencies in locating and cultivating affable members of subverted indigenous groups. These modules can only be penetrated through HumInt and ElInt and on occasions SigInt applications and other tradecraft technologies.

A classical case detection of a long term resident agent related to one Karim Mitahiwala (assumed name), who started a modest sweetmeat shop in a busy market near Halwara in Punjab. An important Air Force Station, Halwara also had a large complement of infantry locations. Nearby Barnala and Sangrur have arrays of radar locations and these are not far away from Ludhiana and Jallandhar which have certain elements of Air Force and infantry units. Karim's establishment located in the flourishing market of Sudharwala was hardly ten kilometers from the AF Station. He surfaced at Sudharwala under the wings of his "uncle" in Ludhiana, a flourishing trader, part of whose family had migrated to Pakistan in 1947. Karim often remained absent from his sweetmeat shop and visited Barnala, Sangrur, Adampur, Jallandhar areas. He never used phone for communication with his handlers. A chance surveillance of a known smuggler and suspected minor ISI agent to Sudharwala presented surprises. His visits were frequent and he mostly spent time in a house owned by the "uncle" of Karim, as grain storage in Sudharwala.

His visit coincided with the visit of Karim to his uncle's grain storage. After four sightings of such coincidental visits an enquiry and surveillance operation was put in procedure. Over three months the counter-intelligence team piled up enough material and located the PCOs, places of his visits and his contacts in different strategic places in Punjab. Certain ElInt operations confirmed the HumInt and surveillance inputs. Karim, the smuggler and "uncle" Osman were lifted and interrogated. The fallout of this detection was followed by arrests of five other sub-agents of Karim who were engaged in collecting intelligence about the Indian armed forces. It was finally revealed that Karim, a resident of Karachi was recruited and trained to be located in India as a long term resident agent. Osman was pressured to work as a frontman through his family members settled in Karachi. The smuggler worked as a cut-out for contacting the resident agent to pass on fresh directives. This one mistake committed by the ISI handlers facilitated the counter-intelligence team to reach Karim, the famous Mithaiwala at Sudharwala town. Obviously for operational safety names of the persons concerned and the greater details of tradecraft technology applied have been suppressed.

There are plenty of such live instances that can be presented to the readers as juicy materials. Since the book relates to tradecraft technology, it does not require espionage stories to thrill them. The thrill is in being a spy and a spymaster. However, it must be mentioned that counter-intelligence sinuses are inadequate in Delhi and major provincial capitals of the country and there is hardly any presence in the vast countryside. India virtually stands exposed in this area of intelligence activity.

Chapter 14

Deception, Disinformation and Propaganda

Deception, disinformation and propaganda in intelligence statecraft and diplomatic parlance are refined science and art for deceiving the adversary. Though these terms sound immoral in common societal and personal relationship ambience, in statecraft these tradecrafts are recognized as highest form of subtle exhibition of wit to misguide, mislead and confuse the adversaries. In military science deception and disinformation are used to confuse the enemy, misguide him to the north by conducting false manoeuvres in the south.

According to Allen W Dulles: "In intelligence, the term 'deception' covers a wide variety of manoeuvres by which a state attempts to mislead another state, generally a potential or rival enemy, as to its own capability and intentions. Its best known use is in war time or just prior to the outbreak of war, when its main purpose is to draw enemy defenses away from a planned point of attack, or to give the impression that there will be no attack at all simply to confuse the opponent about one's plans and purposes." (*The Craft of Intelligence*).

Disinformation, deception and propaganda are not mere mischievous concoctions. These are based on real-life intelligence about the adversary and use of such intelligence as a weapon of counter-intelligence can also be defined as disinformation and deception.

According to Jennifer D Kirbe (Covert Action essay in *Secret Intelligence*), "An important area where intelligence and information can exert a pivotal effect over military operations is deception. Intelligence and deception are not synonymous. However, intelligence is an essential part of deception. Intelligence is important in planning deception, since it is necessary to ascertain at the outset, what the enemy is predisposed to believe. It is important in mounting a counter-intelligence effort to feed enemy intelligence with false information to create and sustain the deception."

Most intelligence departments have departments of disinformation, deception and propaganda, otherwise known as department of Black Arts. While the ancient instance of using the Trojan Horse against Troy is a classical example there are plenty of such instances of use of deception during wartime and also during tense periods of diplomatic relationship between two countries or blocks of countries.

Deception, disinformation and propaganda as well as use of double agent to plant information on the enemy starts with the Intelligence Estimate and political assessment about the status of the adversary. This process is intricate and takes months and years for the intelligence agencies, diplomats, political analysts to formulate concrete bases about the military preparation of the adversaries, their force multiplication, building up international support, forming of alliances, etc. Mind frame of the leaders of the ruling and opposition parties, attitude of the people, economic conditions and the susceptibility to believe in very smart acts of deception and gullibility to swallow a piece of disinformation.

On the other hand certain countries, say the USA, examine its long term geostrategic interest in a country or region and starts collecting intelligence about that country's nuclear ambitions and practical steps taken to enrich uranium. In the case of Pakistan-China-North Korea nuclear axis the US intelligence community were fully aware of Pakistan and China's cooperation. However, no attempt was made to prevent Pakistan from acquiring nuclear capability. There are analysts who believe that the USA had willfully drawn blinkers with a view to build up a parallel nuclear power to checkmate India. On the other hand in the case of Syria, US and Israeli intelligence mounted orchestrated disinformation and finally Israel was allowed to bomb out the fledgling nuclear facility of Syria in Aleppo.

The same drama is now witnessed in Iran, which is on the verge of attaining nuclear capability. Iran claims that it requires nuclear facility for power generation and the USA, Israel and their allies believe that Iran's main objective is to manufacture nuclear weapons and nuclear capable missile systems. During the last ten years serious propaganda and disinformation have been spun to prepare grounds for joint US and Israel strike against Iran's nuclear sites. A nuclear capable Iran will obviously disturb the global power equation in the Middle East, Africa and Central Asian region.

Another recent disinformation and propaganda warfare of the USA is directed at Hugo Chavez Frias, the Venezuelan President, who is a persona non grata with Washington for his oil nationalization policy, communistic attitude and his efforts to establish a pan-Latin block in South America. Major US newspapers, news magazines and several newspapers in Latin America are supplied with news and views directed against the alleged demonic attitude of the Venezuelan President. Covert efforts to unseat Chavez are discernible and distresses suffered by the USA over Fidel Castro-Chavez axis are visible. To evolve disinformation campaign the CIA and other planted agents of the spy agency to gather intelligence about vulnerability of Chavez administration and democratic and extra-democratic efforts made by his opponents to unseat him. There are reports of infiltration of sections of Venezuelan armed forces by the rogue CIA elements.

The process of disinformation, deception and propaganda warfare is the same in India. The tradecrafts and spinning mills are similar, though the structural formation of the Black Arts department is nebulous, back up research is not synchronized and domestic and external targets are not under the constant surveillance of the specialists' weapon systems.

For example, the case of Kashmir can be examined. The Kashmir Valley, Uri, Punch, Sopore and Jammu areas are flooded by Pakistani electronic media barrage. The official and private channels are used to beam programme about alleged atrocities committed by the Indian forces, rape and murder of Muslim women and continuous harassment of the common people and the pro-separatist groups. In these areas certain groups of people tune in for Pakistan TV, as they feel the PTV is the most reliable source of information. They do not trust in contents of Indian TV coverage. Lahore, Islamabad and Muzaffarabad based print media as well as print materials manufactured by jihadi *tanzeems* are smuggled in. Often the vernacular print media in the Valley are also used by Pakistan to publish palpably concocted stories as parts of disinformation campaign by the separatists and Pakistan's intelligence agency. Telephonic communication directly between trusted people in Kashmir and Pakistani intelligence agency's front organizations are analyzed and PTV programme are produced by twisting the truth. Pakistan follows the propaganda tactics of Joseph Goebbels, the German mastermind of propaganda warfare.

Information and intelligence about Pakistani disinformation and propaganda are not systematically gathered by the concerned agencies from print and electronic media and disinformation planted by the religious leaders and separatist stalwarts. There are desks and analysts to examine these materials and evolve certain methodologies to counteract the disinformation and propaganda warfare. But in vast number of cases Pakistani TV channels and cable channels run by individuals in the valley are not systematically covered and recorded.

The simple job can be assigned to certain intelligence agencies. This is done haphazardly and analysis of impact of such disinformation propaganda are not carried out on war footing. The home ministry mysteriously depends on only one production company for producing TV materials which are rather shabby. The allegation that nexus between ministry officials and the production company is questionable, requires independent examination. Examination of the contents of Door Darshan normal channel and the DD Kashir (Kashmir) give impression that portrayal of jihadi activities inside Pakistan, instability of the country do not impact the psychological process of the separatists and common villagers under their sway. DD Kashir programmes are produced crudely and the policy planners and counter-propaganda experts do not apply their minds and evaluate what contents are being beamed and how the programmes are received by the people.

The print media in Kashmiri language and Urdu hardly carry any genuine news item and news analysis prepared by the counter-disinformation and counter-propaganda experts. Journalists who are brave enough to portray the excesses committed by the Pakistan trained terrorists are eliminated. So far over 10 journalists have fallen to the bullets of the terrorists.

Compared to this the readers may like to read a piece reported by *Pakistan Times*, which is a piece of effective disinformation turning the true picture to a believable disinformation:

"Journalists Killed, Arrested, Harassed in Held-Kashmir"

'Pakistan Times' Kashmir Desk

ISLAMABAD: Occupied Kashmir sees no let-up in the killings, illegal detentions and torture of Kashmiri journalists as the world observes the World Press Freedom Day, today.

According to the data several Kashmiri journalists, including a woman scribe, Asia Gilani, have been killed in the occupied territory during Kashmiris' ongoing struggle against India since 1989.

Among others, the journalists who were killed while doing their duties include Shabbir Ahmad Dar, Mushtaq Ali, Ghulam Muhammad Lone, Ghulam Rasool Azad, Muhammad Shaban Wakeel, Pervez Muhammad Sultan and Mushtaq Ahmad.

In the meantime, among those tortured and illegally detained include Muhammad Maqbool Sahil and Rehmattullah Khan and Syed Iftikhar Gilani. Gilani was released after several months of illegal detention during which he was subjected to severe torture. The other two journalists are still languishing in Indian jails.

In the occupied territory, almost routinely, journalists face manhandling by Indian troops, abductions, murder attempts and death threats. All of this has made their everyday work extremely difficult. Manoeuvring blasts in media organizations and banning advertisements of newspapers is also a common phenomenon.

Kashmiri journalists, Muhammad Amin War, Rafique Maqbool and many other scribes were thrashed and injured by the troops when they were performing their professional duties in Rajbagh area of Srinagar in September 2004."

On top of such propaganda Pakistan inspires several journalists in the Valley to write and speak about lack of media freedom. These stories are flashed in print media and WWW sites maintained from Pakistan, the UK, the USA, and the Gulf countries. In comparison to Pakistani efforts, the counter WWW propaganda warfare performance of the Indian Government agencies and other organizations is very inadequate. This obviously means that India is losing the battle of the minds (mass control mechanism), and violation of the rights of the people of Indian Kashmir by the Pakistan trained and based terrorist are not adequately brought to the notice of the world forum. Mere government statistics are not believed by a beleaguered people where pro-Pakistani sentiment generated by religious affinity is stronger than the secular democratic process and constitutional administration. Recent disturbances in the Valley (June-July 2010) prove amply that disinformation and monetary incentive by Pakistan can generate explosive situation any moment. This also proves that Indian intelligence agencies are not completely aware of the designs of Pakistan. In guerrilla warfare the term "mind control and mass control" means destroying faith of the people in the existing governance system and replacing by systems invented and applied by the adversaries. Pakistan has been bombarding Kashmir with such materials (idea, money and weapons) and establishing control on minds of the masses. Unfortunately, India is doing precious little to prepare for war on this front.

We would like to comment on the aspects of disinformation, deception and propaganda practised by Indian intelligence agencies in later paragraphs. Let us look at the global scenario.

Such deception, disinformation and propaganda were launched heavily by the UK, USA and the allies and Germany during the two World Wars. Legends of deception tactics practices by Churchill's government and the US commanders have been recorded in several books.

After German forces were ousted from North Africa the Fuehrer and his planners anticipated that the Allied Forces would target Italy next. To them it appeared that Sicily would be the natural stepping stone for attacking mainland Italy. The Allied Forces wanted to plant convincing deception on the Axis Forces that the attack might come from Spanish coast area. In May 1943 a corpse of a British major was found floating near the southwest coast of Spain, near Spanish town of Huelva, between Portuguese border and Gibraltar. The Germans picked up the body and from the contents of the briefcase deduced that the Allied Forces might attack from Greece side. Believing in this grand disinformation planned by Ewen Montagu (*The Man Who Never Was*) Hitler sent moure armored divisions to Greece. This was a highly sophisticated feat of deception which turned the tide against Mussolini and Hitler.

Operation 'Overlord' was the name of combined Allied invasion of Normandy in June 1944. To deceive the Germans about the real intention of the joint Ally invasion, the British and US planners and executioners planned one of the biggest games of deception to convince Hitler that the Allied Forces were likely to land from Le Havre area of France. A number of fake airports, with faked aircraft were put up in Kent area; several storage locations were built, fake cannons were decked up and some conceited troop movements in the area intensified. They even faked war vessels, planted rumours, sent faked radio signals and used double agents to impress the Berlin war-game planners to bite the bait. Some faked air reconnaissance was carried out in dummy areas to mislead the Germans. Hitler believed in the hoax and it is known that the most important landing had taken place from Normandy coast.

Britain also adopted several deception methodologies to outfox the Luftwaffe, the German air force. They camouflaged airfields, hangars as cultivable fields, decoy cannon battery positions were erected, certain vital areas were blacked out, and certain non-target areas were given shape of heavy industries. Certain false maps were also peddled to the Germans through double agents and misleading radio messages were transmitted after Britain succeeded in breaking the German codes by cloning the Enigma machine and by inventing other deciphering technology. In fact, the tradecraft of disinformation, deception and propaganda attained very high stature during the Second World War. Being a part of the modern concept of spy-war, which incorporates many other elements of tradecraft, sabotage and subversion technologies, the so-called Black Arts of intelligence and military warfare have emerged as classic subjects of research, study and application.

The history of the Second World War is marked by another wild dream of *lebensraum* enunciated by Adolf Hitler in 1925 in his *Mein Kampf*; invasion of Eastern Europe, the Balkans and occupation of Russia. However, in 1939 Russia and Germany concluded an opportunistic treaty that was followed by the attack and occupation of Poland. Since then, especially after cruel purge by Stalin, Germany started massive propaganda campaign in Baltic territories, Georgia, Belarus, Moldavia and even in Russia about Jewish domination of the USSR. Impression was created that unless Jewish influence was eradicated the future of the Aryan and Slavic people would remain bleak. The propaganda blitzkrieg was followed by massive planned attack of the USSR by Hitler despite opposition by some of his close advisers. Operation Barbarosa, attack of the USSR was launched after severe barrage of disinformation; deceptive movements of military resources and propaganda barrage launched by Goering and his gang. As is known, Hitler failed in his scheme of enslaving the Slav people as the Russians fought back valiantly and inflicted irreparable loses on the Germans. Defeat on the Russian and eastern European front had weakened the military juggernaut headed by Hitler, the great psychopathic dictator of modern times.

The Mayak nuclear plant accident in the USSR, near the town of Kalsi was 20% more severe than the accident at Chernobyl. The US had flown U2 spy flights to locate and identify the damage caused in vast territories in Ural catchment area. Gary Power had also flown over the area when he was shot down by USSR missile. The USA knew about the devastating nuclear accident but kept it a secret with the intention of not creating adverse domestic opinion against mushrooming of nuclear plants in the country for gaining superiority in arms race.

CIA disinformation, deception and propaganda campaign against Jacobo Arbenz, the Guatemalan President in the fifties has now been declassified. It is now clear that Arbenz, son of a Swiss pharmacist of the same name had enrolled in Guatemalan army, rose in ranks and had later led a group of army officers and civil groups to oust the pro-US exploitive and corrupt president. The CIA orchestrated publishing of propaganda barrage in Latin newspapers against him, prompted a group of army officers to revolt, CIA pilots bombed parts of the country and all out efforts were made to paint Arbenz as a communist and a lackey of Moscow. He was finally ousted and sent to exile. The same disinformation, deception and propaganda warfare were carried out against the Cuban rebels, in Brazil in 1964, in Dominican Republic in 1965 and Chile in 1973 that led to the fall and assassination of communist cult leader Salvador Allende. It is known that President Nixon had sanctioned $10 million to prevent Allende from capturing power for the second time. The CIA propaganda barrage during that period in Latin and English print media and television prove that the ceremony of killing or neutralizing a strategic rival starts with propaganda and disinformation campaign and the final push is given through orchestrated military uprising or rigging of elections.

Operation Ajax, the well-known story of CIA-MI6 collaboration to oust Mohammad Mossaddegh, Prime Minister of Iran (1951-53) has become a part of modern political history and international intrigue by the CIA and British intelligence. The USA and UK stranglehold on Iran through the Pahlavi regime was symbolized by exploitation of its oil industry by Anglo Iranian Oil Company. As Mossaddegh, loaded with communist and socialist ideas proceeded to nationalize the oil industry Winston Churchill and the US President Dwight D. Eisenhower collaborated and the CIA was tasked to remove Mossaddegh. His ouster was preceded by propaganda barrage, disinformation and deception orchestrated by the CIA and the MI6.

Finally the task was given to the CIA to arrange his removal. On 4 April 1953, CIA director Dulles approved US$1 million to be used "in any way that would bring about the fall of Mossaddegh". Soon the CIA's Tehran station launched propaganda campaign against Mossaddegh. Finally, according to *The New York Times*, in early June, American and British intelligence officials met again in Beirut, and gave the finishing touches on the strategy. Soon afterward, according to his later published accounts, the chief of the CIA's Near East and Africa division, Kermit Roosevelt, Jr. the grandson of US President Theodore Roosevelt, arrived in Tehran to direct it. In 2000, *The New York Times* made partial publication of a leaked CIA document titled, *Clandestine Service History – Overthrow of Premier Mossaddegh of Iran – November 1952-August 1953*. This document describes the point by point planning of the coup by agent Donald Wilbur, and execution conducted by the American and British governments. *The New York Times* published this critical document with the names censored. The newspaper also limited its publication to scanned image (bitmap) format, rather than machine-readable text. This document was eventually published properly — in text form, and fully unexpurgated. The complete CIA document is now web published. It is believed that Director CIA Dulles spent over $1 million only in propaganda warfare against Mossaddegh.

The young monarch Reza Shah Pahlavi succumbed under US pressure and Mossaddegh was forced to resign. He was put under house arrest where he died.

The USSR and its main intelligence tool the KGB also carried out disinformation and propaganda campaigns against the Cold War rival, the USA and other countries. KGB's Service A was generally responsible for conducting active disinformation campaign. The KGB operators posted abroad under diplomatic and other covers were tasked to scrounge the local media, pick up gossip from informed and intellectual circles and industrial cooperators and conceive disinformation campaign on any given subject or event. Their reports were examined in the Department D and by other specialists in a panel. They would examine the originator of the proposal, grill him and when satisfied a report would be prepared by Dezinformatsiya (disinformation) experts. It would then be translated into the languages of the target countries and would be published in print media outside the Soviet Bloc to give credibility about the genuineness of the disinformation.

Some of the major disinformation included reports published about possible involvement of the CIA and the FBI in the killing of John F. Kennedy. Serious cloud of doubt was raised about Lee Harvey Oswald not being the only assassin and possible existence of conspirators in the CIA and the FBI. Lee was a US marine and had defected to the Soviet Union. He returned home and was arrested in a case of assassination of a Dallas police officer. Later he killed JFK on November 22, 1963.

The KGB also circulated sustained disinformation by publishing a report in the *Free Press Journal* of Bombay seemingly by Gordon Goldstein that the US Office of Naval Research had stockpiled biochemical weapons during Vietnam War and these were used against the Vietnamese civilians. These reports were published in Thai, Indian and *Patriot* (USA) newspapers.

Vitriolic propaganda was mounted by the KGB that Rev Martin Luther King Jr. was assassinated by the white supremists-Ku Klux Klan on April 4 at Memphis, Tennessee while he was standing on a motel lobby. The barrage of propaganda had created serious cleavage between the white and black Americans. The USSR had succeeded in creating a strong black lobby in the States.

The USSR had originated and sustained vicious propaganda that USA was responsible for manufacturing AIDS virus to use against people in targeted countries. Though detected in early seventies, it is believed that the disease might have originated from Africa. In early nineties and even thereafter the propaganda was carried out by the KGB and the East German Intelligence that the USA had spread the AIDS virus in Africa, and parts of South Asia. Some reports were published in the *Patriot* (Pennsylvania) that the US Department of Defense was conducting experiments in Zaire in Africa with AIDS virus.

In non-military areas such disinformation campaigns are carried out by most major countries. This is not limited to the USA, UK and other western countries. Israel's spy agency Mossad is regarded as one of the past masters in the game of disinformation and deception. A former Mossad officer has alleged that the Israeli spy agency has its own "passport factory" to create or doctor passports for use in intelligence operations. Relations between Australia and Israel are under strain after three Australian passports were apparently used by Israeli suspects in the killing of top Hamas leader Mahmoud Al Mabhouh in Dubai. Dubai police said they are 99 per cent sure Mossad was behind the operation to smother Mabhouh with a pillow in his hotel room. Victor Ostrovsky, a case officer at Mossad for several years in the 1980s, says he has no doubt that Australian passports have been forged or fraudulently used for similar operations in the past. In recent times this has been the most glaring instance of deception by Israel.

According to William H White (*Global Research,* May 2, 2008) the USA and Israel appeared to be working conjointly to carry out disinformation and propaganda campaign against alleged nuclear programme of Syria and Iran. The case of Syria is now well known. From early 2007 US media and other international media orchestrated reports about Syrian nuclear site at Aleppo. Some reports of 'serious explosion' were also published. The CIA sponsored propaganda campaign were reportedly confirmed by aerial and radar surveillance and reports submitted by Turkish Kurds on payroll of the CIA. Finally, Israel launched Operation Orchid on September 6, 2007 and carried out aerial bombing of the suspected site. Later, reports from IAEA could not conclusively prove if the site was really being used for housing a nuclear reactor, though the CIA and Mossad sponsored reports claimed correctness of their observations and expressed satisfaction over neutralization of the Syrian nuclear facility.

Camouflage, disinformation, deception and propaganda mechanism adopted by the armed forces are parts of the war room exercises and for certain reasons these aspects are kept out of scope of the present discourse. Major armies all over the world have certain rules of business and these are modified from time to time on the basis of intelligence received about the preparation shift of the adversary. Each formation of the army deployed on borders is supposed to make an inventory of preparatory measures adopted by the enemy. Accordingly, complimentary defensive and offensive preparations are conceived, discussed at the war room and certain disinformation and deception measures are adopted to mislead the enemy besides adopting normal offensive/defensive preparations.

On India-Pakistan-Bangladesh borders smuggling is rampant. The habitual smugglers and border-crossers are normally trapped by the MI personnel and debriefed about their links with the MI or intelligence agency of the adversary country. Often they are used as low level double agents to pass on tidbitfalse and manufactured intelligence about location of a particular brigade, radar stations and missile storage locations. The adversary is interested in intelligence about movement of regiments from one location to the other, movements of cavalry units and shifting aircraft squadrons from one location to other. There exist layers of espionage channel to gather such information from informed journalists, intellectuals, army contractors, etc. In addition, strings of low level agents are deployed to collect regimental insignia photos, tag numbers of transport vehicles and tank units. These tactics of the adversary are known to the MI and the counter-intelligence authorities. With a view to mislead the adversary the armed forces adopt certain disinformation tactics and even apply camouflage technology.

Commanders of the armed forces are required to undergo comprehensive training in psychological warfare, disinformation and deception with a view to fog out the enemy on the eve or during a war. Besides adopting defensive camouflage measures several tradecrafts are taught to the officers in misleading the enemy psychologically as well as visually. Experiences have shown that certain planned disinformation broadcast over the radio regarding troop movements in the Line of Control and other border areas with Pakistan had led to selection of infiltration routes by the Pakistani jihadis assuming these to be safe. In fact, these are highly secured routes and in many cases the infiltrators are taken by surprise. On the other hand Pakistan directs certain jihadi groups to make false manoeuvres in the snow bound higher reaches to mislead the armed forces; while they carry out real infiltration in Rajouri, Uri and Punch areas.

Before 1999 attack on Kargil, Pakistan had adopted several camouflage measures to mislead India about road and track construction from Skardu, Satpara and Astore areas. Construction of helipads near the LoC was also overlooked by India and troop build-up at Skardu and Gilgit were done surreptitiously. Movements of the Pakistani army personnel to the higher reaches near the LoC and inside India were also not properly studied and interpreted. In some cases Pakistani infiltration was camouflaged as movements of grazers. Most probably lessons have been learnt by the armed forces and intelligence agencies from the deception tactics adopted by Pakistan army and its intelligence agency.

Unfortunately, in India psychological warfare, tradecrafts on disinformation, deception and propaganda do not form the ingredients of training of an intelligence operative; the higher management and the grassroots operatives. Certain rudimentary lessons are imparted in talks and discussions but these are elementary in nature. Most of the trainers also lack in comprehension and experience in the principles and practice of these tradecraft technologies. There is no organized school of Black Arts, Deception and Disinformation. Certain officers evolve their own methodology in certain specific operations. In government domain certain TV programmes are collaged on affairs in Pakistan. However, Doordarshan is not a popular channel. It is not comprehensible why the policy planners do not create or fund independent TV channels to beam propaganda at Pakistan and people in India loyal to Pakistan. This deficiency only proves that India is not ready with psy-war capability in the civilian domain. The intelligence agencies are also not active in this area and the policy makers are not backed by imaginative bureaucratic support for institutionalizing the concept.

In the absence of a central Directorate of Operations the task of gleaning out intelligence that can be used for disinformation and deception as well as propaganda is devolved by the desk officer and the analyst. They are so much flooded with routine works that their mindset is directed at the completion of the routine drill of producing finished intelligence. From experience it can be concluded that most of the desk officers and analysts are not attuned to comprehend and prepare project reports for psy-war materials.

However, certain individual managers heading segmental operations group often conceive certain propaganda, deception and disinformation operations. But the ideas of using the print and electronic media for progressive disinformation and propaganda are evaluated in conservative manner. Certain operators grab secret money in the name of funding newspapers, pamphlets, etc. Having no knowledge of the value-impact of such tradecraft in a given area, on a given sections of people, the operations officers often fumble and the efforts end up in constricted bureaucratic approach and hesitant implementation. They do not even have a system to gather ground feedback about reception of the disinformation and propaganda, evaluate if these are adequate, and require further honing. Often the entire exercise is lost in bureaucratic quagmire. In case of existence of an elaborate structural arrangement of a Directorate of Operations and sectional operation desks vast improvement can be carried out in this field. This is still an unexplored area of Indian intelligence.

By pleading for a Directorate of Operations in the Intelligence Bureau and other agencies it is not suggested that the government should carry out psy-war against its own people. Tradecraft of intelligence demands such an edifice with a view to carry out operations against the insurgents, terrorists and identified enemies of the country.

At one point of time when the Naga insurgent groups were being sent to China for training and collecting weapons, a scheme was devised to spread amongst the predominantly Christian villagers that Communism was an anathema to Christianity and the Christian youths visiting China would get contaminated by communist ideology and that might harm the very fabric of the Naga society. These ideas were planted amongst the village elders and chiefs through words of mouth and also through certain pastors who were from southern part of the country. Feedback gathered indicated that the society was not ready to embrace communistic ideas and gradually the degree of aversion toward sending groups to China dwindled. Most such operations do not produce 100% result, but even 50% dividend is accepted as good performance.

It is necessary to cite another generalized instance that was experimented in Punjab. Disillusioned Sikh youths were invited to Pakistan for training and supplying arms. The trend had gathered momentum in 1987-88 and continued thereafter. Most of the religiously dedicated Sikhs, particularly those following Jarnail Singh

Bhindranwale and the Dam Dami Taksal were 'amritdharis', those who took a ritual vow for piety, vegetarianism and abstaining from alcohol. Interrogation of certain captured militants indicated that they were forced to eat meat and discard other vows taken by an 'amritdhari.' This point was researched and was adequately propagated amongst the villagers through words of mouth and through certain temple priests. The Sikhs are known for strict allegiance to their religious tenets. This experiment and also the theory floated by Pakistan that Sikhs and Muslims are twins was busted through such subtle propaganda and other psy-war tradecraft implementation.

These tradecrafts have not yet been implemented in organized manner in the states affected by Maoist terrorists. States like Andhra Pradesh and Chhattisgarh have made some experimentation on tribal lines with a view to win over certain tribal groups. But there is no standard model and centralized operational approach. Though Maoist ideology is the common thread and ideology, the people participating in the guerrilla warfare are ethnically, linguistically, culturally and lifestyle-wise different. Except poverty and abject neglect by the tools of governance they have nothing in common. In certain areas some Maoists are Christians and others are Hindus and at best animists. Intelligence operators should be acquainted with these diversities and mount psy-war through disinformation, deception and propaganda to bring about cleavage. This would facilitate the armed police operators in establishing military superiority. With gradual improvement in military superiority the civil administration can address the grievances of the people who were exploited by the Maoists promising good governance and enhanced economic conditions and abolition of exploitation. In some cases printed pamphlets in Hindi are airdropped in the affected areas. In Lalgarh area of West Bengal tragedy is that very few people can read Hindi. Same is the case with Orissa, Jharkhand and Chhattisgarh tribals. It should be possible to print pamphlets in local dialect and reach the people through certain other subtle means, in addition to airdropping.

In these remote areas very few people can afford to have television sets and transistors. Very few of them are exposed to print media even in vernacular language of the concerned state. This vast information gap is filled in by the deception and propaganda materials distributed by the Maoists. For instance, Kishenji, a Maoist leader from Andhra Pradesh can operate easily in west Midnapore district of West Bengal inhabited by mixed ethnic groups like the Bengali, Santhal, Ho, Munda, etc. Kishenji can speak Bengali with an accent and his Hindi and English knowledge is impeccable. He operates a laptop with Internet connection and can communicate with government adversaries on mobile phones. He hogs the media banners. In contrast, efforts of the intelligence operators are limited to their old hackneyed tradecraft of gathering snippets of HumInt. Besides this, the political rivalries between different parties have also segmented the people. The Maoist leader lords over the divided people and the antiquated intelligence system. In a 'military' situation the most harmful interjection comes from feuding political parties. The Maoists take advantage of the divided political structures and the indeterminate forces directed by a constricted government.

Publicity materials containing genuine government actions against forest contractors, loan sharks, Tendu leaf traders and other erring officials should reach the aggrieved people through operational mechanism of the intelligence operators. Such operators may masquerade as teachers, health centre workers, village witch doctors and even NGO operators, some of which are known to be sympathetic to the causes of the guerrillas. What is the harm in floating some such NGOs and plant these in the affected areas? In certain areas village and area pastors, *mahants* and assumed revered saintly persons can also be activated through subtle operational approaches. Every tribe and sub-tribes branching out of it has certain religious functionaries. Besides them the professional Hadia distillers (local brews) have also tremendous influence on the people. In certain pockets the petty baniya (traders of grocery outlets) can be exploited to reach certain sections of the guerrillas and the village elders. Unfortunate part of the whole scenario is that intelligence generation capability of the state governments and the Union Government in these affected areas is highly inadequate. Absence of operational psy-war approach has left the forces to some local initiative and pure and simple hunt or get hunted situation.

In another sensitive area of concern for the country-religion inspired terrorism backed and sponsored by hostile neighbours the psy-war has been hooked up to the WWW domains. Internet domains operated by hardcore Islamists and jihadis (*iMuslim*) and their counterparts in the Hindu community (*iHindu*) have saturated the net-channels. Some of these are horrendous propaganda and blatant exposition of disinformation aimed at misleading the youth of the respective communities. In a couple of cases it was observed that well educated and tech-savvy Muslim youths were drawn to terrorist violence believing that their community can be liberated through armed struggle. At least in one case in Maharashtra *iHindu* propaganda influenced a small group to resort to violence against Muslim targets. This subject has not been studied in India scientifically either by the intelligence community or the scholars, though several books have been written in the west on the subject of *iMuslim*. The jihadi Internet warfare has reached a high pitch. Hindu reaction is gathering momentum and this web warfare is adding to alienation, suspicion and hatred. So far, no tangible operation plans have been adopted by the agencies to block these websites and float portals to promote secular values. Mere affirmative government actions for ameliorating the grievances of the Muslims cannot convince the Hindus that the minorities require protection. These are interpreted by the later as policy of minorityism and appeasement. The borders of differences are increasing dangerously. There is urgent need for psy-war preparations on this front directed at both the aggrieved communities.

Glossary

AASU	All Assam Student's Union
ACIO	Assistant Central Intelligence Officer
AcoustInt	Acoustic Intelligence
ARC	Aviation Research Centre
AWACS	Airborne Early Warning System
BND	Bundesnacharchtendianst (German INT Agency)
CIA	Central Intelligence Agency
CLP	Covert Listening Post
ComInt	Communication Intelligence
Comsec	Communication Security
CryptoInt	Crypto Analogical Intelligence
DCIO	Deputy Central Intelligence Officer
DGFI	Directorate of Forces Intelligence (Bangladesh)
DGSE	Direction Generale de le Securiti Exterieuer (France)
DIA	Directorate of Air Intelligence
DIB	Director Intelligence Bureau
DIS	Defence Intelligence Staff
DLB	Dead Letter Box
DMI	Directorate of Military Intelligence
DNA	Directorate of Naval Intelligence
DOP	Directorate of Operations
DPA	Deep Penetration Agent
ElInt	Electronic Intelligence
ETS	Electronic and Technical Services
FBIS	Foreign Broadcast Information Service
FIS	Foreign Intelligence Services
FSB	Federal Security Bureau (Russian MI5)
GCHQ	Government Communication Headquarters (British)
GRU	General Staff of the Armed Forces of the Russian Federation
HF	High Frequency
HumInt	Human Intelligence
IB	Intelligence Bureau
IO	Intelligence Officer
ISI	Inter Services Intelligence (of Pakistan Army)

JIC	Joint Intelligence Committee
KGB	Committee for State Security (Russian)
LasInt	Laser Intelligence
LLB	Live Letter Box
LTRA	Long Term Resident Agent
MasInt	Measurement and Signature Intelligence
MAV	Micro Air Vehicle
MI5	Security Services (British)
MI6	Secret Intelligence Service (British)
NAV	Nano Air Vehicle
NCS	National Coordination Service
NFG	Naga Federal Government
NIMA	National Imagery and Mapping Service
NNC	Naga Nationalist Council
NSA	National Security Agency/Advisor
NTRO	National Technical Research Organisation
NucInt	Nuclear Intelligence
OCA	Open Contact Agent
OSC	Open Source Centre
OsInt	Open Source Intelligence
PLA	People's Liberation Army
R&AW	Research & Analysis Wing (of the Cabinet Secretariat)
R&D	Research & Development
RadInt	Radiation Intelligence
RRC	Radio Research Centre
RV	Rendezvous
SatInt	Satellite Intelligence
SCA	Social Circuit Agent
SIB	Subsidiary Intelligence Bureau
SigInt	Signals Intelligence
SIO	Suspected Intelligence Officer
SOD	Special Operations Division
SOF	Special Operations Force
SOG	Special Operations Group
SPG	Special Protection Group
STIA	Short Term Itinerant Agent
SVR	Sluzhba Vereshey Razvedki (Russian External Intelligence)
TechInt	Technical Intelligence
UHF	Ultra High Frequency
ULF	Ultra Low Frequency
ULFA	United Liberation Front of Assam
USA	United States of America
VHF	Very High Frequency

Index